Complete Comprehension

Year 5

Contents

Year 5 overview		2
Introduction		4
Skills guide		14

Word meaning	14	Prediction		22
Retrieval	16	Relationship		24
Summarising	18	Word choice		26
Inference	20	Comparison		28

Teaching units and Progress checks	30

Schofield & Sims

Year 5 overview

Unit 1	**Dragonology** by Dugald Steer	Retrieval / Fiction	page 30
Unit 2	**How to Train Your Dragon** by Cressida Cowell	Comparison / Fiction	page 38
Unit 3	**Life in Tudor Britain** by Anita Ganeri	Summarising / Non-fiction	page 46
Unit 4	**Love Letter from Mary Tudor to Her Husband, Philip of Spain** by Brian Moses	Word meaning / Poetry	page 54
Unit 5	**The House with Chicken Legs** by Sophie Anderson	Inference / Fiction	page 62
Unit 6	**The Wizards of Once** by Cressida Cowell	Prediction / Fiction	page 70
Unit 7	**The Polar Bear Explorers' Club** by Alex Bell	Inference / Fiction	page 78
Progress check 1	**A Boy Called Christmas** by Matt Haig	Mixed skills / Fiction	page 86
Unit 8	**The Wolf Wilder** by Katherine Rundell	Retrieval / Fiction	page 90
Unit 9	**The Wolves of Willoughby Chase** by Joan Aiken	Word meaning / Fiction	page 98
Unit 10	**Whale Boy** by Nicola Davies	Word choice / Fiction	page 106
Unit 11	**SeaWorld Decides to Stop Killer Whale Breeding Program** by *The Guardian*	Relationship / Non-fiction	page 114

Schofield & Sims Complete Comprehension 5

Year 5 overview

Unit	Title	Skill / Type	Page
Unit 12	**Beetle Boy** by M.G. Leonard	Summarising — Fiction	page 122
Unit 13	**Beetle Boy: The Beetle Collector's Handbook** by M.G. Leonard	Word meaning — Non-fiction	page 130
Unit 14	**The Boy at the Back of the Class** by Onjali Q. Raúf	Inference — Fiction	page 138
Progress check 2	**Who are Refugees and Migrants? And Other Big Questions** by Michael Rosen and Annemarie Young	Mixed skills — Non-fiction	page 146
Unit 15	**The Jamie Drake Equation** by Christopher Edge	Retrieval — Fiction	page 150
Unit 16	**Once Upon a Star** by James Carter	Word meaning — Poetry	page 158
Unit 17	**Harry Houdini** by Laura Lodge	Retrieval — Non-fiction	page 166
Unit 18	**The Nowhere Emporium** by Ross MacKenzie	Inference — Fiction	page 174
Unit 19	**Plague!** by John Farndon	Retrieval — Non-fiction	page 182
Unit 20	**The Island at the End of Everything** by Kiran Millwood Hargrave	Inference — Fiction	page 190
Unit 21	**The London Eye Mystery** by Siobhan Dowd	Inference — Fiction	page 198
Progress check 3	**The Last Chance Hotel** by Nicki Thornton	Mixed skills — Fiction	page 206

Schofield & Sims Complete Comprehension 5

Introduction

Reading is one of the most important outcomes of a primary school education, and one of the most powerful skills we will ever master, as it is crucial for understanding the world around us. It is no exaggeration to say that the benefits of being an effective reader last a lifetime.

Complete Comprehension is a whole-school programme designed to equip pupils with everything they need to become strong, successful readers. The series, which comprises a book of lesson plans, teaching guidance and photocopiable resources for every year group from Year 1 to Year 6, breaks down the complex process of comprehension into separate **Comprehension skills** (see page 5).

The comprehension skills are signposted throughout the series through the use of child-friendly logos and graphics. Each teaching unit includes a photocopiable **Comprehension text** and a set of **Skills focus questions** that target a single skill, along with detailed guidance to support you, the teacher, to model the relevant skill in context using the **Let's try… questions**.

In addition, a **Skills guide** is provided at the end of this introduction (see page 14). It includes an in-depth **description** of each skill, and explains how the skills relate to each other. It also lists **strategies** to help you develop your pupils' familiarity with each skill and offers advice on how to deal with common difficulties. A selection of resources are also available to download from the Schofield & Sims website (www.schofieldandsims.co.uk/completecomprehension), including a selection of child-friendly **Skills graphics**, which explain the skills in simple terms, and **Skills deskmats**, which function as a reminder of the different skills.

In addition to this skill-specific instruction, **Complete Comprehension** prioritises vocabulary expansion, specifically the pre-teaching of vocabulary, as another prerequisite for successful comprehension. Every teaching unit includes a **Language toolkit**, which contains a set of **Key vocabulary** words from the comprehension text and accompanying activities to boost understanding in advance of reading.

The features outlined above are integrated into each **Complete Comprehension** teaching unit alongside enjoyable activities and discussion opportunities. These have a dual function: first, they promote reading for pleasure; second, they support pupils to engage with the text's features and build their background knowledge by exploring the themes in each text. Children are also encouraged to make comparisons with other texts and to reflect on their personal reactions to the text as readers. See pages 6 to 11 for a complete guide to the teaching unit.

The 21 teaching units in this book are designed to be completed at regular intervals over the course of a year: it is recommended that you work through seven units a term, leaving the remaining weeks free to spend on other reading work.

The comprehension skills

Each **Complete Comprehension** teaching unit targets one of the following skills, which are all essential for meaningful reading. In particular, word meaning, retrieval and inference are seen as cornerstones of comprehension, as children must be confident in these areas before they can master the remaining skills.

Key Stage 2 Comprehension skills

Word meaning
Understand the meaning of vocabulary in the text.

This symbol is used to represent word meaning in the teaching units.

- Go to page 14 to read more about word meaning.
- Word meaning is the target skill in Units 4, 9, 13 and 16.

Prediction
Use details from the text and background knowledge to make plausible predictions based on the text.

This symbol is used to represent prediction in the teaching units.

- Go to page 22 to read more about prediction.
- Prediction is the target skill in Unit 6.

Retrieval
Recall key details from the text.

This symbol is used to represent retrieval in the teaching units.

- Go to page 16 to read more about retrieval.
- Retrieval is the target skill in Units 1, 8, 15, 17 and 19.

Relationship
Comment on the way the text has been structured.

This symbol is used to represent relationship in the teaching units.

- Go to page 24 to read more about relationship.
- Relationship is the target skill in Unit 11.

Summarising
Identify and comment on the text's main points.

This symbol is used to represent summarising in the teaching units.

- Go to page 18 to read more about summarising.
- Summarising is the target skill in Units 3 and 12.

Word choice
Discuss the effect of words and phrases used in the text.

This symbol is used to represent word choice in the teaching units.

- Go to page 26 to read more about word choice.
- Word choice is the target skill in Unit 10.

Inference
Use details from the text and background knowledge to make judgements about aspects of the text.

This symbol is used to represent inference in the teaching units.

- Go to page 20 to read more about inference.
- Inference is the target skill in Units 5, 7, 14, 18, 20 and 21.

Comparison
Make comparisons about events, characters and structure in the text.

This symbol is used to represent comparison in the teaching units.

- Go to page 28 to read more about comparison.
- Comparison is the target skill in Unit 2.

Schofield & Sims Complete Comprehension 5

Structure of the teaching unit

Every **Complete Comprehension** teaching unit contains the same four components, which are explained below.

A short **Introduction** gives a synopsis of the text and highlights links to other texts in the book or to other curriculum subjects.

Teaching is split into five steps.

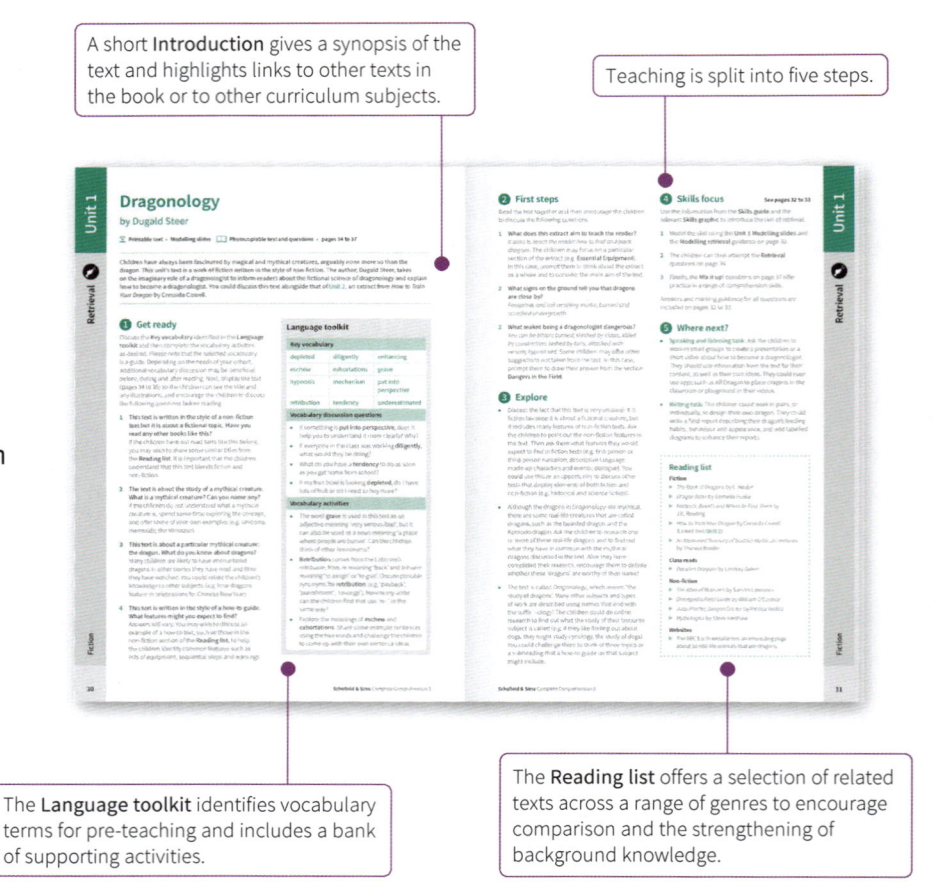

Lesson plan

The first two pages of the teaching unit allow you to see the content of the lesson at a glance. Teaching is divided into five steps to give you the flexibility to make the lesson longer or shorter according to your needs (see **Teaching with Complete Comprehension**, page 8). Taught as a whole, each unit provides the ideal balance of a holistic reading experience and discrete practice of reading skills.

The **Language toolkit** identifies vocabulary terms for pre-teaching and includes a bank of supporting activities.

The **Reading list** offers a selection of related texts across a range of genres to encourage comparison and the strengthening of background knowledge.

The **Target skill** is clearly signposted.

The **Modelling panel** provides detailed guidance for the **Let's try… questions** on the target skill. These questions are also included in the downloadable **Modelling slides**.

Skills focus

These pages support you to model the target skill for your class using the **Let's try… questions**, which are also included in the downloadable **Modelling slides** for easy display. The mark schemes for the **Pupil questions**, which the children can attempt after the modelling session, are also found here.

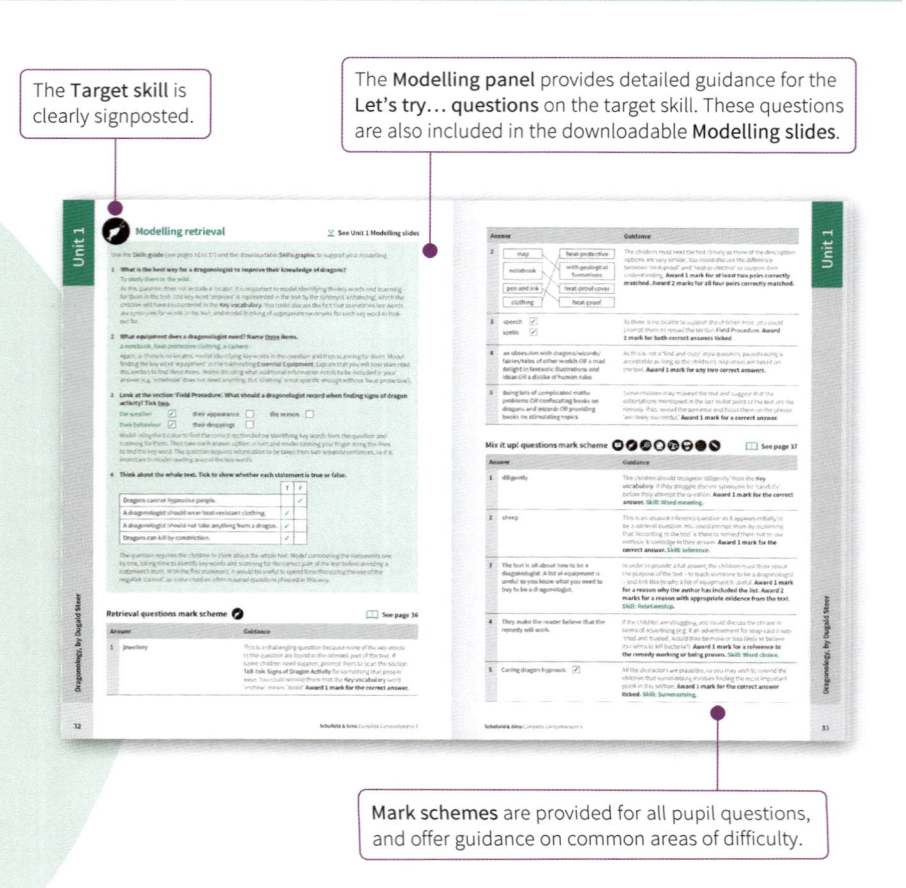

Mark schemes are provided for all pupil questions, and offer guidance on common areas of difficulty.

Schofield & Sims Complete Comprehension 5

The final two parts of each unit are aimed at the pupil. These resources may be photocopied for each child.

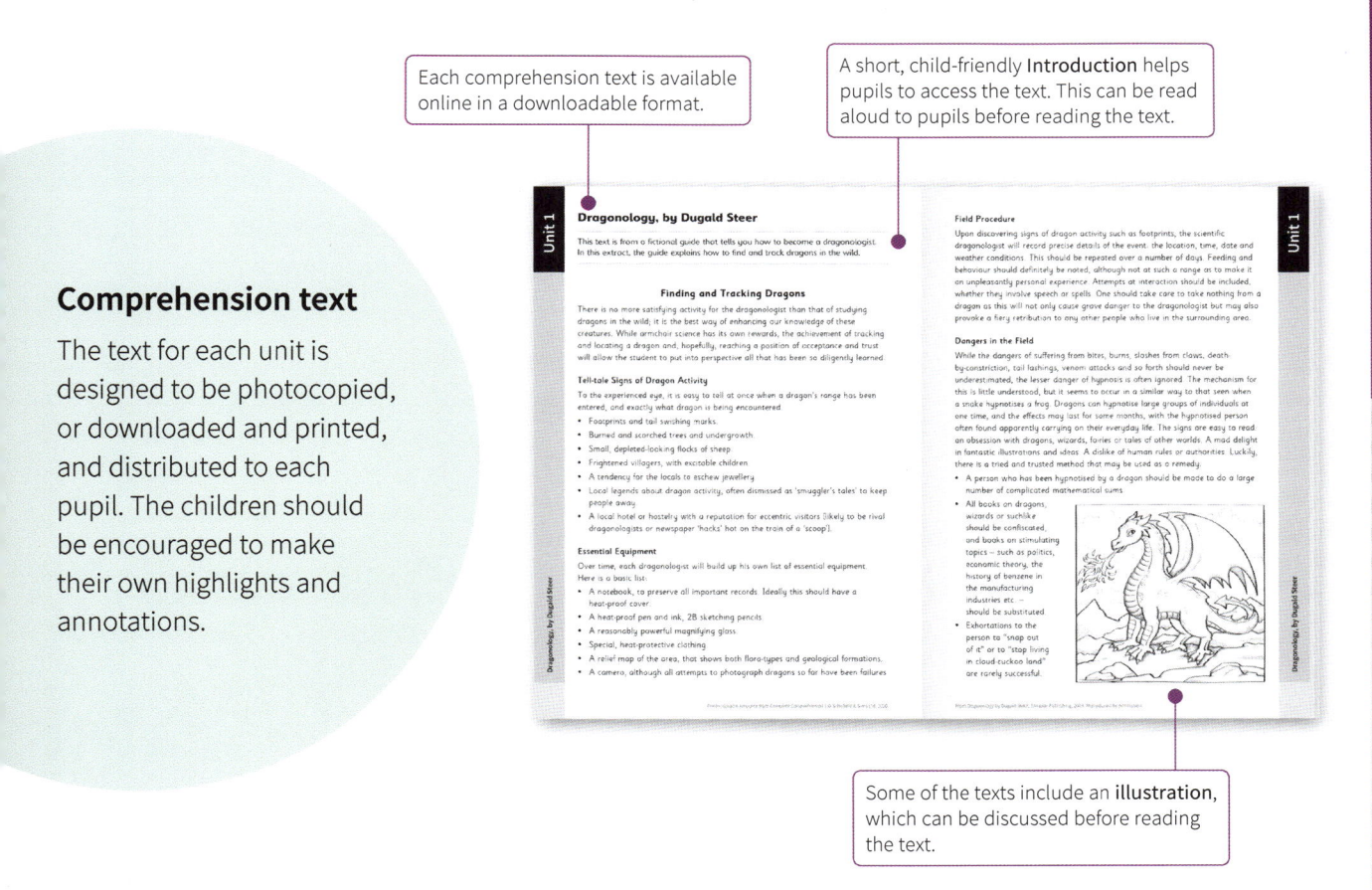

Each comprehension text is available online in a downloadable format.

A short, child-friendly **Introduction** helps pupils to access the text. This can be read aloud to pupils before reading the text.

Comprehension text

The text for each unit is designed to be photocopied, or downloaded and printed, and distributed to each pupil. The children should be encouraged to make their own highlights and annotations.

Some of the texts include an **illustration**, which can be discussed before reading the text.

The **Target skill** is clearly signposted.

The **Mix it up!** questions can be used to practise a range of skills.

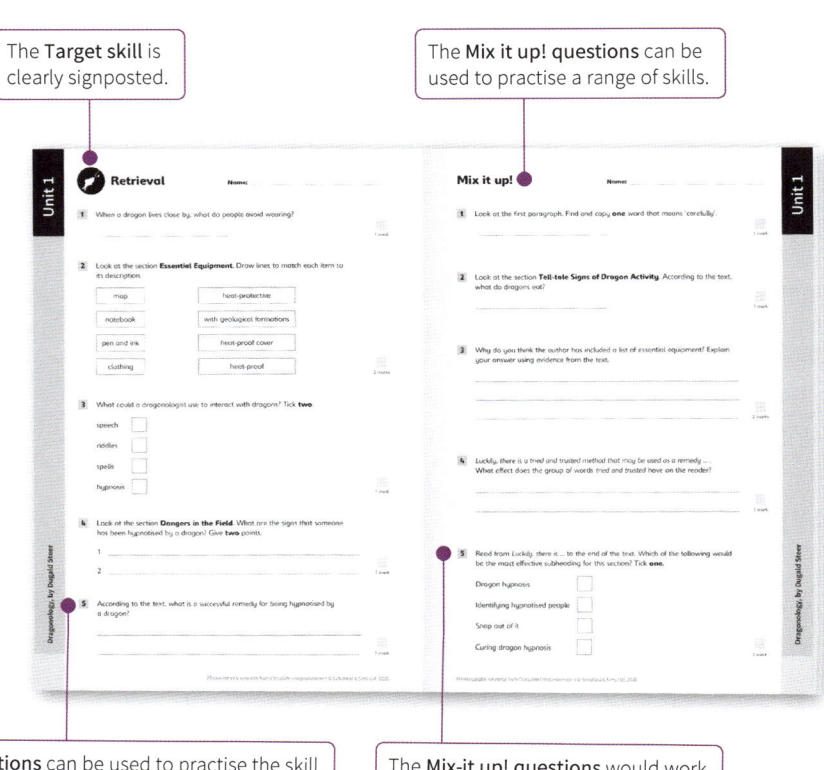

Pupil resources

Each unit includes a set of five **Target-skill questions** to enable the children to practise applying the target skill, as well as a set of **Mix it up! questions** that offer practice in a range of comprehension skills. The resources can be photocopied for each child.

The **Target-skill questions** can be used to practise the skill after modelling the **Let's try… questions** for your class.

The **Mix-it up! questions** would work well as a homework task, if desired.

Schofield & Sims Complete Comprehension 5

Introduction

Structure of the teaching unit

7

Teaching with *Complete Comprehension*

There are 21 teaching units in this book. They can be used flexibly, but it is recommended that they are taught consecutively, as they have been arranged in a specific order to promote discussion and build progression. There are seven units to complete each term, leaving the remaining weeks free to spend on other reading work. Each term's teaching units are followed by one of the three optional **Progress checks** (see **Assessment**, page 11).

Each teaching unit is divided into five steps, which are shown in the diagram below. These could be taught as separate sessions over the course of a week; alternatively, multiple steps could easily be combined into a single session.

The **Get ready**, **First steps** and **Skills focus** steps form the backbone of each teaching unit and should be completed in order. The optional **Explore** and **Where next?** steps are intended to be adapted as necessary to fit the time you have available and the needs of your cohort.

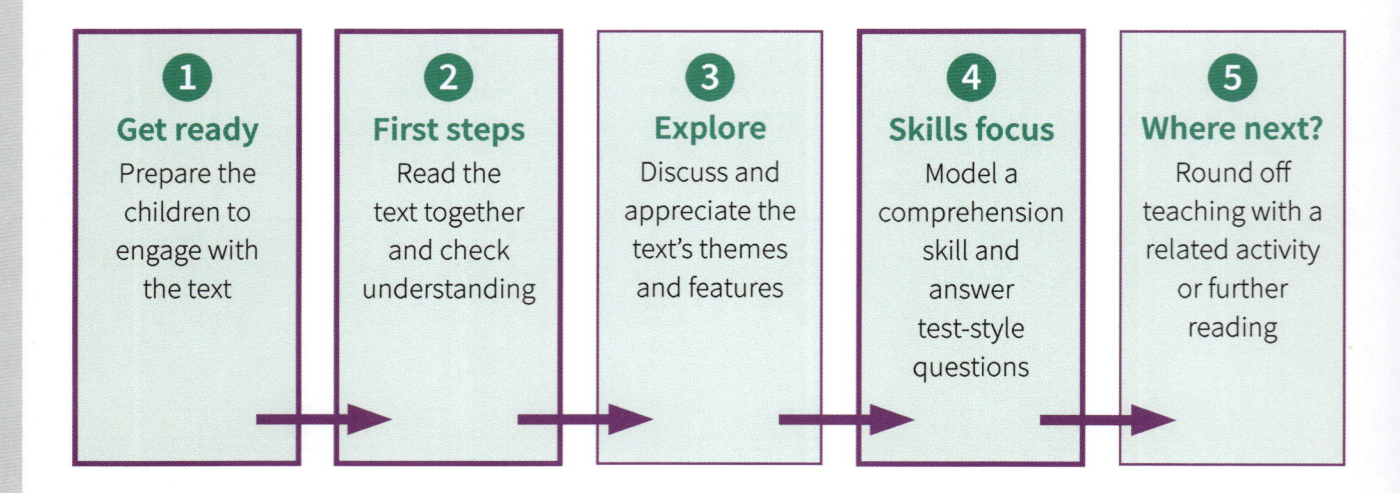

1 **Get ready** Prepare the children to engage with the text	2 **First steps** Read the text together and check understanding	3 **Explore** Discuss and appreciate the text's themes and features	4 **Skills focus** Model a comprehension skill and answer test-style questions	5 **Where next?** Round off teaching with a related activity or further reading

1 Get ready

The **Get ready** session is designed to be carried out verbally as a class.

Start by introducing pupils to the **Key vocabulary** terms in the **Language toolkit**. These are words from the text passage that are unusual or that the children may find difficult to read or understand. Use the **Vocabulary discussion questions** to encourage the children to use the words in context, referring to related or opposite words if desired. You could then use the **Vocabulary activities** to reinforce understanding.

Once your pupils are comfortable with the language in the toolkit, display the comprehension text and accompanying illustration(s) and use the **Get ready questions** to encourage the children to access their existing knowledge of the genre and subject matter. This will ensure that their minds are fully engaged when you come to read the comprehension text together.

In the **Get ready** session, the children will:

- discuss word meanings, linking new meanings to those already known
- draw on what they already know or on background information provided by the teacher
- link what they have read or heard to their own experiences.

2 First steps

Like the **Get ready** session, the **First steps** session is intended to be conducted verbally as a class.

Begin by reading the comprehension text with your class. The **First steps questions**, which should be discussed after reading the text, follow the order of the text and help you to ensure that the children have grasped the basic outline of the passage. The work done in this part of the teaching unit will prepare them to answer more complex questions in the **Skills focus** session (see page 10).

In the **First steps** session, the children will:

- listen to and discuss a wide range of poems, stories and non-fiction
- check that the text makes sense to them as they read, and correct inaccurate reading.

3 Explore

This optional session can be adapted to the needs of your cohort. It offers opportunities for further discussion and enrichment activities to bring the text to life.

The **Explore** discussion questions highlight key themes or literary features of the text. They support the development of analytical skills and encourage the children to express their opinions and listen to the views of their peers, promoting a culture of active reading.

The **Explore** enrichment activities might include using imperative verbs to guide their partner after reading an instructional text. These activities, which represent an enjoyable change of pace within the lesson, will help to build positive attitudes to reading.

In the **Explore** session, the children will:

- learn to appreciate and recite rhymes and poems
- become very familiar with key stories, fairy stories and traditional tales, retelling them and considering their particular characteristics
- participate in discussion of what is read to them, taking turns and listening to what others say.

④ Skills focus

This is the skills-based session of the teaching unit. From Year 2 onwards, the teaching unit is always structured around three sets of questions: modelled target-skill questions (the **Let's try… questions**), practice target-skill questions and mixed skill questions.

1   Model the target skill

First, introduce or recap the target skill, perhaps using one of the downloadable **Skills graphics** to focus the children's attention. The strategies suggested in the relevant pages of the **Skills guide** (see pages 14 to 29) may also be helpful at this point.

Once you have explained the skill, display the **Let's try… questions** (also available as a downloadable resource). Using the answers and modelling guidance provided on the **Skills focus** pages of each unit (see page 6), model the questions for your class. The modelling process is intended to be an interactive experience for the children. The **Modelling panel** contains prompts to help you keep them engaged and highlight the steps in your method.

2   Practise the target skill

Once the **Let's try… questions** have been discussed and completed, the children increase their familiarity with the target skill by working through the **Target-skill questions**. The children could work in small groups to complete these questions, with adult supervision as required. Answers and guidance can be found on the **Skills focus** pages of each teaching unit.

3   Practise a range of comprehension skills

The session ends with a set of **Mix it up! questions**, which offer practice in a range of the Key Stage 2 comprehension skills. These questions are a good way to build the children's confidence in recognising questions from different skill areas. They would also work well as a homework task, if desired.

> In the **Skills focus** session, the children will:
> - discuss the significance of the title and events
> - make inferences on the basis of what is said and done
> - predict what might happen on the basis of what has been read so far
> - explain clearly their understanding of what is read to them.

⑤ Where next?

This optional session includes two useful resources that encourage further engagement with the text. The **Reading list** offers a selection of related texts, categorised by genre, which could be used alongside the main unit text to build background knowledge or provide some interesting contrasts. (See **The comprehension texts**, page 12, for guidance on making contrasts between the texts within this book.)

The **Speaking and listening task** and the **Writing task** can be used to help you round off the unit. Both tasks are closely linked to the themes in the comprehension text, and act as a bridge to other areas of the English curriculum. They also represent an opportunity for the children to apply and strengthen the background knowledge they have gained in the course of the teaching unit.

> In the **Where next?** session, the children will:
> - listen to and discuss a wide range of poems, stories and non-fiction
> - develop pleasure in reading and motivation to read.

Assessment

Each **Complete Comprehension** book contains three **Progress checks** designed to be used at the end of each term. These are informal assessments, in which the children work more independently (without the support of the full teaching unit structure) to answer a set of questions that cover a range of comprehension skills. The Progress checks can be used to boost the children's confidence and provide introductory practice for the reading component of the national tests (SATs). They are designed to be used as a helpful transition towards more formal assessment resources. Full marking guidance is provided for each question.

Running the Progress checks

1. Give each child a copy of the comprehension text and spend a few minutes looking at it together, discussing the title and any illustrations. Read the pupil introduction aloud and discuss any questions the children have. You could also consider dividing the text into shorter sections if some children require further scaffolding.

2. Once all the children have read the text, you could briefly remind them of the different comprehension skills they have worked on and discuss how they can identify the questions in each skill area. You may wish to use the downloadable **Skills graphics** or refer to the **Skills guide** (see pages 14 to 29) to help with this. You could also clarify some of the vocabulary that the children have found tricky during reading, but this discussion should be brief.

3. Encourage the children to reread the text before answering the questions independently. There should be no set time allotted to this activity; allow the children to spend as long as they wish on the Progress check and encourage them to review their answers when they have finished. If they find a question challenging, support them to identify the target comprehension skill and provide them with the relevant **Skills graphic** to remind them what they need to consider when thinking about their answer.

Please note that the Progress check is a tool designed to give a brief snapshot of pupils' comprehension. It should not be used as a formal assessment but can give you an indication of areas your class are finding more challenging, which you can then use to guide your teaching.

Introduction

The comprehension texts

This book contains 24 text passages in total. The texts are arranged in themed pairs, linked by either author or subject matter. These pairings have been planned to facilitate discussion and comparison of related texts as you move through the book. They can be used alongside the external resources in each unit's **Reading list** (see page 10).

In addition to discussing the units in their intended pairs, there are many other links you can make between the texts in each book, including discussing texts of the same genre. As many of the links are cross-curricular, these extra class discussions can be a useful way to strengthen the children's background knowledge. The **Curriculum links chart** below uses shading to show the text pairs and the cross-curricular links for the texts in this book.

Curriculum links in *Complete Comprehension 5*

Unit	Title	Author	Genre	Curriculum links
1	Dragonology	Dugald Steer	Fiction	
2	How to Train Your Dragon	Cressida Cowell	Fiction	History: Vikings
3	Life in Tudor Britain	Anita Ganeri	Non-fiction *Information text*	History: Tudor period
4	Love Letter from Mary Tudor to Her Husband, Philip of Spain	Brian Moses	Poetry	History: Tudor period; Significant individuals
5	The House with Chicken Legs	Sophie Anderson	Fiction *Traditional tale*	
6	The Wizards of Once	Cressida Cowell	Fiction	
7	The Polar Bear Explorers' Club	Alex Bell	Fiction	Geography: The South Pole
Progress check 1	A Boy Called Christmas	Matt Haig	Fiction	
8	The Wolf Wilder	Katherine Rundell	Fiction	Science: Animals
9	The Wolves of Willoughby Chase	Joan Aiken	Fiction *Classic fiction*	

Unit	Title	Author	Genre	Curriculum links
10	Whale Boy	Nicola Davies	Fiction	Science: Animals
11	SeaWorld Decides to Stop Killer Whale Breeding Program	*The Guardian*	Non-fiction *Newspaper article*	Science: Animals PSHE: Caring for living things
12	Beetle Boy	M.G. Leonard	Fiction	
13	Beetle Boy: The Beetle Collector's Handbook	M.G. Leonard	Non-fiction *Narrative non-fiction*	Science: Living things and their habitats
14	The Boy at the Back of the Class	Onjali Q. Raúf	Fiction	PSHE: Respecting self and others
Progress check 2	Who are Refugees and Migrants? And Other Big Questions	Michael Rosen and Annemarie Young	Non-fiction	PSHE: Human rights; Compassion towards others; Diversity within communities
15	The Jamie Drake Equation	Christopher Edge	Fiction	Science: Earth and space
16	Once Upon a Star	James Carter	Poetry	Science: Earth and space
17	Harry Houdini	Laura Lodge	Non-fiction *Information text*	History: Significant individuals
18	The Nowhere Emporium	Ross MacKenzie	Fiction	
19	Plague!	John Farndon	Non-fiction *Information text*	History: The Black Death
20	The Island at the End of Everything	Kiran Millwood Hargrave	Fiction	
21	The London Eye Mystery	Siobhan Dowd	Fiction	
Progress check 3	The Last Chance Hotel	Nicki Thornton	Fiction	

Word meaning

See Units 4, 9, 13 and 16

Understanding word meaning

Without an understanding of words, effective reading is impossible. As Lemov (2016)[1] remarked, 'Successful reading relies on a reader's capacity to understand both a large number of words as well as the subtleties and nuances of those words, even when words change their meaning according to the setting.' Learning to define words in context is an important skill, and one that confident readers use regularly.

It is crucial that children do not simply learn to 'define' individual words, like a dictionary, but that they understand the vocabulary they encounter in the context in which it appears. The National Curriculum (2014) requires children in Key Stage 1 to understand texts by 'drawing on what they already know or on background information or vocabulary provided by the teacher', while children in Key Stage 2 must check that a text makes sense to them by 'explaining the meaning of words in context'. Developing this skill helps children to make links between known and unknown words and teaches them to use the context of a word to interpret its meaning.

Word meaning in *Complete Comprehension*

The teaching of vocabulary can be divided into two key types: explicit and implicit instruction.[2]

Explicit instruction is the teaching of specific words and phrases that are necessary to either comprehend a specific text or comprehend meaning more generally *in advance of reading*.

Implicit instruction is the teaching of strategies that help learners assess their understanding of words *as they read*.

Word meaning is the target skill of several teaching units in each **Complete Comprehension** book. In addition, both types of vocabulary instruction are addressed in every teaching unit: explicit instruction is the focus of the **Get ready** session, in which **Key vocabulary** terms are taught before reading the comprehension passage. Implicit instruction underlies the work done in the subsequent **Explore** and **Skills focus** sessions (see pages 8 to 11 for a full description of the teaching sequence).

Word meaning questions usually require children to make links between synonyms. In **Complete Comprehension**, questions may be worded as follows:

- Which word is closest in meaning to…? Tick **one**.
- Explain what the word(s) … tell(s) you about…
- What does the word … mean in this sentence/line?
- Underline the word which tells you that…
- Draw lines to match each word to its meaning.
- Find and copy **one** word/a group of words that means the same as…

Often, questions that assess the skill of word meaning only require the child to find out one piece of information. However, this information does not usually come directly from the text but must be deduced using vocabulary knowledge. Word meaning questions thus sometimes require the use of other comprehension skills, such as inference (see page 20) to reach the correct answer.

Key challenges

As they read, many children skip over words they do not understand, losing meaning in the process. Teaching children to note down and ask about any vocabulary they do not understand when reading is therefore crucial.

Many children have relatively shallow vocabulary knowledge, only understanding a word when it appears in a familiar context. For example, many will have no trouble with 'It was *raining*' but will struggle with 'The money was *raining down*'. It is important to provide opportunities for children to deepen their knowledge by investigating words in a range of contexts.

Children with less secure vocabularies may also struggle to generate linked vocabulary (e.g. knowing that 'repeat', 'redo' and 'recycle' are all connected by the prefix 're–', which refers to doing something again). Incorporating the etymology and categorisation strategies described on page 15 when you are teaching will support the children to make these connections.

Strategies for developing word meaning

- **Context clues:** Reading around the target word or sentence to gain a general idea of the context can help children make an educated guess about the word's meaning. However, it is important to note that using context clues can also lead to confusion, as authors generally do not write with the primary aim of supporting readers to make meaning. When you use this strategy, the children should only be directed to words with a helpful context. When teaching vocabulary explicitly, it is a good idea to introduce a new word within multiple contexts before modelling how to use the specific context to construct meaning. The vocabulary discussion questions in each unit's **Language toolkit** (see page 6) help the children to understand the **Key vocabulary** terms in context.

- **Substitution:** Encourage the children to make substitutions to help them check the meaning of a word. If the target word is replaced by a new word, does the sentence still make sense? Is the new word a synonym, or has the meaning of the sentence changed? If the sentence still 'works', how does this information help the children to answer the question?

- **Shades of meaning:** When the children are investigating possible synonyms for unfamiliar vocabulary, ensure that they understand that a synonym is similar to, but not the same as, the original word. Asking the children to place a group of synonyms on a scale from the weakest to the strongest can help them to appreciate nuances.

- **Categorisation:** For vocabulary knowledge to become deeper and more securely embedded, the children need to be able to categorise vocabulary. For example, knowing that 'zebra' and 'mongoose' both refer to animals, and that 'angry' and 'exasperated' both describe negative feelings, will support the children to make essential links as they read. Providing them with word cards to sort into categories can help to build up this understanding.

- **Etymology:** Children need to be taught the meanings of root words, prefixes and suffixes, and should be encouraged to use these to help them make educated guesses about word meaning. Throughout **Complete Comprehension**, and especially at Key Stage 2, etymology activities are included in the **Vocabulary activities** section of the **Language toolkit**.

Modelling word meaning

When modelling word meaning for your class using the **Let's try… questions** (see page 6), the steps below may be useful. Specific modelling guidance is also provided in the relevant teaching units.

1. Read aloud. Model reading the whole question carefully.
2. Identify and underline the key words in the question.
3. Model scanning the text efficiently to locate each key word, or related key words, from the question.
4. Demonstrate reading the sentences before and after each key word to look for context clues.
5. Make links aloud between the key words and their synonyms. Model using this knowledge to help you gauge the meaning.
6. Formulate an answer. Model checking that it answers the question.

---

1. Lemov, D. (2016) *Reading Reconsidered*. San Francisco: Jossey Bass, p. 251.
2. Lemov (2016), pp. 253–256.

Retrieval

See Units 1, 8, 15, 17 and 19

Understanding retrieval

Retrieval is the act of efficiently locating, and reproducing, important details in a text. Other reading skills cannot be mastered without a knowledge of retrieval, which is often seen as the most important reading skill.

The National Curriculum (2014) requires children in Key Stage 1 to 'identify/explain key aspects of fiction and non-fiction texts', while children in Key Stage 2 must 'retrieve and record information/identify key details from fiction and non-fiction'. Strong retrieval skills are essential for effective comprehension.

Retrieval in *Complete Comprehension*

Retrieval relies on a secure understanding of the information in a text. The key to successful retrieval is remembering that the information required to answer the question is always stated explicitly in the text. The children must be encouraged to focus on the text rather than relying on memory or on their extrinsic knowledge (in contrast to other comprehension skills, such as inference – see page 20).

Because it is so important, retrieval is the focus skill in many of the units in each **Complete Comprehension** book. This allows the children to practise retrieval in many different contexts. In addition, further retrieval practice is built into every teaching unit through the questions in the **First steps** session (see page 9) of the lesson. These straightforward questions encourage the children to develop the habit of looking back at the text after their initial reading to pick out key details. This helps them to generate a 'mental model' of the text, which will give them a better idea of where to look for answers when they encounter more formal questions in the **Skills focus** session (see page 10).

In **Complete Comprehension**, retrieval questions often begin with a 'question word', such as 'who', 'what', 'where', 'when', 'how' or 'which', that relates to the target information (e.g. 'who' for a character; 'when' for a time). Often, some of the words used in retrieval questions are taken from the text, which provides an important signpost to readers of where in the text the answer is likely to be found. The children should be encouraged to pay attention to the number of details they have been asked to give, as retrieval questions will often ask for more than one piece of information.

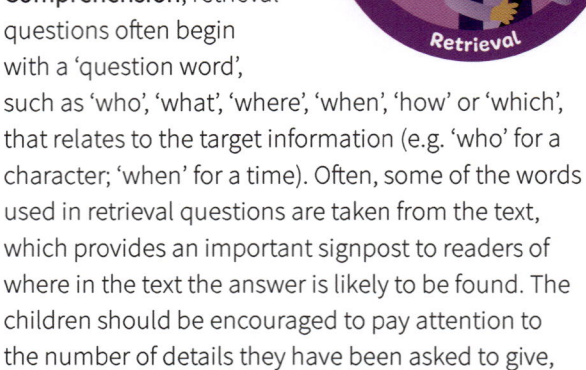

In **Complete Comprehension**, retrieval questions are often worded as follows:

- Who…/What…/When…/ Where…/How…/ Which…?
- Give **two**…
- According to the text…
- Find and copy **two** examples of … from the text.
- Draw lines to match each statement…
- Tick to show whether the statement is true or false.
- Tick to show whether the statement(s) below is/are fact or opinion.

It is important to note that retrieval questions will sometimes require the children to draw on other comprehension skills, such as inference (see page 20), to reach the correct answer.

Key challenges

Some children find retrieval difficult; they try to remember the information or use their extrinsic knowledge to answer questions, instead of referring back to the text. When teaching retrieval, you must emphasise the fact that the information will always be found in the text.

Strategies for developing retrieval

- **Identify key words:** To retrieve information, the children need to be able to identify key words in the question before locating them in the text. This should be modelled explicitly by looking at the question, removing any extraneous information, and then deciding on the key words needed. Sometimes, the key words in the question will be synonymous with words in the text. It is important to model discussing possible synonyms that the text may use instead of the key words.

- **Scanning:** Scanning is the process of rapidly searching the text for specific information, such as a key word. This is a fundamental reading skill that should be prioritised and practised. It is important to model a systematic approach by scanning every line of the text, perhaps using your finger or a ruler on the page. Activities that do not require the children to decode may be helpful for developing scanning skills. The children could use 'search and find' texts, such as the *Where's Wally?* books, to practise scanning. Alternatively, you could provide a section of text and challenge the children to see how many words, letter strings or punctuation marks they can find in it within a given time.

- **Point out the evidence/Fastest finger first:** To emphasise the importance of always referring to the text rather than falling back on extrinsic knowledge, challenge the children to 'point out the evidence' for their answer, for example by highlighting, circling or underlining the text. You could also play games such as 'Fastest finger first', in which players race to physically place their finger on the word(s) in the text that answer a question or provide a relevant detail.

Modelling retrieval

When modelling retrieval for your class using the **Let's try… questions** (see page 6), the steps below may be useful. Specific modelling guidance is also provided in the relevant teaching units.

1. Read the question aloud. Remind the children that they should resist the temptation to draw conclusions based on their own knowledge, and model focusing your attention back to the words in the text.

2. Locate the key words in your concept or question.

3. Scan the text for those key words, or related key words, and highlight or underline them.

4. If necessary, read around the key words to look for context clues.

5. Find the information you need in the text and highlight or underline it.

6. Check that the information you have found answers the question.

Summarising

See Units 3 and 12

Understanding summarising

Once the skill of sequencing has been embedded in Key Stage 1, the children can progress to the Key Stage 2 skill of summarising. To sequence, the children use their knowledge of the whole text to order the events within it. To summarise, they use their knowledge of the whole text and its sequence to identify the most important points and reformulate them concisely. The National Curriculum (2014) requires children to be competent at 'summarising the main ideas drawn from more than one paragraph' and 'identifying key details that support the main ideas'. A confident reader will automatically summarise key information, retaining the most important information and discarding extraneous details.

Summarising in *Complete Comprehension*

Summarising requires a secure understanding of the content of separate sections of a text as well as the text as a whole. Summarising is the target skill for several teaching units across the **Complete Comprehension** series for Key Stage 2. In addition, the **First steps** questions that appear in every unit (see page 9) provide extra summarising practice, as they prompt the children to think about the main events in a text immediately after they first read it. These questions focus on the type of details that the children should look for when attempting to summarise a text (e.g. the number of characters in the extract; their relative importance; main events and their chronology).

In **Complete Comprehension**, summarising questions are often worded as follows:

- What…?/Which…?/Who…?/When…?/Where…?
- Which word best describes…? Tick **one**.
- Which subheading best summarises the content of paragraph X? Tick **one**.
- Look at paragraph X. What is the main point of this paragraph?
- Find and copy/Underline a group of words to summarise the content of paragraph X.
- Which of the following would be the most effective (alternative) title for the whole extract? Tick **one**.
- What is the overall theme of the text?
- Look at the last paragraph. Summarise why…
- Summarise what the first verse tells us about…
- Match each verse/paragraph to its idea/topic.
- What does this sentence tell you about the content of the paragraph?
- Number the statements/events to show the order in which they happen in the text.

Key challenges

Children tend to find summarising a challenge for two main reasons. First, because it requires a good understanding of the entire text: for those who have poor working memories, or who find decoding a challenge, the cognitive load of summarising this much material can be too heavy. Some children also find it difficult to sum up the key points concisely once they have identified them because they struggle to eliminate extraneous detail.

Strategies for developing summarising

- **Skim-reading:** Skim-reading means reading a text quickly to assimilate the main ideas. It enables the children to gain an overview of what each paragraph of a text is about. This helps them to generate a mental map of the text and predict where information is most likely to be found. This strategy is particularly helpful when reading non-fiction. You could introduce skim-reading by showing the children the text with most lines blacked out, so that only the title and the first sentence of each paragraph are visible. Discuss what this content tells the reader about the paragraph. Encourage the children to use the first line of a paragraph to 'get the gist' of the text before reading it in more detail. It is also worth reminding them to look at titles, subheadings, illustrations, captions and words that are formatted in bold or italics.

- **Captions:** Children often struggle to retain the sequence and content of a text while reading. Model annotating each paragraph with a brief caption. This method will support the children to summarise as they read and help them to order events and information.

- **'Somebody Wanted But So Then':** This is a useful structure to use when summarising the events in a story, because it is easy to remember. Model the technique using a well-known story, as in the example below:
    - **Somebody:** Cinderella.
    - **Wanted:** To go to the ball and escape her evil stepmother.
    - **But:** The magic ran out before she could live happily ever after.
    - **So:** She went back to her ordinary life.
    - **Then:** The prince found her and they lived happily ever after.

- **Cut it down:** Once the children have learnt how to write a summary, challenge them to make it more concise by removing all unnecessary information. Using a summary you have prepared yourself or one written by a pupil, work as a group to remove any extraneous detail. As you read through, make sure that you also draw attention to any examples of particularly concise writing.

- **Limits:** When the children have developed some confidence in using this skill, you could add another level of challenge by giving them a limit to the number of words or characters they can use to summarise a text or concept.

Modelling summarising

When modelling summarising for your class using the **Let's try… questions** (see page 6), the steps below may be useful. Specific modelling guidance is also provided in the relevant teaching units.

1. Read the question aloud.

2. Model deciding whether the question is asking you to give a summary of the whole text or of a specific part of the text.

3. If the question asks for a general summary, model skim-reading the whole text to remind yourself of the key points. If you are summarising part of a text, model scanning the text to find that part, using the key words and/or the locator from the question, and reminding yourself of the main points.

4. Model formulating a concise summary or answering the question using your summarising skill.

5. Model checking your summary for non-essential details and removing them.

6. Finally, model checking that your final answer matches the question.

Inference

See Units 5, 7, 14, 18, 20 and 21

Understanding inference

Inference skills are essential for understanding our world: we use them whenever we gauge other people's emotions using their facial expressions or tone of voice. Children will therefore have some ability to infer even before they learn to decode.

Inference is often described as the ability to 'read between the lines' or 'find clues' in a text. However, it can be more helpfully defined as the skill of using both evidence from the text and our background knowledge to come to a reasonable conclusion.

Academics have separated inference-making into a number of distinct categories (Kispal, 2008).[3] However, most recognise two main categories of inference:

Coherence inferences are necessary for basic comprehension. They can be formulated from understanding a text's cohesive devices, such as pronouns, or from linking background knowledge to the text. For example, from the sentence 'Maggie loved playing catch but sometimes she refused to bring the ball back', we could infer that 'Maggie', 'she' and 'her' are the same (using cohesive devices), and that Maggie is probably a dog (using background knowledge).

Elaborative inferences are not necessary for basic comprehension, but they make a text more interesting. An elaborative inference might be a prediction or speculation that the reader makes about a character or the consequences of an action. For example, from the sentence 'Maggie loved playing catch but sometimes she refused to give the ball back to her owner', we could infer that, because she sometimes refused to bring back the ball, Maggie might be a puppy. Elaborative inferences depend on background knowledge and are thus more demanding than coherence inferences.

The National Curriculum (2014) requires pupils in Key Stage 1 to be 'making inferences on the basis of what is being said and done'. At Key Stage 2, learners must rely on their background knowledge, 'drawing inferences such as inferring characters' feelings, thoughts and motives'.

Inference in *Complete Comprehension*

Inference is the focus skill in a high proportion of the units in each **Complete Comprehension** book, to allow the children to practise inference in different contexts.

In **Complete Comprehension**, inference questions often include the phrase 'How/Why do you think…?'. It is a good idea to draw the children's attention to this wording to help them remember that they need to make a judgement using their own knowledge *in addition to* the text, rather than limiting themselves to details explicitly mentioned in the text, as they would when answering a retrieval (see page 16) or summarising (see page 18) question. Once the children's inference skills have begun to embed, most questions will require them to provide evidence to support their inferences. You should explore the expectations of these questions with the children.

In **Complete Comprehension**, inference questions are often worded as follows:

- Why…/How…/Which…?
- Why/How/What do you think…? Explain your answer.
- How can you tell…?
- Explain why…
- Give two reasons…
- True or false…
- Think about the whole text. What impression do you get of…? Give **one** impression and **one** piece of evidence.

More demanding inference questions are sometimes structured using a grid format to support children's responses. It is also important to note that inference questions always require the use of other comprehension skills, such as retrieval (see page 16), to reach the correct answer.

Key challenges

For many children, inference is a real challenge. This is because they are required to make an intuitive leap to move from what they *know* (direct evidence that they can see in the text) to what they *think* (the conclusion they come to after locating and assessing the evidence). An understanding of the text, robust vocabulary skills and strong background knowledge are essential prerequisites for successful inference-making. The skills of word meaning (see page 14) and retrieval (see page 16) must therefore be embedded before inference skills can fully develop.

Strategies for developing inference

- **Think-alouds:** Confident readers make inferences automatically as they read. However, when teaching children to infer, you should slow down and model your thought process. 'Think-alouds' (statements that verbalise your thought process) can be useful. For example, you could think aloud to model dividing your thoughts into two types: 'what I know' and 'what I think' (e.g. 'From the text, I know that… This makes me think…'). Think-alouds can also be used to model refining an inference (e.g. 'I thought that… because… but… so…'), and can be incorporated into the strategies below.

- **Inference check:** Marzano (2010)[4] suggested that teachers could support inference-making by modelling asking the following four questions:

    1. 'What is my inference?'
    2. 'What did I use to make my inference?'
    3. 'How good was my thinking?'
    4. 'Do I need to change my thinking?'

    These questions could be used in the strategy above.

- **Objects and visual representations:** Using objects and images that relate to the text can be helpful when exploring inference, as this eliminates the need to decode and therefore reduces cognitive load. You could use images to represent characters or scenes from the text, and model inference by adding thought or speech bubbles to them. Alternatively, you could assign objects to characters from a text. For example, if you were reading 'The Three Bears', you could provide different porridge bowls and ask the children to decide which character each bowl is most likely to belong to.

- **Real-life scenarios:** Many children will need prompting to connect the inferences they make in everyday life with inferences made while reading. One strategy is to use models such as 'think-alouds' to explore real-life scenarios, using clues to make inferences about people's preferences, location or relationship. For instance, you could listen to a conversation or watch a video clip showing two people and ask the children what they can infer about their relationship (e.g. 'Do you think these people are friends or enemies? How can you tell from what they do and what they say?').

- **Graphic organisers:** These are especially helpful when the children are asked to provide evidence or an explanation for their inferences. For example, the children could complete a 'I can see…I know…I think' chart: a table with three columns in which they first record what they can see in the text or image. They then record what they know from the text, and use this to write what they think (the inference). It is important to explicitly model the thinking process behind this strategy.

Modelling inference

When modelling the skill of inference for your class using the **Let's try… questions** (see page 6), the steps below may be useful. Specific modelling guidance is also provided in the teaching units.

1. Read the question aloud.
2. Locate the key words in the question. Scan the text for those key words, or related key words, and highlight or underline them.
3. Read around the key words to look for context clues.
4. Discuss what the text tells you about the key words.
5. Model using this information to make an inference. This might involve relating the ideas in the question to your own experiences to model the use of background knowledge.
6. Model justifying your inference with evidence from the text.
7. Check that the information answers the question.

---

3 Kispal, A. (2008) 'Effective Teaching of Inference Skills for Reading'. *Literature Review*. Research Report DCSF-RR031, National Foundation for Educational Research.

4 Marzano, R.J. (2010) 'The Art and Science of Teaching/Teaching Inference'. *Educational Leadership,* 67(7), 80–81.

Prediction

See Unit 6

Understanding prediction

Prediction is the skill of being able to make inferences (see page 20) about what is likely to happen later in a text. In a fiction extract, this might relate to a character's actions; in a non-fiction extract, it might be about the type of information that will be found in the next part of the text. A skilled reader makes predictions automatically, finding links between known and new information as they read. The National Curriculum (2014) requires pupils in Key Stage 1 to predict 'what might happen on the basis of what has been read so far' while Key Stage 2 children need to predict 'what might happen from details stated and implied'. The ability to make predictions requires a thorough understanding of a passage. To make a plausible prediction, the reader must be able to select details from the text and use these, and their own background knowledge, to decide what is likely to happen.

Prediction in *Complete Comprehension*

One teaching unit in each **Complete Comprehension** book focuses on prediction. In addition, the children's prediction skills are engaged in the **Get ready** session of every unit. These questions encourage the children to use the title and any subheadings, illustration(s) and their own background knowledge to help them predict what a passage will be about. Following on from this, the **Mix it up! questions** in the **Skills focus** session offer frequent opportunities to practise and refine this important skill. (See pages 6 to 11 for a complete guide to the teaching unit.)

As prediction requires the use of inference skills, it is not surprising that prediction questions are often worded similarly to inference questions. Once the children's prediction skills have begun to embed, most questions will require them to justify their predictions using the text. In **Complete Comprehension**, prediction questions may be worded as follows:

- Who…/What…/When…/Where…/How…/Which…?
- Predict…
- Imagine…
- Which is most likely…?

The skill of prediction is usually assessed through tick-box or extended response questions: however, on occasion, it may also be assessed through other question types, which may require additional teacher modelling.

Key challenges

Often, children with poor comprehension skills will be able to formulate a prediction, but their predictions will not be sufficiently plausible, and may not be linked to the original text. You should remind all children to use the text to inform any prediction and underlying inference; this can also help when answering prediction questions that require additional justification, which can be challenging. (For more information on the challenges of teaching and using inference, see page 20.)

Strategies for developing prediction

- **'Think-alouds':** One way to support children to predict is to use 'think-alouds' (statements that verbalise your thought process). You can use think-alouds at different points to model prediction:
  - Before reading (e.g. 'I've found this book and when I look at the title/illustrations I think… because… so that might mean… I could predict…').
  - While reading (e.g. 'I wonder what's going to happen next. I know… So that makes me think… I could predict…').
  - After reading (e.g. 'While I was reading I predicted… I was right because/I was incorrect because…').

- **Multiple predictions:** Confident readers not only make predictions, but they also constantly re-evaluate and adjust their predictions as they read. One way to help the children develop this skill is to start from a narrow viewpoint: for example, you could show them a small part of an illustration or a phrase from the text and ask them to make a prediction based on what they can see, then show them more of the picture/text and ask them to make another prediction. This will help them to adjust their first prediction as they read.

- **Making links:** Making plausible predictions involves making links to other known texts, characters and information. Although predictions should be made with reference to a specific text, extrinsic knowledge relating to the wider genre or subject matter of the text is also important. For instance, if you are reading 'Cinderella' with your class and the children have read other fairy tales, they will know that in a fairy tale the main character usually lives happily ever after, and this could have a bearing on any predictions they make. As part of the 'think-aloud' process detailed above, you could model making links to known texts and different types of text. In **Complete Comprehension**, each extract has at least one linked text; listed on pages 12 to 13 and often referred to in each unit's introduction, these links are designed to help you make connections with the children's existing knowledge. Each unit also includes a **Reading list** of related texts.

- **Graphic organisers:** Once the children have started to make predictions, you could use graphic organisers to help them organise their ideas and scaffold their justifications. It is important to explicitly model the thinking process behind this strategy. Examples of useful graphic organisers for prediction include:

    - 'I predict… because': The children complete a chart that asks them to record their predictions and their justification.

    - 'What has happened… What will happen… What actually happened': The children complete a chart by recording event(s) from the text and their predictions about what will happen next. You could then give them copies of the source text and allow them to read beyond the extract and record what actually happened.

Modelling prediction

When modelling the skill of prediction for your class using the **Let's try… questions** (see page 6), the steps below may be useful. Specific modelling guidance is also provided in the teaching units.

1. Read the question aloud. Point out the need to look back at the text rather than making a hasty prediction that does not relate closely enough to the text – the children need to think about what is *likely* to happen rather than what they *want* to happen.

2. Identify the key words in the question. Scan the text for those key words, or related key words, and highlight or underline them.

3. Read around the key words to look for context clues.

4. Discuss what you know already.

5. Discuss what you think may happen next, linking this back to the text.

6. Model justifying your prediction. This might involve relating the ideas in the question to your own experiences to model using your background knowledge.

7. Check that the information in your answer matches the question.

Relationship

See Unit 11

Understanding relationship

Understanding the relationship between elements of a text and the overall text structure is one of the skills of a confident reader. The children must be able to understand the structure and theme of a text in order to derive meaning from it – for example, through appreciating how the organisation of the text helps the reader to understand its content; or how the author builds up atmosphere in a suspenseful narrative. The National Curriculum (2014) requires Key Stage 2 pupils to read 'books that are structured in different ways' to become accustomed to 'identifying and discussing themes and conventions' and 'how language, structure and presentation contribute to meaning'. As Oakhill et al. (2015) notes, an understanding of the relationships within a text 'supports comprehension, especially that of new texts, [and] helps the reader to establish critical relations between information'.[5]

Relationship in *Complete Comprehension*

This skill of relationship requires a secure overall understanding of the text. Children must possess a deep knowledge of a range of text structures and themes: they need to be able to appreciate that a quest story or a mystery will be structured differently from other fiction narratives, and that a non-fiction, instructional text will have a different effect on the reader than that of a traditional information text. The building blocks for understanding relationship are incorporated into every **Complete Comprehension** book through regular opportunities for discussing theme and structure in the **Get ready** and **Explore** sessions of each unit (see pages 8 to 9). In addition, relationship is the target skill of one unit in each **Complete Comprehension** book aimed at Key Stage 2. It is also regularly tested in the **Mix it up! questions**.

Relationship questions can be structured in a variety of ways. The children should be encouraged to justify their responses with evidence. In **Complete Comprehension,** relationship questions are often worded as follows:

- Who…?/What…?/When…?/Where…?/How…?/Which…?/Why…?
- At this point…
- At what point in the text…?
- Who do you think this information is for?
- Why do you think the first sentence in paragraph X was included?
- What does this sentence tell you about…?
- What do you think is the author's opinion of…?
- How has the text been written to make you want to find out more? Give **one** point and **one** piece of evidence.
- Why has the author structured the text in this way?
- Which event in the text led to…?
- How do X's feelings change over the course of the story? Give **two** changes.
- How does the author encourage you to read on at the end of this extract? Explain your answer using evidence from the text.
- Why do you think this text has been written?
- Look at the first sentence. What effect do you think the author is trying to create?

Relationship is most often assessed through extended response questions. However, sometimes question types that require additional teacher modelling will be used. It is important to note that relationship questions require the use of other comprehension skills, such as inference (see page 20), to reach the correct answer.

Key challenges

Although readers automatically make judgements about the relationship between different elements of a text as they read, these can be challenging to articulate, as they require a solid understanding of the content of the whole text. Children often find relationship challenging because they do not understand the text well enough. Overall understanding should therefore be prioritised before attempting to introduce the analysis of relationship. There is also a correlation between poor overall comprehension and a person's understanding of text structures.[6] To remedy this, teachers should explicitly teach and make reference to a variety of text structures (e.g. for fiction texts: quest/mystery stories versus fairy tales/comic stories; for non-fiction texts: information texts as compared to instructional texts), both when teaching with **Complete Comprehension** and elsewhere across the curriculum.

Strategies for developing relationship

- **Remembering content:** In order to make an informed judgement about the relationship between parts of a text, the children must understand the structure of the text itself. Research by Paris and Paris (2007)[7] shows that when pupils are taught techniques to remember the key elements of narrative, such as the 'five-finger trick' (thumb – 'who', first finger – 'where', second finger – 'beginning', third finger – 'middle', fourth finger – 'end'), they can retell stories more fully and show improved narrative comprehension. It is important to discuss the structure of narrative and non-narrative texts, both in the **Get ready** and **First steps** sessions of **Complete Comprehension** and whenever you read texts as a class.

- **Plotting points:** Relationship questions sometimes focus on a character's actions at a particular point in the text. While this relies on the ability to sequence and structure the text, you can support the skill of relationship by modelling how to plot key points on a graph. You could plot a character's emotions throughout the text on an axis of emotion, or use a graph to show how one character's actions affect another.

- **Graphic organisers:** Once the children can recognise different text structures, they may find it helpful to use a graphic organiser to explore these structures. These can range from the more general (e.g. sequencing story plot points on a storyboard) to the more specific (e.g. making a plan for a non-chronological report). It is important to explicitly model both the thinking process behind this strategy, and the activity itself. Examples of useful graphic organisers for relationship include:
  - Storyboards: The children draw six key events from the story and write captions for them.
  - Mind maps: The children create a branching diagram to show related ideas in a text.
  - Flowcharts: The children create a diagram to show cause and effect in the text.
  - Top hat diagram: The children complete a hat-shaped chart to compare and contrast what they know about two texts. They summarise the differences in the 'brim', and then note any similarities in the raised part of the 'hat'.
  - Genre-specific skeleton: The children create a graphic representation to show the structure of the text (e.g. for a non-chronological report, they might include boxes for the introduction, each subheading and the conclusion).

Modelling relationship

When modelling the skill of relationship for your class using the **Let's try… questions** (see page 6), the steps below may be useful. Specific modelling guidance is also provided in the relevant teaching units.

1. Read the question aloud.
2. Locate the key words in the question. At this point, you could talk about the genre and theme of the text and about how what you know could help you to answer the question.
3. Scan the text for those key words, or related key words, and highlight or underline them.
4. Read around the key words for context clues.
5. Discuss how the information relates to the text as a whole. Does it help to communicate a certain theme?
6. Discuss why it relates to the text.
7. Check that the information in your answer matches the question.

---

5   Oakhill, J., Cain, K. & Elbro, C. (2015) *Understanding and Teaching Reading Comprehension*. London: Routledge, p. 92.
6   Oakhill et al. (2015), p. 90.
7   Paris, A. & Paris, S. (2007) 'Teaching narrative comprehension strategies to first-graders'. *Cognition and Instruction, 25*(1), 1–44.

Word choice

See Unit 10

Understanding word choice

Word choice is the skill of understanding why an author has chosen to use specific words or phrases, and of being able to comment on the effect that this language has on the text and the reader. The National Curriculum (2014) requires pupils to be adept at 'discussing words and phrases that capture the reader's interest and imagination' and able to 'discuss and evaluate how authors use language, including figurative language, considering the impact on the reader'. Understanding word choice is a key reading skill and one that is crucial for developing pupils' writing abilities.

Word choice in *Complete Comprehension*

Word choice relies on a good understanding of the vocabulary in a text. Once the children have grasped the meaning of the words used in a text, they can then be supported to think about why those particular words were used: what was the author hoping to achieve? This skill can be developed through carefully modelled discussion of the effect of words and phrases in every text you share in the classroom. The children should be encouraged to focus on the *effect* of the word choice, rather than on the meaning created by that choice (see page 14 for more about the skill of word meaning).

In **Complete Comprehension**, the **Explore** and **Where next?** sessions (see pages 9 to 11) often relate to the author's use of language. Discussion questions are provided to help you and your class examine the effect of figurative language and atmosphere on the reader.

Often, the words used in a word choice question will be found in the text itself. Sometimes, a quotation will be given for pupils to find in the text. The author or writer is often referred to directly in the question (e.g. 'Why does the poet use the word … to describe…').

In **Complete Comprehension**, word choice questions are often worded as follows:

- Give **two** things this word/group of words tells you about…
- The author often uses the word … to describe… Why do you think the author does this?
- What impression does the group of words … give you of…? Give **one** impression and **one** piece of evidence.
- Find and copy **one** word/group of words that tells you…
- What is the effect of using repetition in this line/paragraph/text?
- What does the group of words … tell you about how … is feeling?
- What does the word/group of words … tell you about the character of…?
- What does this group of words tell us about…? Tick **one**.
- What effect does this choice of words have on the reader?
- How does the author's choice of words here add to the atmosphere at the end of the story?
- What impact does this sentence have on the reader? Explain your answer using evidence from the text.

Sometimes word choice questions require the use of other comprehension skills, such as inference (see page 20), to reach the correct answer.

Key challenges

The skill of word choice relies on robust vocabulary knowledge: after all, one cannot make a judgement about the effect of the author's choice of language without understanding its meaning. If the children are finding vocabulary challenging, you could refer to the word meaning strategies on page 15.

Even pupils with large vocabularies often find discussing the impact of language challenging. However, by reading widely in class and discussing the literary effects in a wide range of texts, you can support them to become more familiar with this kind of analysis.

Strategies for developing word choice

- **Discussion and think-alouds:** The children need to become comfortable with exploring the effect of words and phrases in the text. Providing regular opportunities to discuss texts, including modelling thinking aloud about why a text is effective and what impact certain word choices have on the reader, will help them to grow in confidence. You can do this with every text you explore as a class, including all the texts in **Complete Comprehension**.

- **Categorisation by effect:** For vocabulary knowledge to become deeper and more secure, the children need to be able to categorise vocabulary *by effect*. For example, they might collect adjectives that show that a character is elderly, or vocabulary that builds tension. Providing them with word cards to sort into categories can help to build their understanding.

- **Figurative language:** Although word choice questions often deal with the effect of single words, the focus can sometimes be on the effect of figurative language, including alliteration, metaphor, personification and simile. It is crucial that the children are exposed to numerous examples of each of these concepts so that they learn to identify them in new texts.

- **'What I know' and 'What I think':** To reach a conclusion about a word's impact, the children should always use the sentences before and after the target word or phrase for context. A useful strategy to help with this is the 'What I know…What I think' model (similar to the chart mentioned on page 21). When using this strategy to explore word choice, 'what I know' refers to the word(s) and who/what they are about, while 'what I think' encourages the children to make an inference about the words' effect on the text.

Modelling word choice

When modelling the skill of word choice for your class using the **Let's try…** questions (see page 6), the steps below may be useful. Specific modelling guidance is also provided in the teaching units.

1. Read the question aloud.
2. Identify the key words in your question, including the target word(s).
3. Discuss what you already know about the word(s), including generating synonyms if applicable.
4. Scan the text for the target word(s) and highlight or underline them.
5. Read the sentences before and after the target word(s) to get a sense of the context.
6. Discuss the effect the words have on the surrounding sentence(s) or paragraph.
7. Formulate your answer, checking that the information in your answer matches the question.

Comparison

See Unit 2

Understanding comparison

Comparison is the act of identifying the similarities and differences between two things. We make comparisons every day, from comparing the options on a menu to comparing films at the cinema – it is a key life skill. The National Curriculum (2014) requires pupils in Key Stage 2 to know 'how to compare characters, settings, themes and other aspects' so they can 'mak[e] comparisons within and across books'. Comparison is a higher-order thinking skill, and fluent comparison of texts is a key attribute of a confident reader. Moreover, research has shown that teaching comparative thinking leads to significant gains in pupil achievement across the curriculum.[8]

Comparison in *Complete Comprehension*

Each teaching unit in **Complete Comprehension** provides a number of opportunities for the children to make comparisons. The **Get ready** questions encourage them to use their knowledge of texts that may be linked to the unit's text by subject matter. The **Where next?** reading list provides related books to allow them to compare texts that share a theme but are generically different. Finally, every text in each **Complete Comprehension** book is linked to another text in the same book, which enables you to easily build in comparison discussions every time you teach a unit (see **The comprehension texts**, page 12).

In **Complete Comprehension**, comparison questions are often worded as follows:

- Who…?/What…?/Where…?/When…?/How…?/Which…?
- Compare…
- Compare and contrast…
- How does/are/is…?
- Give **one**/**two** way(s) in which … is/are similar to/different from…
- What impression does the text give you of…? Give **one** impression and **one** piece of evidence.
- Compare how … and … feel about… Give **two** points and evidence from the text.
- How are … and … different from…?
- What do … and … have in common?
- Compare the characters of … and… Give **one** difference and explain your answer using the text.
- At first … feels… How do their emotions change straight after that?
- Look at the first two paragraphs. What was similar about … and…?
- What is the main difference between … and…?

The skill of comparison is most often assessed through short and open-ended questions. However, on occasion, questions may be structured in other ways, including in gridded formats. These questions may require additional teacher modelling.

Key challenges

Comparison is a complex skill to master and must be modelled carefully. Often, children find comparison challenging when they have not understood the content of the text as a whole. Overall understanding should therefore be prioritised before you attempt to introduce comparison. The children also need to be familiar with the concepts of 'similarity' and 'difference', and be comfortable describing what they can see or have read in two different texts or two parts of the same text. They can then look for similarities or differences between the two.

Strategies for developing comparison

- **Spot the difference:** One of the best ways to demonstrate the skill of comparison is by using images: you could start by comparing pictures of familiar animals or objects, and then look at more complex images: for example, different depictions of the same events. You could also play games such as 'spot the difference'. Once the children can confidently compare more complex images, you can move on to written texts. It is often easiest to begin by making comparisons between two very different texts before attempting more nuanced comparisons. For example, if you are working with children in lower Key Stage 2, you could compare hero and villain characters in fairy tales. In upper Key Stage 2, you might progress to comparing two characters' reactions to the same event, or examining how one character's mood or behaviour changes throughout a text.

- **Graphic organisers:** Once the children have some understanding of comparison, they may find it helpful to use a graphic organiser to structure their ideas. It is important both to explicitly model the thinking process behind this strategy, and to show the pupils how to complete it. Examples of useful graphic organisers for comparison include:
  - Top hat diagram: The children complete a hat-shaped chart to compare and contrast what they know about two texts. They summarise the differences in the 'brim', and then note any similarities in the raised part of the 'hat'.
  - Venn diagram: The children complete a diagram composed of two overlapping circles, writing similarities in the overlapping central section and differences in the two outer sections.

Modelling comparison

When modelling the skill of comparison for your class using the **Let's try… questions** (see page 6), the steps below may be useful. Specific modelling guidance is also provided in the teaching units.

1. Read the question aloud.
2. Locate the key words in the question.
3. Scan the text for the key words, or related key words, and highlight or underline them.
4. Read around the key words and look for context clues.
5. Use the text to describe and discuss each of the elements being compared. Draw attention to any contrasts you notice.
6. Make comparisons between the two elements, thinking about the similarities and differences, depending on the focus of the question.
7. Use your comparison to form a conclusion.
8. Model checking that your conclusion answers the question.

---

8 Manzano, R.J., Pickering, D. & Pollock, J.D. (2001) *Classroom Instruction that Works: Research-based Strategies for Increasing Student Achievement*. ASCD: Alexandria, VA, pp. 17–19.

Dragonology
by Dugald Steer

▽ Printable text • Modelling slides   📖 Photocopiable text and questions • pages 34 to 37

Children have always been fascinated by magical and mythical creatures, arguably none more so than the dragon. This unit's text is a work of fiction written in the style of non-fiction. The author, Dugald Steer, takes on the imaginary role of a dragonologist to inform readers about the fictional science of dragonology and explain how to become a dragonologist. You could discuss this text alongside that of Unit 2, an extract from *How to Train Your Dragon* by Cressida Cowell.

1 Get ready

Discuss the **Key vocabulary** identified in the **Language toolkit** and then complete the vocabulary activities as desired. Please note that the selected vocabulary is a guide. Depending on the needs of your cohort, additional vocabulary discussion may be beneficial before, during and after reading. Next, display the text (pages 34 to 35) so the children can see the title and any illustrations, and encourage the children to discuss the following questions before reading.

1. **This text is written in the style of a non-fiction text but it is about a fictional topic. Have you read any other books like this?**
   If the children have not read texts like this before, you may wish to share some similar titles from the **Reading list**. It is important that the children understand that this text blends fiction and non-fiction.

2. **The text is about the study of a mythical creature. What is a mythical creature? Can you name any?**
   If the children do not understand what a mythical creature is, spend some time exploring the concept, and offer some of your own examples (e.g. unicorns; mermaids; the Minotaur).

3. **This text is about a particular mythical creature: the dragon. What do you know about dragons?**
   Many children are likely to have encountered dragons in other stories they have read and films they have watched. You could relate the children's knowledge to other subjects (e.g. how dragons feature in celebrations for Chinese New Year).

4. **This text is written in the style of a how-to guide. What features might you expect to find?**
   Answers will vary. You may wish to discuss an example of a how-to text, such as those in the non-fiction section of the **Reading list**, to help the children identify common features such as lists of equipment, sequential steps and warnings.

Language toolkit

Key vocabulary

depleted	diligently	enhancing
eschew	exhortations	grave
hypnosis	mechanism	put into perspective
retribution	tendency	underestimated

Vocabulary discussion questions

- If something is **put into perspective**, does it help you to understand it more clearly? Why?
- If everyone in the class was working **diligently**, what would they be doing?
- What do you have a **tendency** to do as soon as you get home from school?
- If my fruit bowl is looking **depleted**, do I have lots of fruit or do I need to buy more?

Vocabulary activities

- The word **grave** is used in this text as an adjective meaning 'very serious/bad', but it can also be used as a noun meaning 'a place where people are buried'. Can the children think of other homonyms?
- **Retribution** comes from the Latin verb *retribuere*, from *re* meaning 'back' and *tribuere* meaning 'to assign' or 'to give'. Discuss possible synonyms for **retribution** (e.g. 'payback'; 'punishment'; 'revenge'). How many verbs can the children find that use 're–' in the same way?
- Explore the meanings of **eschew** and **exhortations**. Share some example sentences using the two words and challenge the children to come up with their own sentence ideas.

Schofield & Sims Complete Comprehension 5

2 First steps

Read the text together and then encourage the children to discuss the following questions.

1 **What does this extract aim to teach the reader?**
It aims to teach the reader how to find and track dragons. The children may focus on a particular section of the extract (e.g. **Essential Equipment**). In this case, prompt them to think about the extract as a whole and to consider the main aim of the text.

2 **What signs on the ground tell you that dragons are close by?**
Footprints and tail swishing marks; burned and scorched undergrowth.

3 **What makes being a dragonologist dangerous?**
You can be bitten; burned; slashed by claws; killed by constriction; lashed by tails; attacked with venom; hypnotised. Some children may offer other suggestions not taken from the text. In this case, prompt them to draw their answer from the section **Dangers in the Field**.

3 Explore

- Discuss the fact that this text is very unusual: it is fiction because it is about a fictional creature, but it includes many features of non-fiction texts. Ask the children to point out the non-fiction features in the text. Then ask them what features they would expect to find in fiction texts (e.g. first-person or third-person narration; descriptive language; made-up characters and events; dialogue). You could use this as an opportunity to discuss other texts that display elements of both fiction and non-fiction (e.g. historical and science fiction).

- Although the dragons in *Dragonology* are mythical, there are some real-life creatures that are called dragons, such as the bearded dragon and the Komodo dragon. Ask the children to research one or more of these real-life dragons and to find out what they have in common with the mythical dragons discussed in the text. After they have completed their research, encourage them to debate whether these 'dragons' are worthy of their name!

- The text is called *Dragonology*, which means 'the study of dragons'. Many other subjects and types of work are described using names that end with the suffix '–ology'. The children could do online research to find out what the study of their favourite subject is called (e.g. if they like finding out about dogs, they might study cynology, the study of dogs). You could challenge them to think of three topics or a subheading that a how-to guide on that subject might include.

4 Skills focus See pages 32 to 33

Use the information from the **Skills guide** and the relevant **Skills graphic** to introduce the skill of retrieval.

1 Model the skill using the **Unit 1 Modelling slides** and the **Modelling retrieval** guidance on page 32.

2 The children can then attempt the **Retrieval** questions on page 36.

3 Finally, the **Mix it up!** questions on page 37 offer practice in a range of comprehension skills.

Answers and marking guidance for all questions are included on pages 32 to 33.

5 Where next?

- **Speaking and listening task:** Ask the children to work in small groups to create a presentation or a short video about how to become a dragonologist. They should use information from the text for their content, as well as their own ideas. They could even use apps such as AR Dragon to place dragons in the classroom or playground in their videos.

- **Writing task:** The children could work in pairs, or individually, to design their own dragon. They could write a field report describing their dragon's feeding habits, behaviour and appearance, and add labelled diagrams to enhance their reports.

Reading list

Fiction
- *The Book of Dragons* by E. Nesbit
- *Dragon Rider* by Cornelia Funke
- *Fantastic Beasts and Where to Find Them* by J.K. Rowling
- *How to Train Your Dragon* by Cressida Cowell (Linked text: **Unit 2**)
- *An Illustrated Treasury of Scottish Mythical Creatures* by Theresa Breslin

Class reads
- *Darwin's Dragons* by Lindsay Galvin

Non-fiction
- *The Atlas of Monsters* by Sandra Lawrence
- *Dracopedia Field Guide* by William O'Connor
- *Joan Procter, Dragon Doctor* by Patrica Valdez
- *Mythologica* by Steve Kershaw

Websites
- The BBC Earth website has an interesting page about 10 real-life animals that are dragons.

Modelling retrieval

▽ See Unit 1 Modelling slides

Use the **Skills guide** (see pages 16 to 17) and the downloadable **Skills graphic** to support your modelling.

1 **What is the best way for a dragonologist to improve their knowledge of dragons?**
To study them in the wild.

As this question does not include a locator, it is important to model identifying the key words and scanning for them in the text. The key word 'improve' is represented in the text by the synonym 'enhancing', which the children will have encountered in the **Key vocabulary**. You could discuss the fact that sometimes key words are synonyms for words in the text, and model thinking of appropriate synonyms for each key word to look out for.

2 **What equipment does a dragonologist need? Name three items.**
a notebook, heat-protective clothing, a camera

Again, as there is no locator, model identifying key words in the question and then scanning for them. Model finding the key word 'equipment' in the subheading **Essential Equipment**. Explain that you will now skim-read this section to find three items. Model deciding what additional information needs to be included in your answer (e.g. 'notebook' does not need anything, but 'clothing' is not specific enough without 'heat-protective').

3 **Look at the section 'Field Procedure'. What should a dragonologist record when finding signs of dragon activity? Tick two.**

| the weather | ✓ | their appearance | ☐ | the season | ☐ |
| their behaviour | ✓ | their droppings | ☐ | | |

Model using the locator to find the correct section before identifying key words from the question and scanning for them. Then take each answer option in turn and model running your finger along the lines to find the key word. The question requires information to be taken from two separate sentences, so it is important to model reading around the key words.

4 **Think about the whole text. Tick to show whether each statement is true or false.**

	T	F
Dragons cannot hypnotise people.		✓
A dragonologist should wear heat-resistant clothing.	✓	
A dragonologist should not take anything from a dragon.	✓	
Dragons can kill by constriction.	✓	

The question requires the children to think about the whole text. Model considering the statements one by one, taking time to identify key words and scanning for the correct part of the text before deciding a statement's truth. With the first statement, it would be useful to spend time discussing the use of the negative 'cannot', as some children often misread questions phrased in this way.

Retrieval questions mark scheme

See page 36

Answer		Guidance
1	jewellery	This is a challenging question because none of the key words in the question are found in the relevant part of the text. If some children need support, prompt them to scan the section **Tell-tale Signs of Dragon Activity** for something that people wear. You could remind them that the **Key vocabulary** word 'eschew' means 'avoid'. **Award 1 mark for the correct answer.**

Unit 1 — Dragonology, by Dugald Steer

	Answer	Guidance
2	map — with geological formations notebook — heat-proof cover pen and ink — heat-proof clothing — heat-protective	The children must read the text closely as three of the description options are very similar. You could discuss the difference between 'heat-proof' and 'heat-protective' to support their understanding. **Award 1 mark for at least two pairs correctly matched. Award 2 marks for all four pairs correctly matched.**
3	speech ✓ spells ✓	As there is no locator to support the children here, you could prompt them to reread the section **Field Procedure**. **Award 1 mark for both correct answers ticked.**
4	an obsession with dragons/wizards/fairies/tales of other worlds OR a mad delight in fantastic illustrations and ideas OR a dislike of human rules	As this is not a 'find and copy'-style question, paraphrasing is acceptable as long as the children's responses are based on the text. **Award 1 mark for any two correct answers.**
5	doing lots of complicated maths problems OR confiscating books on dragons and wizards OR providing books on stimulating topics	Some children may misread the text and suggest that the exhortations mentioned in the last bullet point of the text are the remedy. If so, reread the sentence and focus them on the phrase 'are rarely successful.' **Award 1 mark for a correct answer.**

Mix it up! questions mark scheme See page 37

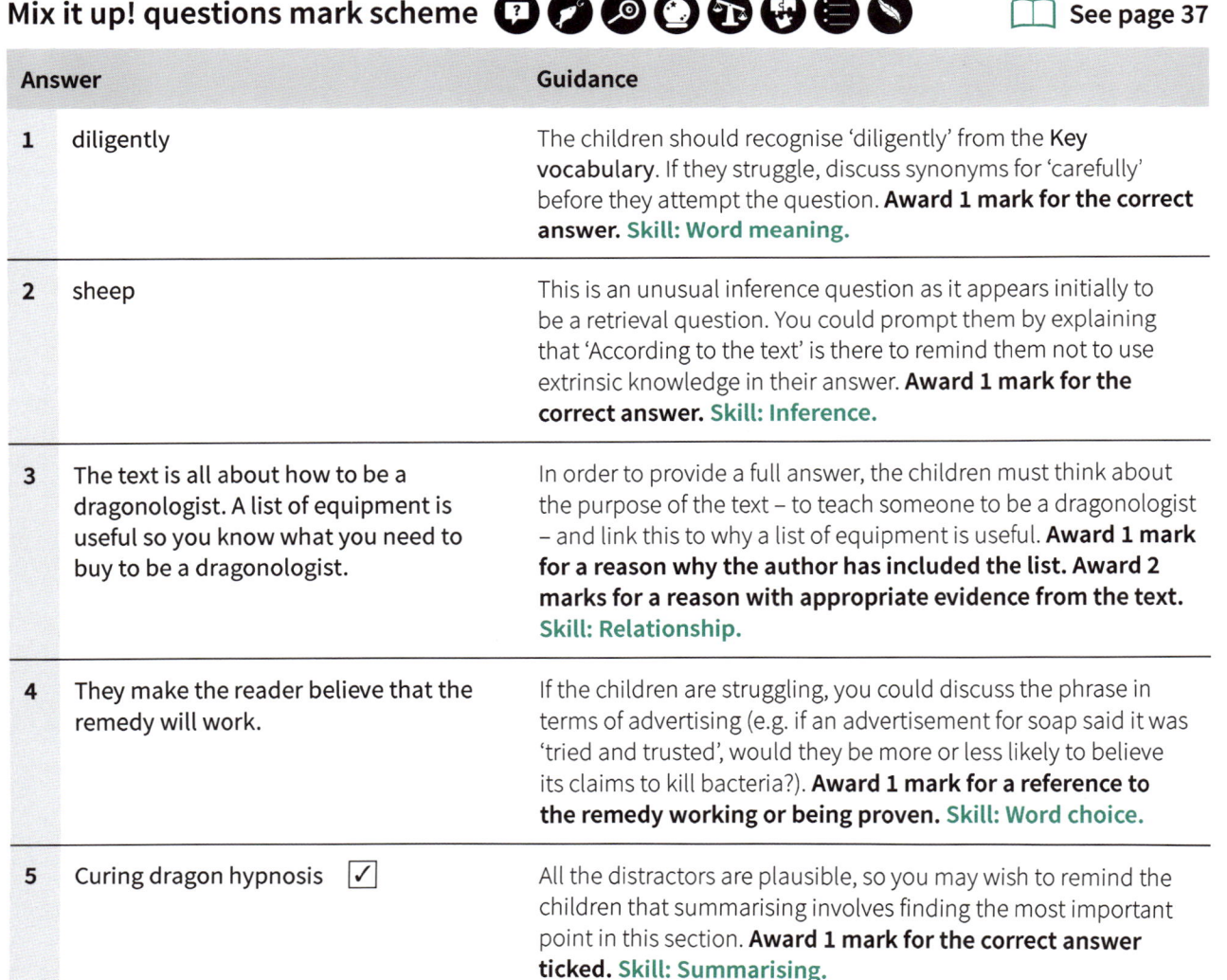

	Answer	Guidance
1	diligently	The children should recognise 'diligently' from the **Key vocabulary**. If they struggle, discuss synonyms for 'carefully' before they attempt the question. **Award 1 mark for the correct answer. Skill: Word meaning.**
2	sheep	This is an unusual inference question as it appears initially to be a retrieval question. You could prompt them by explaining that 'According to the text' is there to remind them not to use extrinsic knowledge in their answer. **Award 1 mark for the correct answer. Skill: Inference.**
3	The text is all about how to be a dragonologist. A list of equipment is useful so you know what you need to buy to be a dragonologist.	In order to provide a full answer, the children must think about the purpose of the text – to teach someone to be a dragonologist – and link this to why a list of equipment is useful. **Award 1 mark for a reason why the author has included the list. Award 2 marks for a reason with appropriate evidence from the text. Skill: Relationship.**
4	They make the reader believe that the remedy will work.	If the children are struggling, you could discuss the phrase in terms of advertising (e.g. if an advertisement for soap said it was 'tried and trusted', would they be more or less likely to believe its claims to kill bacteria?). **Award 1 mark for a reference to the remedy working or being proven. Skill: Word choice.**
5	Curing dragon hypnosis ✓	All the distractors are plausible, so you may wish to remind the children that summarising involves finding the most important point in this section. **Award 1 mark for the correct answer ticked. Skill: Summarising.**

Dragonology, by Dugald Steer

This text is from a fictional guide that tells you how to become a dragonologist. In this extract, the guide explains how to find and track dragons in the wild.

Finding and Tracking Dragons

There is no more satisfying activity for the dragonologist than that of studying dragons in the wild; it is the best way of enhancing our knowledge of these creatures. While armchair science has its own rewards, the achievement of tracking and locating a dragon and, hopefully, reaching a position of acceptance and trust will allow the student to put into perspective all that has been so diligently learned.

Tell-tale Signs of Dragon Activity

To the experienced eye, it is easy to tell at once when a dragon's range has been entered, and exactly what dragon is being encountered.

- Footprints and tail swishing marks.
- Burned and scorched trees and undergrowth.
- Small, depleted-looking flocks of sheep.
- Frightened villagers, with excitable children.
- A tendency for the locals to eschew jewellery.
- Local legends about dragon activity, often dismissed as 'smuggler's tales' to keep people away.
- A local hotel or hostelry with a reputation for eccentric visitors [likely to be rival dragonologists or newspaper 'hacks' hot on the train of a 'scoop'].

Essential Equipment

Over time, each dragonologist will build up his own list of essential equipment. Here is a basic list:

- A notebook, to preserve all important records. Ideally this should have a heat-proof cover.
- A heat-proof pen and ink, 2B sketching pencils.
- A reasonably powerful magnifying glass.
- Special, heat-protective clothing.
- A relief map of the area, that shows both flora-types and geological formations.
- A camera, although all attempts to photograph dragons so far have been failures.

Field Procedure

Upon discovering signs of dragon activity such as footprints, the scientific dragonologist will record precise details of the event: the location, time, date and weather conditions. This should be repeated over a number of days. Feeding and behaviour should definitely be noted, although not at such a range as to make it an unpleasantly personal experience. Attempts at interaction should be included, whether they involve speech or spells. One should take care to take nothing from a dragon as this will not only cause grave danger to the dragonologist but may also provoke a fiery retribution to any other people who live in the surrounding area.

Dangers in the Field

While the dangers of suffering from bites, burns, slashes from claws, death-by-constriction, tail lashings, venom attacks and so forth should never be underestimated, the lesser danger of hypnosis is often ignored. The mechanism for this is little understood, but it seems to occur in a similar way to that seen when a snake hypnotises a frog. Dragons can hypnotise large groups of individuals at one time, and the effects may last for some months, with the hypnotised person often found apparently carrying on their everyday life. The signs are easy to read: an obsession with dragons, wizards, fairies or tales of other worlds. A mad delight in fantastic illustrations and ideas. A dislike of human rules or authorities. Luckily, there is a tried and trusted method that may be used as a remedy:

- A person who has been hypnotised by a dragon should be made to do a large number of complicated mathematical sums.

- All books on dragons, wizards or suchlike should be confiscated, and books on stimulating topics – such as politics, economic theory, the history of benzene in the manufacturing industries etc. – should be substituted.

- Exhortations to the person to "snap out of it" or to "stop living in cloud-cuckoo land" are rarely successful.

From *Dragonology* by Dugald Steer, Templar Publishing, 2003. Reproduced by permission.

Retrieval

Name: _____

1 When a dragon lives close by, what do people avoid wearing?

_____

1 mark

2 Look at the section **Essential Equipment**. Draw lines to match each item to its description.

map	heat-protective
notebook	with geological formations
pen and ink	heat-proof cover
clothing	heat-proof

2 marks

3 What could a dragonologist use to interact with dragons? Tick **two**.

speech ☐

riddles ☐

spells ☐

hypnosis ☐

1 mark

4 Look at the section **Dangers in the Field**. What are the signs that someone has been hypnotised by a dragon? Give **two** points.

1 _____

2 _____

1 mark

5 According to the text, what is a successful remedy for being hypnotised by a dragon?

_____

_____

1 mark

Mix it up!

Name: _____

1 Look at the first paragraph. Find and copy **one** word that means 'carefully'.

_____

1 mark

2 Look at the section **Tell-tale Signs of Dragon Activity**. According to the text, what do dragons eat?

_____

1 mark

3 Why do you think the author has included a list of essential equipment? Explain your answer using evidence from the text.

_____

_____

_____

2 marks

4 *Luckily, there is a tried and trusted method that may be used as a remedy ... .*
What effect does the group of words *tried and trusted* have on the reader?

_____

_____

1 mark

5 Read from *Luckily, there is ...* to the end of the text. Which of the following would be the most effective subheading for this section? Tick **one**.

Dragon hypnosis ☐

Identifying hypnotised people ☐

Snap out of it ☐

Curing dragon hypnosis ☐

1 mark

How to Train Your Dragon
by Cressida Cowell

▽ Printable text • Modelling slides   📖 Photocopiable text and questions • pages 42 to 45

The well-known and beloved franchise, *How to Train Your Dragon*, continues to fascinate children across the globe with its depiction of life on the imaginary Viking island of Berk. In this extract from the first book, the main character Hiccup and his adversaries, Dogsbreath and Snotlout, are about to begin a daring challenge. Cressida Cowell builds an intricate picture of the characters' appearance and motivations, contrasting their differences in the build-up to the challenge and emphasising the boys' differing personalities. This extract can be linked to Unit 1, which focused on dragons and the imaginary vocation of 'dragonology'.

1 Get ready

Discuss the **Key vocabulary** identified in the **Language toolkit** and then complete the vocabulary activities as desired. Please note that the selected vocabulary is a guide. Depending on the needs of your cohort, additional vocabulary discussion may be beneficial before, during and after reading. Next, display the text (pages 42 to 43) so the children can see the title and any illustrations, and encourage the children to discuss the following questions before reading.

1. **The author of this story uses detailed descriptions of the characters to highlight the differences between them. What type of language would you expect to see in a character description?**
   Answers will vary depending on the children's understanding of the question. Encourage them to think about how an author would write about and compare characters (e.g. by using lots of adjectives in a row; expanded noun phrases; strong verbs and adverbs to describe movement; metaphors and similes to help readers to imagine what a character looks like).

2. **This story is set in a fantasy Viking world. What do you know about the Vikings?**
   The children may be able to make links to things they have learnt as part of the history curriculum. A basic understanding of Viking life is useful when reading this text, so you could spend some time building up the children's background knowledge. See the Reading list for ideas for resources.

3. **This story is set in the Viking age and features dragons. Do you think real-life Vikings would have encountered dragons?**
   Although the answer here is no, as dragons are mythical creatures, the children may challenge this opinion, especially given the quasi non-fiction style of the Unit 1 text, *Dragonology*. You could refer back to your discussions about dragons from that unit.

Language toolkit

Key vocabulary

average	consisted	easy to overlook
fashion	for instance	menacing
oblige	perilous	squint
the beginnings of	unmemorable	unremarkable

Vocabulary discussion questions

- If something is **easy to overlook** is it **unmemorable**? Why?
- When you **oblige**, are you being helpful or not? What might you be doing?
- If you **squint** at something, is that the same as having a squint?

Vocabulary activities

- **For instance** is used to introduce examples in a text or conversation. How many other ways of doing this can the children think of?
- The words **squint** and **fashion** can be used as both nouns and verbs in different situations. Can the children name any other words that can be used as two different word classes?
- **Unmemorable**, **average** and **easy to overlook** are all synonymous. Challenge the children to find additional words and phrases that are synonymous and order them in a 'Shades of meaning' activity (see **Skills guide** page 15).

Schofield & Sims *Complete Comprehension 5*

Unit 2 • Comparison • Fiction

38

2 First steps

Read the text together and then encourage the children to discuss the following questions.

1. **Who are the main characters in the story?**
   Hiccup, Dogsbreath, Snotlout and Fishlegs. You may wish to discuss who the overall main character is (Hiccup) and why the children think this.

2. **Who decides that they are the leader of the group?**
   Snotlout.

3. **What are the boys doing?**
   Preparing to climb something as part of a team challenge. You could discuss what the children think the boys are about to climb. Many of the children will have seen the film version of the story, so you may need to remind them that they should use the text, not their memories of the film, to answer.

4. **Did you enjoy the story? Why? Why not?**
   Answers will vary. The children should be able to justify their responses (e.g. *I liked the fact that there are lots of characters and they all have different personalities*).

3 Explore

- This extract is about a group of boys – Hiccup, Dogsbreath, Snotlout and Fishlegs – working together to complete a challenge. Ask what different challenges the children have completed together at school and what made these challenges easy or difficult. Decide, as a class, on some helpful steps for working together. You could even set the children a challenge to complete and encourage them to use the steps discussed.

- In the story, Hiccup and the other boys are completing a rite of passage – capturing and training a dragon – in order to be able to stay on the island of Berk. In real life, many people go through rites of passage at different points in their lives, which can be religious, cultural or due to their choice of profession. Research what rites of passage people go through across the world (e.g. Jewish children will celebrate their bar or bat mitzvah; people from some Bantu ethnic groups practise Okuyi; and Australian Aboriginal boys complete Walkabout).

- In the first three paragraphs, the text discusses what we expect heroes to look like and how we expect them to behave. Ask the children to tell you how they think a hero should look and act. Depending on their responses, you may want to challenge their opinions and look together at heroes of all different physical appearances and personalities.

4 Skills focus See pages 40 to 41

Use the information from the **Skills guide** and the relevant **Skills graphic** to introduce the skill of comparison.

1. Model the skill using the **Unit 2 Modelling slides** and the **Modelling comparison** guidance on page 40.

2. The children can then attempt the **Comparison** questions on page 44.

3. Finally, the **Mix it up!** questions on page 45 offer practice in a range of comprehension skills.

Answers and marking guidance for all questions are included on pages 40 to 41.

5 Where next?

- **Speaking and listening task:** The story features four very different characters: Hiccup, Dogsbreath, Snotlout and Fishlegs. Divide the children into pairs and ask one child in each pair to role-play one of the characters, using information from the text. As one child acts, the other could ask them questions, trying to guess who their partner is pretending to be by using clues from the text.

- **Writing task:** The children could work in small groups to transform the extract into a script to be used in the film version of the story, paying special attention to stage directions and narration. They could then compare their script with a clip from the film.

Reading list

Fiction
- *Odd and the Frost Giants* by Neil Gaiman
- *Riddle of the Runes* by Janina Ramirez
- *The Time-Travelling Cat and the Viking Terror* by Julia Jarman

Class reads
- *Viking Boy* by Tony Bradman

Non-fiction
- *Dragonology* by Dugald Steer (Linked text: **Unit 1**)
- *The Incomplete Book of Dragons* by Cressida Cowell
- *Vicious Vikings (Horrible Histories)* by Terry Deary
- *Vikings in 30 Seconds* by Philip Steele

Films
- *How to Train Your Dragon* (Dreamworks, 2010)

Music
- Viking Saga Songs, BBC Teach

Modelling comparison

See Unit 2 Modelling slides

Use the **Skills guide** (see pages 28 to 29) and the downloadable **Skills graphic** to support your modelling.

1. **Look at the first and second paragraphs. What is the main point of these paragraphs? Tick <u>one</u>.**

    to describe Hiccup ☐
    to compare Hiccup and Snotlout ☑
    to describe Snotlout ☐
    to compare Hiccup and Dogsbreath ☐

    This question includes a locator, so it is important to model using it to find the correct paragraphs. This is a challenging question as it requires the children to use some elements of the summarising skill in order to answer. You could use the strategies in the **Skills guide** to recap summarising (see pages 18 to 19). Many of the children may assume that the point of the paragraphs is to describe one of the characters. You could model considering each option in relation to the text in turn, before discounting those which are incorrect.

2. **Snotlout and Dogsbreath work together as a team but they each have different roles. What is different about their roles?**

    Snotlout leads the team but Dogsbreath makes sure everybody does what they are told.

    Model identifying key words in the question and then scanning for them in the text. Discuss how Snotlout and Dogsbreath rely on one another – Snotlout relies on Dogsbreath to make sure everyone does as he tells them, while Dogsbreath relies on Snotlout for his position in the group. Discuss each character in turn, perhaps using a graphic organiser, then model deciding on their differences.

3. **Compare Hiccup and Snotlout's appearance. Give <u>two</u> differences between them.**

    Snotlout is tall but Hiccup is small. Hiccup has an unmemorable face but Snotlout's looks like a hero's.

    There is no locator for this question, so it is advisable to spend extra time identifying key words and scanning for them in the text. Some children may respond with only a difference (e.g. 'Snotlout is tall') without explicitly stating the difference between the two characters. Model amending an answer like this to demonstrate making a true comparison. Again, as there are a number of possible responses, discuss these and then model choosing the most effective points for your final answer.

4. **What do Hiccup and Fishlegs have in common? Give <u>two</u> points.**

    They are both ordered around by the others and they are both unsure about the challenge ahead of them.

    Model identifying key words in the question and scanning for them. There are a number of possible responses to this question, including simple retrieval (e.g. 'They were both tied on last'). Discuss all the possible responses and then model choosing the most effective points for your final answer.

Comparison questions mark scheme

See page 44

	Answer	Guidance
1	They are both tall/bossy/strong/bullies.	Some children may answer vaguely (e.g. 'They look the same'). This should not be accepted and the children should be prompted to draw their answer directly from the text. **Award 1 mark for a similarity taken from the text.**
2	Hiccup ignores them/stays quiet/gets pushed around but Fishlegs makes fun of them/speaks up/is sarcastic.	Some children may only provide an implicit, rather than a direct comparison (e.g. 'Hiccup ignores them'). If so, remind them that a comparison needs to refer to both characters to be fully correct. **Award 1 mark for reference to Hiccup ignoring them while Fishlegs makes fun of them.**

	Answer	Guidance
3	*At the beginning of the challenge*: Dogsbreath pushes everybody around. *During the challenge*: Dogsbreath helps Clueless and stops him from falling.	The question format scaffolds the children's answers. If you wish to provide more of a challenge, present this as an open question. **Award 1 mark for a reference to Dogsbreath's behaviour at either the beginning or during the challenge. Award 2 marks for two clear references to Dogsbreath's behaviour at the beginning and during the challenge.**
4	The tone in this paragraph makes you feel like the challenge is dangerous, but before the tone was more light-hearted because it was about friends having an argument without danger or stress.	This is an interesting question as it involves some understanding of relationship as well as comparison. If the children struggle, recap the skill of relationship using the strategies in the **Skills guide** (pages 24 to 25). **Award 1 mark for a reference to the tone of the paragraph. Award 2 marks for a reference to the tone plus a direct comparison between this paragraph and the preceding paragraphs.**
5	Snotlout likes to be in charge but Hiccup follows the rest of the group.	The children should be encouraged to give both sides of the difference where possible. However, a response such as 'Snotlout likes to be in charge' should still be accepted. **Award 1 mark for a difference taken from the text.**

Mix it up! questions mark scheme

See page 45

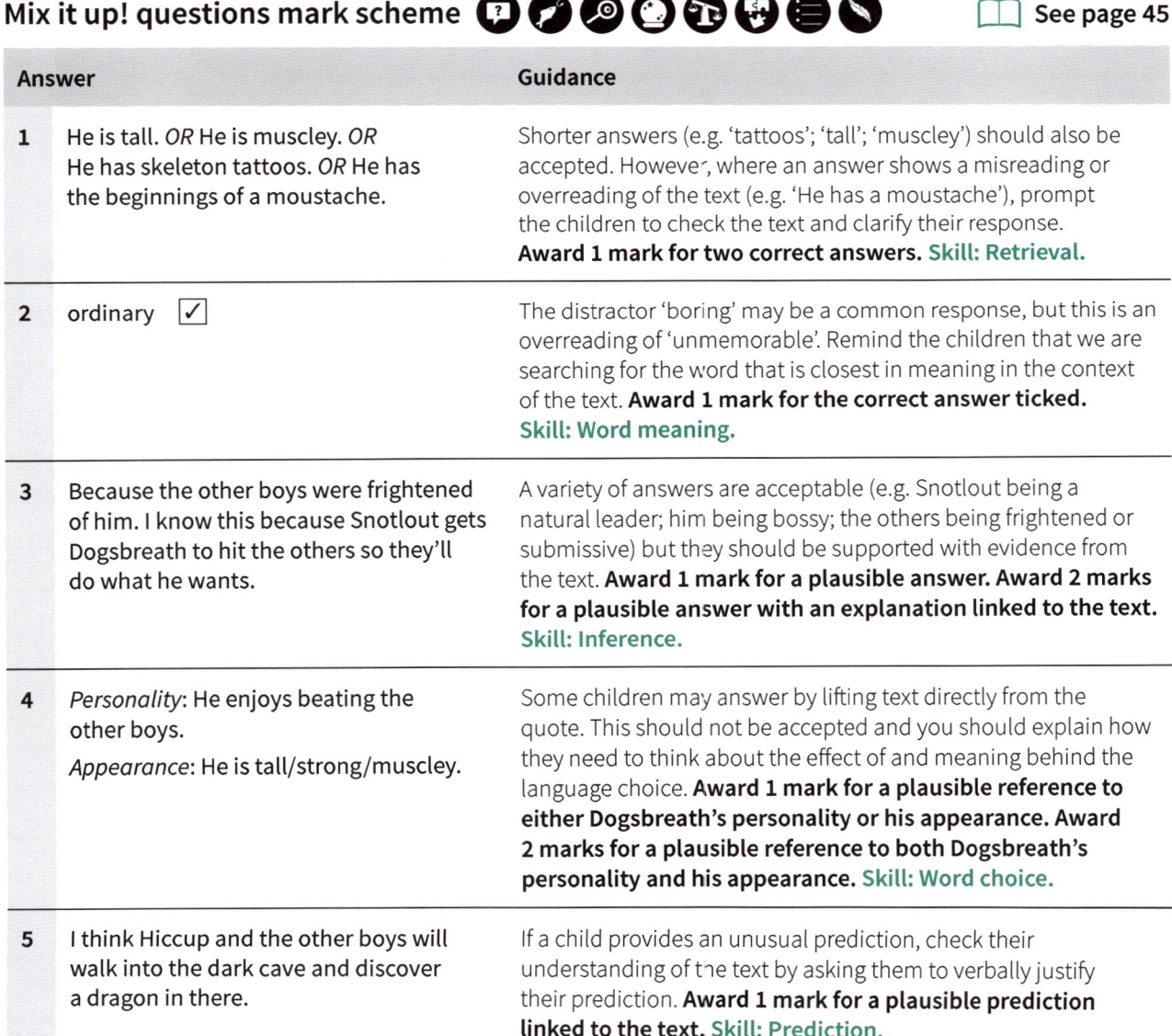

	Answer	Guidance
1	He is tall. *OR* He is muscley. *OR* He has skeleton tattoos. *OR* He has the beginnings of a moustache.	Shorter answers (e.g. 'tattoos'; 'tall'; 'muscley') should also be accepted. However, where an answer shows a misreading or overreading of the text (e.g. 'He has a moustache'), prompt the children to check the text and clarify their response. **Award 1 mark for two correct answers. Skill: Retrieval.**
2	ordinary ✓	The distractor 'boring' may be a common response, but this is an overreading of 'unmemorable'. Remind the children that we are searching for the word that is closest in meaning in the context of the text. **Award 1 mark for the correct answer ticked. Skill: Word meaning.**
3	Because the other boys were frightened of him. I know this because Snotlout gets Dogsbreath to hit the others so they'll do what he wants.	A variety of answers are acceptable (e.g. Snotlout being a natural leader; him being bossy; the others being frightened or submissive) but they should be supported with evidence from the text. **Award 1 mark for a plausible answer. Award 2 marks for a plausible answer with an explanation linked to the text. Skill: Inference.**
4	*Personality*: He enjoys beating the other boys. *Appearance*: He is tall/strong/muscley.	Some children may answer by lifting text directly from the quote. This should not be accepted and you should explain how they need to think about the effect of and meaning behind the language choice. **Award 1 mark for a plausible reference to either Dogsbreath's personality or his appearance. Award 2 marks for a plausible reference to both Dogsbreath's personality and his appearance. Skill: Word choice.**
5	I think Hiccup and the other boys will walk into the dark cave and discover a dragon in there.	If a child provides an unusual prediction, check their understanding of the text by asking them to verbally justify their prediction. **Award 1 mark for a plausible prediction linked to the text. Skill: Prediction.**

How to Train Your Dragon, by Cressida Cowell

This is an extract from a story about a Viking boy called Hiccup who needs to capture and train a dragon in order to live on the island of Berk. At this point in the story, Hiccup is about to start his challenge with other boys from the island.

You have probably guessed by now that Hiccup was not your natural Viking Hero. For a start, he didn't LOOK like a Hero. Somebody like Snotlout, for instance, was tall, muscley, covered in skeleton tattoos, and already had the beginnings of a small moustache. This consisted of a few straggly yellow hairs clinging to his upper lip and was deeply unpleasant to look at, but still impressively manly for a boy not yet thirteen.

Hiccup was on the small side and had the kind of face that was almost entirely unmemorable. He DID have Heroic Hair, which was a very bright red and stood up vertically however much you tried to wet it down with sea-water. But nobody ever saw that because it was hidden under his helmet most of the time.

You would NEVER have picked Hiccup out of those ten boys to be the Hero of this story. Snotlout was good at everything and a natural leader. Dogsbreath was as tall as his father and could do amusing things like farting to the tune of the Berk National Anthem.

Hiccup was just absolutely average, the kind of unremarkable, skinny, freckled boy who was easy to overlook in a crowd.

So when Gobbler blew the horn and moved out of sight to find a comfortable rock to sit on and eat his mussel-and-tomato sandwich, Snotlout pushed Hiccup out of the way and took charge.

"OK, listen up, boys," he whispered in a menacing fashion. "I'M in charge, not the Useless. And anybody who objects gets a knuckle sandwich from Dogsbreath the Duhbrain."

"Ugh," grunted Dogsbreath, pounding his fists together in happy excitement. Dogsbreath was Snotlout's chief sidekick and a great, big gorilla of a boy.

"Bash him, Dogsbreath, to show what I mean…"

Dogsbreath was delighted to oblige. He gave Hiccup a shove that sent him sprawling head first into the snow, then ground his face in it.

"Pay attention!" hissed Snotlout. The boys dragged their eyes away from Dogsbreath and Hiccup and paid attention. "Rope yourselves together. The best climber should go first…"

"Well, that's YOU of course, Snotlout," said Fishlegs. "You're the best at everything, aren't you?"

Snotlout looked at Fishlegs suspiciously. It was difficult to tell whether Fishlegs was laughing at him or not, because of his squint.

"That's right, Fishlegs," said Snotlout. "I AM."

And, just in case he *had* been laughing at him: "Bash him, Dogsbreath!"

While Dogsbreath pushed Fishlegs down to join Hiccup in the snow, Snotlout bossily ordered everybody to rope themselves together.

Hiccup and Fishlegs were the last to be tied on, just behind a flushed and triumphant Dogsbreath.

"Oh brilliant," muttered Fishlegs. "I'm about to enter a cave full of man-eating reptiles tied up to eight complete maniacs."

"If we *get* to the cave…" said Hiccup nervously, looking up at the sheer black cliff.

Hiccup put the lighted torch between his teeth to leave his hands free, and started climbing after the others.

It was a perilous climb. The rocks were slippery with snow and the other boys were thoroughly over-excited, making the ascent far too quickly. At one point Clueless missed his footing and fell – luckily on to Dogsbreath, who caught him by the back of the trousers and heaved him back on to the rock again, before he brought the whole lot of them down.

When they finally made it to the mouth of the cave, Hiccup looked down briefly at the sea pounding the rocks way below, and swallowed very hard…

From *How to Train Your Dragon*, by Cressida Cowell. Text and illustrations copyright © Cressida Cowell, 2003. Reproduced by permission of Hodder Children's Books, an imprint of Hachette Children's Books, Carmelite House, 50 Victoria Embankment, London imprint, EC4Y 0DZ.

Comparison

Name: _____

1 How are Snotlout and Dogsbreath the same? Give **one** similarity.

_____

_____

1 mark

2 How do Hiccup and Fishlegs react differently to Snotlout and Dogsbreath?

_____

_____

1 mark

3 Compare how Dogsbreath acts at the beginning of the challenge with how he reacts during the challenge itself.

At the beginning of the challenge	_____ _____
During the challenge	_____ _____

2 marks

4 Look at the paragraph beginning *It was a perilous climb*. How is the tone of the story different in this paragraph?

_____

_____

_____

2 marks

5 Think about the whole text. Compare the personalities of Hiccup and Snotlout. Give **one** difference between them.

_____

_____

_____

1 mark

Mix it up!

Name: _____

1 What does Snotlout look like? Give **two** features.

1 _____

2 _____

1 mark

2 Look at the second paragraph. Which word is closest in meaning to *unmemorable*? Tick **one**.

interesting ☐   ordinary ☐   boring ☐   uncommon ☐

1 mark

3 Why was Snotlout in charge? Explain your answer using evidence from the text.

_____
_____
_____

2 marks

4 "Ugh," grunted Dogsbreath, pounding his fists together in happy excitement. Dogsbreath was Snotlout's chief sidekick and a great, big gorilla of a boy.
What does this description tell you about Dogsbreath? Give **one** point about his personality and **one** point about his appearance.

Personality	_____ _____
Appearance	_____ _____

2 marks

5 What do you think might happen next in the story?

_____
_____

1 mark

Photocopiable resource from *Complete Comprehension 5* © Schofield & Sims Ltd, 2020.

Unit 3

Summarising

Non-fiction

Life in Tudor Britain
by Anita Ganeri

Printable text • Modelling slides • Photocopiable text and questions • pages 50 to 53

Although the Tudor period is not covered in detail in the primary curriculum, many of the children will be familiar with aspects of it, such as Henry VIII and his six wives and the Tudors' penchant for grisly executions. This text explores childhood in Tudor England, discussing the differences between family life, clothing and food then and now. The Tudor period is also the setting for the poem in Unit 4. After completing both units, you could compare how the two texts convey historical information in different ways.

1 Get ready

Discuss the **Key vocabulary** identified in the **Language toolkit** and then complete the vocabulary activities as desired. Please note that the selected vocabulary is a guide. Depending on the needs of your cohort, additional vocabulary discussion may be beneficial before, during and after reading. Next, display the text (pages 50 to 51) so the children can see the title and any illustrations, and encourage the children to discuss the following questions before reading.

1. **This text encourages readers to imagine what life would be like for them in the past. Have you read any other texts that do this?**
   The children's responses are likely to include both fiction and non-fiction texts. Some of them may mention fictional texts that feature time travel. You may wish to explain that the text in this unit is non-fiction.

2. **If you could travel to any historical period, which would you choose? Why?**
   You could provide some options for the children to pick from, perhaps taken from the time periods they have studied as part of the history curriculum. It is important to ask them to justify their opinions using their historical knowledge and you could encourage them to thoughtfully challenge each other's choices.

3. **This text is about the Tudor period. What do you know about this period?**
   Many of the children will have some knowledge of the Tudors, but you may need to supplement this by discussing famous figures (e.g. Henry VIII) or locations (e.g. the Tower of London).

4. **How do you think childhood in Tudor times might have been different from now?**
   Encourage a broad discussion. As the text will introduce key facts on this subject, it is more important for the children to grasp a general sense of what might be different.

Language toolkit

Key vocabulary

afford	breeches	cure
embroidered	fine	gentry
household	luxury	marzipan
nobles	obey	prevent

Vocabulary discussion questions

- What bad things would you like to **prevent** from happening?
- What is the difference between a medicine and a **cure**?
- How many people are in your **household**?
- Who do you have to **obey**?
- How do you know whether or not you can **afford** something?
- What makes something a **luxury**?

Vocabulary activities

- **Prevent** begins with the prefix 'pre–', which means 'before'. How many other words can the children think of that begin with the prefix 'pre–'?
- **Nobles** and **gentry** are both words that can be applied to groups of people. Can the children think of other historical words that describe groups of people from different parts of society (e.g. 'aristocrats'; the 'elite'; 'royalty'; 'peasants'; 'commoners')? Which of these would we still say today?
- This text includes a number of unusual terms relating to historical clothing and food (e.g. **breeches**; 'hose'; 'doublets'; 'ruffs'; 'rye'; 'pottage'). You could spend some time discussing these terms with the children.

Schofield & Sims Complete Comprehension 5

2 First steps

Read the text together and then encourage the children to discuss the following questions.

1 **Which children went to school?**
   Some wealthy boys. You could discuss the fact that children from poorer families had to go to work rather than go to school, and that girls from wealthy families were only taught skills for running a home.

2 **How would wealthy Tudors decorate their clothing?**
   With jewels and gold and silver embroidery.

3 **What is marzipan? What shapes was it made into?**
   It is a paste made of sugar and almonds. It was shaped into castles, animals and fruit, then decorated with real gold. You may wish to point out that marzipan was the Tudor equivalent of the sweets we have today.

4 **Did you enjoy the text? Why? Why not?**
   Answers will vary. The children should be able to justify their responses (e.g. *I liked working out what I'd be made to do during Tudor times, but I don't think I'd like to live then!*).

3 Explore

- This text discusses family life, clothing and food in the Tudor period. You could discuss what other aspects of Tudor life the children would like to find out about (e.g. school; games played; the types of houses they lived in; medicine). The children could use the school library or the internet to research an aspect of Tudor life or childhood that interests them, and then share their findings with the class.

- The author of this text encourages children to think about what their own lives would be like in Tudor England. Using information from the text and the research they did in the previous activity, ask the children to compare and contrast their childhood now with the one they would have had in Tudor England. They could work in small groups to create illustrated posters to present the differences, structuring their work using similar headings to the ones in the text (e.g. school; food and drink; clothing; houses).

- The beginning of the Tudor period was over 500 years ago, so we would expect everyday life to have been very different. However, lifestyles are continually changing and the children may be surprised by how different their parents' or grandparents' childhoods were to their own. The children could ask their older relatives about key aspects of life when they were growing up (e.g. family life; clothing; food; hobbies; school), finding out what is similar and different between now and then.

4 Skills focus See pages 48 to 49

Use the information from the **Skills guide** and the relevant **Skills graphic** to introduce the skill of summarising.

1 Model the skill using the **Unit 3 Modelling slides** and the **Modelling summarising** guidance on page 48.

2 The children can then attempt the **Summarising** questions on page 52.

3 Finally, the **Mix it up!** questions on page 53 offer practice in a range of comprehension skills.

Answers and marking guidance for all questions are included on pages 48 to 49.

5 Where next?

- **Speaking and listening task:** In small groups, the children could create a presentation recounting key information about childhood in Tudor England. This could be shared with younger classes in your school.

- **Writing task:** The children could each write an information booklet that could be given to a time-travelling Tudor child, introducing them to childhood in the 21st century. They should think carefully about how to structure and present their information (e.g. clear subheadings; bullet points; key words in bold) as well as deciding what content would be most useful for a Tudor child.

Reading list

Fiction
- *The Boy and the Globe* by Tony Bradman
- *Cue for Treason* by Geoffrey Trease
- *Eliza Rose* by Lucy Worsley
- *Katie Watson and the Painter's Plot* by Mez Blume
- *Treason* by Berlie Doherty
- *Tudor Tales* by Terry Deary

Class reads
- *Spy Master: First Blood* by Jan Burchett and Sara Vogler

Non-fiction
- *Discover the Tudors: Everyday Life* by Moira Butterfield
- *Step Inside Homes Through History* by Goldie Hawk
- *Terrifying Tudors (Horrible Histories)* by Terry Deary
- *Tudors and Stuarts* by Fiona Patchett

Poetry
- 'Love Letter from Mary Tudor to Her Husband, Philip of Spain' by Brian Moses (Linked text: **Unit 4**)

Modelling summarising

See Unit 3 Modelling slides

Use the **Skills guide** (see pages 18 to 19) and the downloadable **Skills graphic** to support your modelling.

1   Look at the section 'What would my family be like?'. Draw lines to match each paragraph to its main topic.

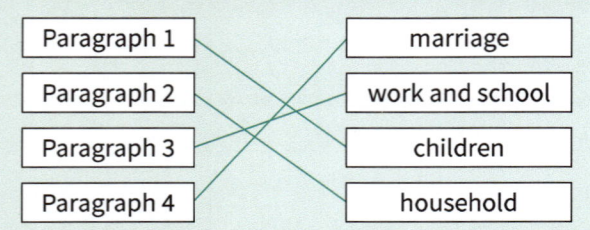

Paragraph 1	—	marriage
Paragraph 2	—	work and school
Paragraph 3	—	children
Paragraph 4	—	household

This question includes a locator, so it is important to model using this to find the correct section in the text. Model identifying the key words from the question, focusing on 'match' and 'main topic' – you could remind the children what a 'main topic' is before continuing. This is an unusual question, as it asks them to match the main content to its appropriate paragraph. Model numbering the paragraphs in the text, then working through each individually to identify the main point. Finally, model matching each paragraph to its main topic, including drawing a clear line.

2   Look at the section 'What clothes would I wear?'. What would be an effective alternative subheading for this section?

Clothing in Tudor times

This question includes a locator, so it is important to model finding the correct section in the text. When identifying the key words from the question, focus on 'effective', 'alternative' and 'subheading'. The children could think of their own ideas for subheadings, sharing them in a whole-class discussion. You could encourage them to challenge each other's suggestions before voting on the most effective one.

3   Look at the paragraph beginning *Towards the end of Tudor times, …* . What is the main point of this paragraph?

Tudor people started to eat new foods from around the world.

Model using the locator to find the correct paragraph. Draw the children's attention to the fact that we are looking for the 'main' point of this paragraph. Model underlining key points as you read through the paragraph and then identify the main point after discussing the possible options with the children.

4   Think about the whole text. What is the main theme of the text?

what life was like for Tudor children

It is important to emphasise to the children that they need to think about everything the text has told them. Once again, the word 'main' should be identified and discussed. This question also includes the word 'theme', which may be unfamiliar to the children, so you could discuss its meaning before modelling an answer.

Summarising questions mark scheme

See page 52

	Answer	Guidance
1	Family life	The children are likely to respond in many ways, from single-word subheadings (e.g. 'Family'), which would be acceptable, to more developed subheadings. Any plausible subheading which focuses on the main point of the section should be accepted. **Award 1 mark for any plausible subheading.**
2	<u>Tudor parents were very strict.</u>	The correct answer can be underlined in a range of ways (e.g. <u>Tudor parents</u>, <u>Tudor parents strict</u>, <u>Tudor parents were strict</u>). If 'Tudor' is not underlined, the answer should not be accepted. **Award 1 mark for a correct answer underlined.**

	Answer	Guidance
3	Wealthy people's clothing ✓	The correct option includes a synonym for 'rich' used in the text. If some children find this question challenging, you could use the word 'rich' in place of 'wealthy' in the options. Some of them may choose 'Noble people's clothing' because noble people tend to be wealthy. If so, explain that this answer is too specific. **Award 1 mark for the correct answer ticked.**
4	Paragraph 1 — poor people's food Paragraph 2 — new foods Paragraph 3 — marzipan Paragraph 4 — rich people's food (Paragraph 2 ↔ rich people's food, Paragraph 4 ↔ marzipan cross-matched)	Some children may benefit from being prompted to look at each paragraph individually, giving each a caption, before matching the statements in the question. **Award 1 mark for at least two pairs correctly matched. Award 2 marks for all four pairs correctly matched.**
5	Life as a Child in Tudor England	The children's responses to this question may or may not include reference to childhood. As long as the response includes reference to life *or* childhood in Tudor times, it should be accepted. **Award 1 mark for a plausible title linked to the content of the text.**

Mix it up! questions mark scheme   See page 53

	Answer	Guidance
1	obey	This is an unusual 'find and copy' question as it asks about the meaning of a phrase rather than a single word. If necessary, remind the children that they should still find and copy only one word in their response. **Award 1 mark for the correct answer.** **Skill: Word meaning.**
2	when they were in their twenties ✓	To increase the challenge in this question, you could give it in an open-response format, perhaps also removing the locator. **Award 1 mark for the correct answer ticked. Skill: Retrieval.**
3	to show off how rich they were	A certain degree of background knowledge is needed here. Although you will already have discussed this part of the text, you could provide the children with a graphic organiser to support their inference-making. **Award 1 mark for a reference to showing their wealth, importance or getting attention.** **Skill: Inference.**
4	Rich people ate white bread and poor people ate dark bread. Rich people ate a lot of meat but poor people could only eat it occasionally as a treat.	Some children will give an implicit comparison (e.g. 'Rich people ate meat'), therefore implying that poor people didn't. If so, remind them that for comparison they always need to write down both sides. You could provide any children who are struggling with some sentence prompts (e.g. 'Rich people … but poor people …'). **Award 1 mark for a reference to one difference taken from the text. Award 2 marks for a reference to two differences taken from the text. Skill: Comparison.**
5	What games would I play?	This question does not require the children to justify their prediction. However, in order to check the depth of their understanding, you could ask them to verbally explain their choice. **Award 1 mark for a plausible prediction linked to the text. Skill: Prediction.**

Life in Tudor Britain, by Anita Ganeri

The Tudors reigned in England from 1485 to 1603. Back then, life was very different. This text tells us about some of the things that were different.

What would my family be like?

In Tudor times, your family was very important, whether you were rich or poor. People often had more children than they do today. They needed children to look after them in their old ages and to carry on the family name. Sadly, many children died at a young age because the Tudors knew little about how to prevent and cure diseases.

Your household probably included your parents, your grandparents, aunts, uncles and cousins. Wealthy families also had plenty of servants to look after them. Tudor parents were very strict. You were expected to obey your parents and might be beaten if you did something wrong.

Up to the age of seven, most children were looked after by their mothers or older brothers and sisters. After this, if you came from a poor family, you had to start work. In wealthy families, some boys went to school. Girls were expected to learn the skills they needed to run a home.

In Tudor times, children could get married when they were as young as 12, though most people married in their twenties. All Tudor couples got married in church.

What clothes would I wear?

If you were poor, you wore hard-wearing clothes made from rough wool cloth. Boys wore breeches tucked into woollen leggings, with a wool or linen shirt. Girls wore a fitted top and long skirt over linen petticoats. Both girls and boys covered their heads when they went out. Girls tucked a linen cap over their hair. Boys had woollen caps.

In rich families, people could afford clothes made from fine woollen cloth, cotton, or silk. At court, nobles wore the latest and most expensive fashions. Men wore tight-fitting breeches, called hose, with silk shirts and doublets (jackets). Women wore full skirts over frames made of whalebone or wood. Both men and women wore frilly linen collars, called ruffs, around their necks.

There were strict laws in Tudor times about what people could wear. For example, only the gentry or nobles were allowed to wear velvet or silk.

Wealthy Tudors wore clothes decorated with jewels, and embroidered with gold and silver. These fabulous outfits were a way of showing off how rich and important they were. We know a lot about these clothes from the paintings of the time.

What would I eat and drink?

In Tudor times, you ate what your family could afford. As a poor child, your food was very plain. You mostly ate heavy, dark bread made from barley or rye, cheese, and a thick vegetable soup, called pottage. You had weak beer to drink.

For most ordinary people, meat was a luxury. But if you came from a wealthy family, meat made up a large part of your diet. It came from deer, cows, pigs, wild boar, birds and rabbits. You usually ate fresh meat, but some was preserved by rubbing salt into it. On Fridays, you ate fish instead of meat. You also ate white bread made from wheat.

Towards the end of Tudor times, people started to eat some new foods. Turkeys, potatoes, and tomatoes were brought back to England by explorers sailing to the New World of the Americas. Cauliflowers came from Asia.

Sugar was very expensive and you only had sweets if you were rich. A favourite treat was marzipan, a paste made from almonds and sugar. It was made into the shapes of castles, animals, and fruit, and decorated with real gold.

Excerpted from the work entitled: *Life in Tudor Britain* © 2014 by Capstone Global Library Limited. All rights reserved.

Summarising

Name: _____

1 Look at the first section. What would be an effective alternative subheading for this part of the text?

_____

1 mark

2 Look at the sentences below. Underline the main point of these sentences.

> Tudor parents were very strict. You were expected to obey your parents and might be beaten if you did something wrong.

1 mark

3 Look at the paragraph beginning *In rich families, people could afford ...* . Which of the following would be the most effective subheading for this paragraph? Tick **one**.

Tudor people's clothing ☐   Wealthy people's clothing ☐

Noble people's clothing ☐   Women's clothing ☐

1 mark

4 Look at the section **What would I eat and drink?** Draw lines to match each paragraph to its main topic.

Paragraph 1	poor people's food
Paragraph 2	new foods
Paragraph 3	marzipan
Paragraph 4	rich people's food

2 marks

5 Think about the whole text. What would be an effective title for the extract?

_____

1 mark

Mix it up!

Name: _____

1 Look at the paragraph beginning *Your household ...* . Find and copy **one** word that means 'do what someone says'.

_____

1 mark

2 Look at the first section. When did most Tudor people get married? Tick **one**.

when they were 12 ☐

when they were in their teens ☐

when they were 20 ☐

when they were in their twenties ☐

1 mark

3 *At court, nobles wore the latest and most expensive fashions.*
Why do you think the nobles did this?

_____

_____

1 mark

4 Look at the section **What would I eat and drink?** Compare what rich people and poor people ate. Give **two** differences.

1 _____

_____

2 _____

_____

2 marks

5 Imagine you could read on. What might the next section in the text be called?

_____

1 mark

Photocopiable resource from *Complete Comprehension 5* © Schofield & Sims Ltd, 2020.

Unit 4

Love Letter from Mary Tudor to Her Husband, Philip of Spain by Brian Moses

▽ Printable text • Modelling slides   📖 Photocopiable text and questions • pages 58 to 61

Many of the children will have heard about Henry VIII and his multiple marriages, but how many will know about his daughter, Mary? Mary I's reputation is that of a cruel monarch, but the truth is more complex. The extract for this unit is a poem by Brian Moses, who is known for his humorous style. In the poem, Mary is cast as a lovelorn wife, desperate for her long-distance husband's return to her. The text provides wonderful opportunities to discuss different portrayals of Mary I, as well as how the poet has played with history when writing this. You could discuss this text alongside that of Unit 3, an information text about childhood in Tudor England.

1 Get ready

Discuss the **Key vocabulary** identified in the **Language toolkit** and then complete the vocabulary activities as desired. Please note that the selected vocabulary is a guide. Depending on the needs of your cohort, additional vocabulary discussion may be beneficial before, during and after reading. Next, display the text (pages 58 to 59) so the children can see the title and any illustrations, and encourage the children to discuss the following questions before reading.

1. The text for this unit is a poem. What different types of poems do you know? What features do poems tend to have?
   You could have some examples of different types of poetry available to show the children and to prompt discussion. Examples of poetry that you could discuss include: haikus; tankas; cinquains; sonnets; limericks; narrative poetry; shape poems; calligrams; blackout poetry. The children should all be able to comment on general features of poetry (e.g. rhyming; verses; atypical punctuation).

2. In this poem, the poet writes as Queen Mary I of England, who was a Tudor queen. What do you know about Tudor times?
   The children should be able to recall some of the facts learnt in the Unit 3 text. If the children have a limited understanding of this period, you could spend some additional time discussing life in Tudor England. See the **Reading list** for ideas for resources.

3. What do you know about Queen Mary I of England or her husband King Philip of Spain?
   It is important for the children to know who Mary and Philip were, and what their relationship was like, in order to understand the poem fully. Spend some time summarising the key facts for the children. See the **Reading list** for helpful resources.

Language toolkit

Key vocabulary

alight	double billing	equal to none
forsake	heir	reignited
relate	send a pigeon	senorita
the state	turtle dove	united

Vocabulary discussion questions

- If you are the **heir** to something, when will you own it?
- What does it mean if you **relate** to someone or something?
- In the UK, is the king/queen or the prime minister in charge of **the state**?
- When something is **united** does it want to break apart or stay together?
- What are you doing if you **forsake** something?

Vocabulary activities

- The author uses idioms and other plays on words (e.g. **double billing** and **equal to none**). Discuss what these mean. Can the children think of any words or groups of words that mean the same?
- **Alight** and **reignited** are both used in connection with fires and burning. Can the children think of any other words that are linked to fires and burning?
- The poem is written as if by Queen Mary I during the 1500s, and contains some old-fashioned references (e.g. **send a pigeon**; 'burn/all those plotting against the state') as well as the Spanish word **senorita**, which you may wish to explain.

Schofield & Sims Complete Comprehension 5

2 First steps

Read the text together and then encourage the children to discuss the following questions.

1. **The poem is set in the 1500s. What does Mary ask Philip to do that couldn't be done in the 1500s?**
   Phone her. This relies on the children's background knowledge, so you may wish to discuss this in more detail.

2. **What does Mary want Philip's help with?**
   To burn all those plotting against the state. The children may also refer to the fact that Mary needs Philip to give her an heir. You could discuss what this means with the children.

3. **What does Mary want Philip to do at the end of the poem?**
   Leave Spain and come back to live in England with her. The children need to know the meaning of 'forsake' to be able to fully understand the last verse. If they find this challenging, you could remind them of the **Key vocabulary**. You could also run one of the vocabulary activities in the **Skills guide** to support discussion (see page 15).

4. **Did you enjoy the poem? Why? Why not?**
   Answers will vary. The children should be able to justify their responses (e.g. *I like the fact that the poet tells us facts about history in a funny way*).

3 Explore

- Mary I is often regarded as a cruel queen and is only remembered for executing her subjects on the grounds of their religion. The children could research the story of the real Mary I, using the books on the **Reading list**, to decide whether Mary was indeed just a cruel queen, or whether there are two sides to the story.

- This poem is a humorous take on the relationship between Queen Mary I of England and her husband, King Philip of Spain. Although Mary is known as 'Bloody Mary', in this poem the poet makes her seem more human, as he suggests what she might have felt about her marriage to Philip. Discuss what the poem tells the reader about how Mary felt. Do the children think she was happy?

- The poet, Brian Moses, uses a range of different language features to make his poem interesting for the reader. Discuss with the children what features and patterns they can find, and what the effect is on the reader (e.g. the number of verses there are and whether the poet uses rhyme). The poet also combines the past and the present – why do the children think he does this?

4 Skills focus   See pages 56 to 57

Use the information from the **Skills guide** and the relevant **Skills graphic** to introduce the skill of word meaning.

1. Model the skill using the **Unit 4 Modelling slides** and the **Modelling word meaning** guidance on page 56.

2. The children can then attempt the **Word meaning** questions on page 60.

3. Finally, the **Mix it up!** questions on page 61 offer practice in a range of comprehension skills.

Answers and marking guidance for all questions are included on pages 56 to 57.

5 Where next?

- **Speaking and listening task:** The children could work in pairs to rehearse and perform the poem, with one child playing Mary, reading the letter before she sends it, and another child playing Philip, reading the letter when he receives it. They could focus on portraying emotion through tone of voice and body language, recognising that the emotions of the sender and the recipient are likely to be different.

- **Writing task:** Split the class into groups and assign each group a different historical figure, known for a key event. Each group should then research a key point in that person's life and create their own poem or rap to explain it, using this unit's poem as inspiration.

Reading list

Fiction
- *Queen of the Sea* by Dylan Meconis
- *Tangled in Time: The Burning Queen* by Kathryn Lasky

Class reads
- *Lady Mary* by Lucy Worsley

Non-fiction
- *Bloody Mary: Cruel Queen or Good Catholic?* by Josh Brooman
- *Kings and Queens* by Tony Robinson
- *Life in Tudor Britain* by Anita Ganeri (Linked text: **Unit 3**)
- *The Tudors: Kings, Queens, Scribes and Ferrets!* by Marcia Williams
- *You Wouldn't Want to Be Married to Henry VIII!* by Fiona Macdonald

Websites
- The Horrible Histories video 'Mary Tudor Vlogs from the 1500s' is available on the CBBC YouTube channel.

Schofield & Sims Complete Comprehension 5

Unit 4

Modelling word meaning

See Unit 4 Modelling slides

Use the **Skills guide** (see pages 14 to 15) and the downloadable **Skills graphic** to support your modelling.

1. Look at the first verse. Find and copy a group of words that means 'destined to be'.

   meant to be

   This question includes a locator, so it is important to model using this to locate the correct verse in the poem. Although the children will have encountered 'find and copy' questions before, you may wish to recap the steps for answering this type of question. It is important to note that this question requires a group of words; you could model discounting individual words, such as 'not', until you reach the required response.

2. Look at the third verse. Which word is closest in meaning to *plotting*? Tick <u>one</u>.

   playing ☐
   mapping ☐
   conspiring ☑
   pushing ☐

   Model using the locator to find the correct verse in the poem. You could discuss the meaning of 'plotting' with the children and gather synonyms before modelling how to look systematically at each of the options. You may find it helpful to model substituting each option into the verse, as detailed in the strategies section of the **Skills guide** (page 15).

3. *Dear Philip, I'm willing to share double billing, …*
   What does the group of words *share double billing* **mean?**

   Mary is willing for her husband to be king and be just as important as her.

   This question includes a quotation, so it is important to model scanning for the quote within the poem, then reading around the quote to gain deeper understanding. As this phrase is idiomatic, you could recap its meaning – the children may recall this from the **Key vocabulary**. Point out that your answer must relate to the context of the poem rather than simply providing a standard definition of the phrase.

4. *Forsake sunny Spain … .* **What does the word** *forsake* **mean in this line?**

   Mary wants Philip to leave Spain.

   Model scanning for the quote within the poem and reading around it to learn more. The target word 'forsake' is challenging. You could refer back to the **Key vocabulary** and discuss the standard definition to strengthen the children's understanding. Again, it is important to emphasise the need to relate the definition to the context (i.e. what Mary would like Philip to do).

Word meaning questions mark scheme

See page 60

	Answer	Guidance
1	their marriage will become exciting/successful/happy	Some children may focus on the literal meaning of 'alight' (i.e. 'on fire'). If so, explain that this is an example of poetic language being used to describe a strong, positive emotion. Some may answer without referring to Mary and Philip's relationship. This should be accepted but prompt them to link their vocabulary understanding back to the context. **Award 1 mark for reference to excitement, success or happiness.**
2	against	If the children do not understand the meaning of 'versus', discuss the standard definition of the word or show the children that it can be abbreviated to 'vs' (e.g. Manchester United vs Manchester City). **Award 1 mark for the correct answer.**

Love Letter from Mary Tudor to Her Husband, Philip of Spain, by Brian Moses

	Answer	Guidance
3	heir	If the children find this challenging, you could provide a more specific locator (e.g. the lines 'Everybody I know/says you should go,/but I need you/to give me an heir'). **Award 1 mark for the correct answer.**
4	their reign will be better than anyone else's	Some children may answer without referring to Mary and Philip's reign. This should be accepted but you could prompt the children to link their vocabulary understanding back to the context of the poem. **Award 1 mark for a reference to the reign being better than others'/the best.**
5	(joined)	You could remind the children of the meaning of 'united', from the **Key vocabulary**, or gather synonyms for the word before they attempt this question. **Award 1 mark for the correct answer circled.**

Mix it up! questions mark scheme — See page 61

	Answer	Guidance
1	She's anxious/upset/heartbroken because she thinks Philip doesn't want to be married to her any more.	Some children may provide vague answers in their responses to this question (e.g. 'ill' or 'sad'). These should be accepted, but the children should be reminded that the question is for 2 marks and requires them to give an explanation using evidence from the text. **Award 1 mark for a plausible emotion. Award 2 marks for a plausible emotion plus appropriate evidence from the text. Skill: Inference.**
2	by phone OR by sending a pigeon OR by writing	This question does not include a locator. You could provide one for some children if they are finding the question challenging. **Award 1 mark for two correct answers. Skill: Retrieval.**
3	She feels she has things in common with him. OR She understands him.	To correctly answer this question, the children must understand the definition of 'relate'. If necessary, remind them of the discussion you had about this word in the **Key vocabulary** section. **Award 1 mark for a reference to having a connection with Philip. Skill: Word choice.**
4	Mary wants a child. ✓ Mary wonders whether Philip likes someone else. ✓	This question requires summarising skills, but the children also have to understand the meaning of the text. If some find this question challenging, you could discuss each distractor in turn with them. **Award 1 mark for one correct box ticked. Award 2 marks for two correct boxes ticked. Skill: Summarising.**
5	No ✓ Mary says he's made it clear he doesn't want to be married to her. He wouldn't want to leave Spain because he lives there/it is sunny there, whereas it is cold and rainy in England.	If necessary, remind the children of the definition of 'forsake'. Accept positive answers as long as appropriate reasons are given to justify the opinion. **Award 1 mark for an answer ticked plus one piece of appropriate evidence. Award 2 marks for an answer ticked plus two pieces of appropriate evidence. Skill: Prediction.**

Love Letter from Mary Tudor to Her Husband, Philip of Spain, by Brian Moses

This is a poem by Brian Moses where he writes as if he is Queen Mary I of England in the 1500s. The poem is a love letter to Mary's husband, Philip, who lives in Spain.

Dear Philip, my Phil
it's making me ill
to think that
you don't love me.
I love you my dear
but you're making it clear
that this marriage was not meant to be.

I'm here all alone,
if only you'd phone,
send a pigeon
or simply just write.
Invite me, please do,
Ibiza with you
would soon set
our marriage alight.

Dear Philip, my love,
my sweet turtle dove,
I know it's with you
I relate.
I wish you'd return
and help me to burn
all those plotting against the state.

Everybody I know
says you should go,
but I need you
to give me an heir.
Do you think that I'm neater
than a sweet senorita
or do your eyes
wander elsewhere?

Dear Philip, I'm willing
to share double billing,
if our love could be
reignited.
Then our reign as one
will be equal to none,
King and Queen of
two countries united.

So Philip, my Phil,
come home, say you will,
without you it's really
quite scary.
Forsake sunny Spain
for the cold English rain
and the arms of
your loving wife, Mary.

'Love Letter from Mary Tudor to Her Husband Philip of Spain' by Brian Moses. From *Lost Magic: The Very Best of Brian Moses* (Macmillan, 2016). Copyright © Brian Moses.

Word meaning

Name: _____

1 *... would soon set
our marriage alight.*
What does Mary mean by *alight*?

_____
_____

1 mark

2 Look at the third verse. Find and copy **one** word that means the same as 'versus'.

_____

1 mark

3 Look at the fourth verse. Find and copy **one** word that means 'successor'.

_____

1 mark

4 *Then our reign as one
will be equal to none, ...*
What does the group of words *equal to none* tell you about Mary's plans for their reign?

_____
_____

1 mark

5 Look at the fifth verse. Which word is closest in meaning to *united*? Circle **one**.

| similar | joined | divided | uniform |

1 mark

Unit 4

Love Letter from Mary Tudor to Her Husband, Philip of Spain, by Brian Moses

Photocopiable resource from *Complete Comprehension 5* © Schofield & Sims Ltd, 2020.

Mix it up!

Name: _____

1 Look at the first verse. How does Mary feel about her marriage? Explain your answer using evidence from the text.

_____
_____
_____

2 marks

2 How does Mary suggest Philip contact her? Give **two** ways.

1 _____

2 _____

1 mark

3 ... I know it's with you
I relate.
What do these lines tell you about how Mary feels about Philip?

_____
_____

1 mark

4 Look at the fourth verse. What are the **two** main points? Tick **two**.

Mary's friends think Philip should leave. ☐

Mary wants to know whether she is neat. ☐

Mary wants a child. ☐

Mary wonders whether Philip likes someone else. ☐

2 marks

5 Do you think Philip will *forsake sunny Spain*? Tick **one**.

Yes ☐   No ☐

Give **two** reasons to explain your answer.

1 _____

2 _____

2 marks

Photocopiable resource from *Complete Comprehension 5* © Schofield & Sims Ltd, 2020.

Unit 4 — Love Letter from Mary Tudor to Her Husband, Philip of Spain, by Brian Moses

Unit 5

The House with Chicken Legs
by Sophie Anderson

▽ Printable text • Modelling slides   📖 Photocopiable text and questions • pages 66 to 69

Inference

Many people know the traditional tale about the witch Baba Yaga and her house with chicken legs, travelling around the countryside deciding whether to help or hinder those who visit her. This text is a reinterpretation of the story and focuses on a girl called Marinka, who helps Baba to guide dead people through The Gate. Marinka's thoughts about her life provide a wealth of opportunities for inference and deduction. You could discuss this text alongside Unit 6 (*The Wizards of Once*), which also features a magical setting.

① Get ready

Discuss the **Key vocabulary** identified in the **Language toolkit** and then complete the vocabulary activities as desired. Please note that the selected vocabulary is a guide. Depending on the needs of your cohort, additional vocabulary discussion may be beneficial before, during and after reading. Next, display the text (pages 66 to 67) so the children can see the title and any illustrations, and encourage the children to discuss the following questions before reading.

1. **This story is based on a folk tale. What do you know about folk tales?**
   Discuss which folk tales the children know, especially from other countries and cultures, and explore the features of folk tales (e.g. a hero overcoming a villain).

2. **Have you ever read an alternative version of a folk tale? How was that version different from the original story?**
   It is likely that the children will have read an alternative version of a folk tale or fairy tale before (e.g. *Snow White in New York* – see **Reading list**. However, they may need some prompting to see the links between the text they have read and the original story.

3. **This story is an alternative version of the tale of Baba Yaga. Have you heard of Baba Yaga before?**
   This would be an ideal time to share the original story with the children. You might like to use *Vasilisa the Beautiful and Baba Yaga* by Alexander Afanasyev from the **Reading list**.

4. **Baba Yaga is a witch. Can you name any texts you have read that feature witches?**
   Encourage the children to say whether the witches they have read about are similar or different to the traditional image of an old, haggard woman doing evil deeds.

Language toolkit

Key vocabulary

at the edge of civilisation	bagels	barren
bleak	carcass	hinge
jackdaw	nestles	perched
tundra	ungainly	weathered

Vocabulary discussion questions

- Most doors have a **hinge**. What does the **hinge** allow the door to do?
- Where would something be if it was **perched**?
- What are **bagels**? When would you eat them?
- Can you give an example of an animal that is **ungainly** when it is on land?
- What is the **carcass** of an animal?

Vocabulary activities

- **Bleak** and **barren** are adjectives used to describe a **tundra**. Explore what sort of environment a **tundra** is and ask the children to think of other synonyms that could be used to describe this type of setting.
- The adjective **weathered** is formed by taking the verb 'to weather' and adding the suffix '–ed'. Ask the children if they can think of any other adjectives that are formed this way.
- Places are described as being **at the edge of civilisation** when they are far away from normal life and home comforts. Ask the children where the edge of civilisation might be for them.

Fiction

Schofield & Sims Complete Comprehension 5

2 First steps

Read the text together and then encourage the children to discuss the following questions.

1. **How often does the house with chicken legs move?**
   Two or three times a year. It is important that the children are specific in their response to this question.

2. **Why does the fence keep falling down?**
   The wind, wild animals or clumsy dead people.

3. **Who are the characters in the story?**
   A girl (called Marinka) who tells the story; a woman/witch called Baba; and Jack, a jackdaw. Although Marinka is not named in the text, the children's introduction to the extract gives her name and explains that she is a young girl. The children may not realise that Jack is a jackdaw. If this is the case, read the penultimate paragraph of the text together.

3 Explore

- If you have shared the original story of *Baba Yaga* during **Get ready**, you could challenge the children to compare the original version with this extract. The children could work in groups to discuss the similarities and differences between the texts, particularly in the portrayal of Baba Yaga.

- The extract mentions that Baba helps to guide the souls of dead people through The Gate. Ask the children what they think The Gate is and what they think is on the other side. This could be used as a starting point for the children to research approaches and beliefs of different religions and cultures to death and life after death. For instance, people who practise the Buddhist religion believe in reincarnation, while those who are Christian often believe in Heaven.

- The narrator of this extract, Marinka, dreams of being able to have a different life, where her house doesn't move and she can play with other children. Discuss with the children the difficulties of always moving around and never settling in one place. The children could work in groups to list the positives and negatives of moving to a new place every few months.

4 Skills focus   See pages 64 to 65

Use the information from the **Skills guide** and the relevant **Skills graphic** to introduce the skill of inference.

1. Model the skill using the **Unit 5 Modelling slides** and the **Modelling inference** guidance on page 64.

2. The children can then attempt the **Inference** questions on page 68.

3. Finally, the **Mix it up!** questions on page 69 offer practice in a range of comprehension skills.

Answers and marking guidance for all questions are included on pages 64 to 65.

5 Where next?

- **Speaking and listening task:** Split the children into two groups. One group should represent the narrator, Marinka, and the other should represent Baba. Ask the group who represent Marinka to prepare arguments for visiting the village and mixing with the living. The group who represent Baba should prepare arguments for staying in the house with chicken legs. The two groups should come together for a class debate. Which is preferable: staying in the house or visiting the village?

- **Writing task:** The children could each create an estate agent's listing for the house with chicken legs. You could print out some examples of listings from estate agent websites and show them to the children. They should use persuasive features to try to sell the house to the highest bidder and think carefully about the way their advert is presented on the page.

Reading list

Fiction
- *Babushka Baba Yaga* by Patricia Polacco
- *Folk Tales for Bold Girls* by Fiona Collins
- *A Pinch of Magic* by Michelle Harrison
- *The Sleeper and the Spindle* by Neil Gaiman
- *Snow & Rose* by Emily Winfield Martin
- *Snow White in New York* by Fiona French
- *Vasilisa the Beautiful and Baba Yaga* by Alexander Afanasyev
- *The Witches* by Roald Dahl
- *The Wizards of Once* by Cressida Cowell (Linked text: **Unit 6**)
- *A Wolf for a Spell* by Karah Sutton
- *A World Full of Spooky Stories* by Angela McAllister
- *A Year Full of Stories* by Angela McAllister

Class reads
- *The Girl Who Speaks Bear* by Sophie Anderson

Non-fiction
- *Goddesses and Heroines* by Xanthe Gresham-Knight
- *Journey through Russia* by Anita Ganeri
- *Russia: The Land and the People* by Cath Senker
- *Your Passport to Russia* by Douglas Hustad

Unit 5

🔍 Modelling inference

▽ See Unit 5 Modelling slides

Use the **Skills guide** (see pages 20 to 21) and the downloadable **Skills graphic** to support your modelling.

1. **Look at the first paragraph. How do you think Marinka feels about her house moving around? Explain your answer using evidence from the text.**

    Frustrated/annoyed because the house moves in the middle of the night without warning. *OR* Unhappy because it always moves to a lonely and bleak place.

    Model using the locator to find the correct paragraph in the text. It is important to make it clear that this question requires the children to provide both a feeling and an explanation using the text. You could discuss what Marinka's feelings might be, then model choosing the strongest and most appropriate feeling for your answer.

2. *Maybe if it was summer a few of them could wander up here, … .* **Why does Marinka want people to visit?**

    Because she doesn't have anyone else other than Baba/she's lonely. *OR* Because she never gets to see living people, only dead people.

    As this question includes a quotation, model scanning for it in the text, before reading around it to gain deeper understanding. This is particularly important here because Marinka mentions things in both preceding paragraphs that could be used to answer this question.

3. *"Thanks, Jack."* **Is Marinka really thankful that Jack has given her a dead spider? Explain your answer using the text.**

    No. She's saying thank you because she knows he's trying to share his food, but she's sick of dead things.

    Model scanning for the quote in the text, then reading around it to learn more. This is a tricky inference as there is an element of sarcasm to Marinka's response. You could encourage the children to read the section of text aloud to ascertain whether they have understood the nuance of Marinka's response. If not, prompt them to put themselves in Marinka's shoes. How would they feel if their pet brought them something dead?

4. **Think about the whole text. What impression do you get of Baba? Give <u>one</u> impression and <u>one</u> piece of evidence from the text.**

Impression	Evidence
caring	She has made a feast for Marinka and her pet Jack.

    It is important to emphasise that this question is about the whole text. Model scanning the text for mentions of Baba and discuss what impression the children get of her at each point in the story. Model choosing the strongest of these impressions. Write your answer with evidence from the text.

Inference questions mark scheme 🔍

📖 See page 68

	Answer		Guidance
1	It is gloomy. ✓ It is isolated. ✓		The distractors here are all referenced in the text. If the children choose an incorrect option, refer them to the word 'always' in the question. Is it always 'snowy' in every place the house goes to? **Award 1 mark for both correct answers ticked.**
2	Because she doesn't have anyone other than Baba to talk to.		Some children may answer vaguely (e.g. 'He's her pet'). If so, prompt them to make their answer more specific and relate it closely to the text. **Award 1 mark for a reference to Marinka not having other people to talk to/being lonely.**

The House with Chicken Legs, by Sophie Anderson

64

Schofield & Sims Complete Comprehension 5

	Answer	Guidance
3	He loves her/trusts her because he sits on her shoulder.	This is an interesting question as it requires the children to make an inference about an animal's feelings. If they find this challenging, prompt them to think about important animals in their lives; if those animals behaved like Jack does, how would the children interpret this? **Award 1 mark for a plausible reference to Jack liking or trusting Marinka.**
4	*Impression*: helpful *Evidence*: She always fixes the fence for Baba.	If the children find this challenging, prompt them to look in the text for their evidence first. Once they have found something Marinka does, discuss what this makes them think about her. **Award 1 mark for a plausible impression. Award 2 marks for a plausible impression with appropriate evidence from the text.**
5	It has chicken legs so it can move. OR It is surrounded by a fence made out of human bones. OR It is always in an isolated place away from towns.	The two reasons provided must be clearly different. Many of the children will answer that the house has chicken legs and it moves. This should only be awarded 1 mark as both points are about the same feature. Encourage the children to see if they can think of anything else that is unusual about the house. **Award 1 mark for each plausible reason, up to a maximum of 2 marks.**

Mix it up! questions mark scheme

See page 69

	Answer	Guidance
1	a number of times per year ✓ at night ✓	This is a fairly straightforward question, but the lack of a locator adds to the challenge. You could provide the children with a locator if necessary. **Award 1 mark for both correct answers ticked. Skill: Retrieval.**
2	crumbling	The children may not initially see 'crumbling' and 'collapsing' as synonyms. If so, discuss the idea of a range of things crumbling or collapsing (e.g. cakes; buildings; walls). **Award 1 mark for the correct answer. Skill: Word meaning.**
3	It's on the edge of the rocky ledge.	Some children may focus on the fact that the house is high up or on a ledge, but they must expand their answer to take into account the meaning of the word 'perched'. If necessary, remind them of your discussion in the **Key vocabulary**. **Award 1 mark for a reference to the house being on the edge of the mountain. Skill: Word choice.**
4	to tell us why Marinka fixes the fence ✓	Some children may focus on Marinka's feelings, which do form a significant part of this paragraph, but they are not the main point. If necessary, prompt them to look at the first sentence of the paragraph for any clues. **Award 1 mark for the correct answer ticked. Skill: Summarising.**
5	I think she'll run away and go down the mountain because she keeps saying how much she wishes she could have a normal house.	The children will need to use the text and their background knowledge of similar stories to create their prediction. Many of them may provide a prediction similar to the example answer. You could share some other ideas to widen discussion. **Award 1 mark for a plausible prediction. Award 2 marks for a plausible prediction plus an explanation linked to the text. Skill: Prediction.**

The House with Chicken Legs, by Sophie Anderson

This is an extract from an alternative version of the traditional tale of Baba Yaga. In this extract, a girl called Marinka dreams of being a normal child in a normal house, instead of living in a house with chicken legs.

My house has chicken legs. Two or three times a year, without warning, it stands up in the middle of the night and walks away from where we've been living. It might walk a hundred miles or it might walk a thousand, but where it lands is always the same. A lonely, bleak place at the edge of civilisation.

It nestles in dark forbidden woods, rattles on windswept icy tundra, and hides in crumbling ruins at the far edge of cities. At this moment, it's perched on a rocky ledge high in some barren mountains. We've been here two weeks and I still haven't seen anyone living. Dead people, I've seen plenty of those of course. They come to visit Baba and she guides them through The Gate. But the real, live, living people, they all stay in the town and villages far below us.

Maybe if it was summer a few of them could wander up here, to picnic and look at the view. They might smile and say hello. Someone my own age might visit – maybe a whole group of children. They might stop near the stream and splash in the water to cool off. Perhaps they would invite me to join them.

"How's the fence coming?" Baba calls through the open window, pulling me from my daydream.

"Nearly done." I wedge another thigh bone into the low stone wall. Usually I sink the bones straight into the earth, but up here the ground is too rocky, so I built a knee-high stone wall all the way around the house, pushed the bones into it and balanced the skulls on top. But it keeps collapsing in the night. I don't know if it's the wind, or wild animals, or clumsy dead people, but every day we've been here I've had to rebuild a part of the fence.

Baba says the fence is important to keep out the living and guide in the dead, but that's not why I fix it. I like to work with the bones because my parents would have touched them once, long ago, when they built fences and guided the dead. Sometimes I think I feel the warmth of their hands on the cold bones, and I imagine what it might have been like to hold my parents for real. This makes my heart lift and ache all at the same time.

The house creaks loudly and leans over until the front window is right above me. Baba pokes her head out and smiles. "Lunch is ready. I've made a feast of *shchi** and black bagels. Enough for Jack too."

My stomach rumbles as the smell of cabbage soup and freshly baked bread hits my nose. "Just the gate hinge, then I'm done." I lift up a foot bone, wire it back into place, and I look around for Jack.

He's picking at a weathered piece of rock underneath a dried-up heather bush, probably hoping to find a woodlouse or beetle. "Jack!" I call and he tilts his head up. One of his silver eyes flashes as it catches the light. He bounds towards me in an ungainly cross between flying and jumping, lands on my shoulder, and tries to push something into my ear.

"Get off!" My hand darts up to cover my ear. Jack's always stashing food to save for later. I don't know why he thinks my ears are a good hiding place. He forces the thing into my fingers instead; something small, dry and crispy. I pull my hand down to look. It's a crumpled, broken spider. "Thanks, Jack." I drop the carcass into my pocket. I know he means well, sharing his food, but I've had enough of dead things. "Come on." I shake my head and sigh. "Baba's made a feast. For two people and a jackdaw."

I turn and look at the town far below us. All those houses, snuggled close together, keeping each other company in this cold and lonely place. I wish my house was a normal house, down there, with the living.

---

* *shchi* is a traditional Russian cabbage soup.

From *The House with Chicken Legs* by Sophie Anderson, copyright © 2018 by Sophie Anderson. Reproduced by permission of Usborne Publishing, 83–85 Saffron Hill, London EC1N 8RT, UK. www.usborne.com

Inference

Name: _____

1 Look at the second paragraph. What is always the same about the location of the house with chicken legs? Tick **two**.

It is snowy. ☐   It is isolated. ☐

It is busy. ☐   It is windy. ☐

It is gloomy. ☐

1 mark

2 Why do you think Marinka talks to Jack, even though he is a bird?

_____
_____

1 mark

3 Look at the paragraph beginning *He's picking at a weathered piece of rock …* . How do you think Jack feels about Marinka?

_____
_____

1 mark

4 Think about the whole text. What impression do you get of Marinka? Give **one** impression and **one** piece of evidence from the text.

Impression	Evidence

2 marks

5 Think about the whole text. Give **two** reasons why Marinka's house is not *a normal house*.

1 _____

2 _____

2 marks

The Wizards of Once
by Cressida Cowell

▽ Printable text • Modelling slides   📖 Photocopiable text and questions • pages 74 to 77

Set long ago in a magical version of Britain, *The Wizards of Once* revolves around the relationship between a boy and girl who have been taught to hate each other. This extract sets the scene and describes what happened to make their world so divided. You could make links between the magical setting of this text and that of Unit 5. You could also discuss this text alongside the Unit 2 text, as they are by the same author.

1 Get ready

Discuss the **Key vocabulary** identified in the **Language toolkit** and then complete the vocabulary activities as desired. Please note that the selected vocabulary is a guide. Depending on the needs of your cohort, additional vocabulary discussion may be beneficial before, during and after reading. Next, display the text (pages 74 to 75) so the children can see the title and any illustrations, and encourage the children to discuss the following questions before reading.

1. **This story is set in a magical version of Britain, long ago. What type of characters might you expect to find in a magical or supernatural setting?**
   The children should be able to draw upon the texts from Units 1, 2 and 5. They may suggest witches, wizards, dragons, vampires, werewolves, mermaids, fairies, elves, unicorns, ogres or trolls.

2. **In this story, a group of people invade the country, taking it over from its native inhabitants. Has Britain ever been invaded in real life? By whom?**
   The children should be able to comment on some invasions they have learnt about in history lessons (e.g. the Roman, Saxon, Viking or Norman invasions). You could also talk about how countries within Britain have invaded each other (e.g. the English invasion of Wales).

3. **In this story, one group of people disagrees with another group and so they try to get rid of them. Have you ever read other stories like this?**
   Answers will vary. If the children have not read texts with a similar theme, you could share a fictional text from the **Reading list**.

4. **The extract ends on a cliffhanger. What is a cliffhanger? Why might an author use one?**
   The children should understand that a cliffhanger is where a text ends at a dramatic or exciting point to make the reader want to read on. You could share examples of cliffhangers from other texts or TV programmes.

Language toolkit

Key vocabulary

empire	extinction	intending
invaded	larks	mammoths
peaceable	perhaps	powerless
quarrelling	sprites	territory

Vocabulary discussion questions

- If you say you are **intending** to do something, what do you mean?
- How can someone who is **powerless** ever defeat their enemies?
- Have you ever tried to stay **peaceable** even when someone was **quarrelling** with you?
- What is the difference between an **empire** and a **territory**?

Vocabulary activities

- The verb 'invade' is usually used to describe a group of people taking over a country or **territory**. It can also describe something uninvited entering a space. Challenge the children to think of some sentences that show the different meanings of **invaded**.
- The suffix '–able' changes a verb or noun (e.g. 'peace') into an adjective (e.g. **peaceable**). How many other adjectives can the children think of that share this suffix? What nouns and verbs do they come from?
- **Mammoths** were prehistoric creatures. We now use the word 'mammoth' as an adjective to describe something that is huge in size. Explore some other adjectives which come from a comparison with an animal (e.g. 'canine'; 'equine'; 'feline'; 'ratty'; 'sluggish').

Mix it up!

Name: _____

1 When does the house with chicken legs move? Tick **two**.

once a year ☐

during the day ☐

a number of times per year ☐

at night ☐

a thousand times ☐

1 mark

2 Look at the second paragraph. Find and copy **one** word that means 'collapsing'.

_____

1 mark

3 *At this moment, it's perched on a rocky ledge high in some barren mountains.* What does the word *perched* tell you about the location of the house?

_____

_____

1 mark

4 Look at the paragraph beginning *Baba says the fence is important ...* . What is the main point of this paragraph? Tick **one**.

to tell us why Marinka fixes the fence ☐

to tell us why Baba wants the fence to be fixed ☐

to tell us that Marinka misses her parents ☐

to tell us that Marinka's parents also built fences ☐

1 mark

5 What do you think Marinka will do later in the story? Explain your prediction using evidence from the text.

_____

_____

_____

2 marks

2 First steps

Read the text together and then encourage the children to discuss the following questions.

1 **What did the Warriors do first after they invaded Britain?**
   They fought the Witches and drove them into extinction.

2 **What did Queen Sychorax ban from the Iron Warrior Empire?**
   All magic (and magical creatures, including sprites, giants, rogrebreaths, snowcats, werewolves, greenteeths). You may find it helpful to discuss the creatures mentioned on the poster in the text, to ensure that the children understand what each is.

3 **What has been discovered at the end of the extract? Why is it important?**
   A gigantic black feather. It's important because it could be the feather of a Witch, which means they might have come back. The children may need to discuss the second part of the answer with you, as it requires inference in addition to retrieval skills.

4 **Did you enjoy the story? Why? Why not?**
   Answers will vary. The children should be able to justify their responses.

3 Explore

- The story focuses on the Warriors' invasion of the dark forests and their attempts to eradicate all magical creatures. Discuss whether the children think that the Warriors' behaviour is right or wrong. Should someone be killed or exiled because of their beliefs or opinions? You could relate this situation to current or historical events.

- At the end of the extract, two characters are introduced. The Wizard boy and Warrior girl have been taught to hate each other since they were born because they belong to different groups. Discuss with the children how they can welcome people with different beliefs or who come from different countries. What can be done to ensure that everyone, whatever their background, is treated equally?

- In the extract, the author provides a backstory for the reader. A backstory explains what happened before the events of the text and can shed light on what is happening in the main story. Discuss another magical story that the children know well such as the fairy tale 'Hansel and Gretel'; what might the backstory be for the witch in the gingerbread house? What has happened to her to make her want to eat Hansel and Gretel?

4 Skills focus   See pages 72 to 73

Use the information from the **Skills guide** and the relevant **Skills graphic** to introduce the skill of prediction.

1 Model the skill using the **Unit 6 Modelling slides** and the **Modelling prediction** guidance on page 72.

2 The children can then attempt the **Prediction** questions on page 76.

3 Finally, the **Mix it up!** questions on page 77 offer practice in a range of comprehension skills.

Answers and marking guidance for all questions are included on pages 72 to 73.

5 Where next?

- **Speaking and listening task:** 'The Warriors thought that just because *some* Magic was bad, *that* meant that ALL Magic was bad.' Divide the class into two groups: the Warriors and the Wizards. Each group should put together some arguments for their cause. Representatives from the two groups could then argue for or against the Warriors' point of view in a mock courtroom debate.

- **Writing task:** Ask the children to reread the second paragraph and then write their own paragraph to describe the setting, using a range of descriptive language to show the complete darkness, both literal and metaphorical, of the forests of the past.

Reading list

Fiction
- *The Apprentice Witch* by James Nicol
- *Arthur: High King of Britain* by Michael Morpurgo
- *The Girl Who Drank the Moon* by Kelly Barnhill
- *The House with Chicken Legs* by Sophie Anderson (Linked text: Unit 5)
- *The Tales of Beedle the Bard* by J.K. Rowling

Class reads
- *A Wizard of Earthsea* by Ursula K. Le Guin

Non-fiction
- *Cut-Throat Celts (Horrible Histories)* by Terry Deary
- *The Genius of the Stone, Bronze, and Iron Ages* by Izzi Howell
- *Iron Age (Found!)* by Moira Butterfield
- *Stone, Bronze and Iron Ages (Explore!)* by Sonya Newland

TV series
- *Merlin* (BBC, 2008–2012)

Unit 6

Modelling prediction

▽ See Unit 6 Modelling slides

Use the **Skills guide** (see pages 22 to 23) and the downloadable **Skills graphic** to support your modelling.

1 If the Witches come back, what might the Warriors use to defeat their magic?

They might use their iron because the magic of the Witches is powerless against it.

This question does not include a locator because prediction questions require the children to use what they know from the whole text to answer. It is important to model identifying the key words in the question and scanning the text for helpful sections. You may also wish to discuss the children's other predictions, which may be plausible but are likely to be less well signposted by the text.

2 Will the Warriors always rule the wildwoods? Explain your answer using evidence from the text.

No, because the Wizards and magical creatures will rise up and work together to make the Warriors leave the wildwoods.

Again, this question does not include a locator. It is important to model identifying key words and locating them in the text. You could point out that the question focuses on the wildwoods, not the whole of Britain or the Iron Warrior Empire. Explain that this would be a 2-mark question so you will need to make two points in your answer as well as answering 'yes' or 'no'. You could use a graphic organiser to support your modelling (see page 23 of the **Skills guide**). Alternative predictions are acceptable as long as they are linked to the text.

3 Look at the last paragraph. How do you think the boy Wizard and girl Warrior will feel when they meet? Explain your answer using evidence from the text.

I think they will feel disgusted because they have been taught by all their people to hate each other.

As this question includes a locator, it is important to model identifying the correct part of the text. You should also model noting the expectations of the question – that your answer will include both a feeling and an explanation of that feeling linked to the text. As this question requires the children to make an inference about emotion as part of their prediction, you could refer to the inference strategies listed in the **Skills guide** (see page 21).

4 Look at the last paragraph. Do you think the black feather belongs to a Witch? Explain your answer using evidence from the text.

Yes, because the author uses questions like 'Could that feather really be the feather of a Witch?'.

Again, model using the locator and focusing on the same paragraph. The children are likely to share a range of predictions and reasoning for this question, depending on their understanding of the text. It is important to note that any prediction, as long as it is rooted in the text, is valid (e.g. 'No, I think it belongs to one of the other banned magical creatures.'). You could model reviewing a number of predictions and discounting weaker examples before choosing your final answer.

Prediction questions mark scheme

See page 76

	Answer	Guidance
1	No, because they will have had time to work out how to battle against the iron and defeat the Warriors. Last time, they didn't know what iron was so they didn't know how to defeat it.	The children are likely to use some extrinsic knowledge to answer prediction questions such as these. As long as the prediction clearly links to events in the text, it should be accepted. **Award 1 mark for a plausible prediction with one piece of evidence from the text. Award 2 marks for a plausible prediction with two pieces of evidence from the text.**
2	No, because the Witches were evil and the Wizards are not. I think the Wizards will help the Warriors to defeat the Witches and then they will become friends.	As in the previous question, the children are likely to use some extrinsic knowledge. This should be accepted as long as the prediction clearly links to events in the text. **Award 1 mark for a plausible prediction with one piece of evidence from the text. Award 2 marks for a plausible prediction with two pieces of evidence from the text.**

	Answer	Guidance
3	He will have his head chopped off.	Some children may make predictions not linked to the poster. If so, remind them to use the locator and to base their prediction on information from the poster only. **Award 1 mark for a reference to Wizards having their heads chopped off.**
4	Evil Returns ✓	If some children choose another response, ask them to verbally justify their answer using the text. If the justification is plausible and text-led, their answer may be acceptable. **Award 1 mark for the correct answer ticked.**
5	I predict that even though they hate each other they will have to work together to save their people from the Witches.	Some children may focus on short- or long-term events. Either are acceptable as long as they link closely to the text. **Award 1 mark for a plausible prediction linked to the text.**

Mix it up! questions mark scheme

See page 77

	Answer	Guidance
1	The author is trying to show the reader that the forest is darker than anything they have seen before.	Some children will only refer to how dark the forest is, without going further. Although this is acceptable, you could discuss as a class how to make the response more specific. **Award 1 mark for a reference to the author trying to show how the forest is darker than anything the reader may have seen before or to show that the forest is a mysterious/imaginary place.** Skill: Word choice.
2	powerless	The paragraph includes the phrase 'iron was the only thing that Magic would not work on' – some children may use this phrase to answer the question. If so, remind them that the question asks for one word only and prompt them to read further into the paragraph to find the correct word. **Award 1 mark for the correct answer.** Skill: Word meaning.
3	devastated because the dark forest was their home and the Warriors were destroying it	The children need to read around the quote to understand what the Warriors were chopping down. You could prompt them to do this before they write their answer. **Award 1 mark for a plausible emotion (e.g. sadness; frustration; anger). Award 2 marks for a plausible emotion plus an explanation linked to the text.** Skill: Inference.
4	No Magic/Magical Creatures Allowed OR Wizards Enter on Pain of Death	Encourage the children to use synonyms to differentiate their title from the original wording in the poster. **Award 1 mark for a plausible title linked to the contents of the poster.** Skill: Summarising.
5	wizards — use good magic sprites — burn like stars giants — are peaceful and slow witches — use magic for evil warriors — came from across the seas	This is a difficult question because there are a lot of competing statements to work through and the children need to locate information from multiple paragraphs. One line has been drawn to help the children. You could provide additional support by supplying them with locators. **Award 1 mark for at least two pairs correctly matched. Award 2 marks for all four pairs correctly matched.** Skill: Retrieval.

The Wizards of Once, by Cressida Cowell

This story is set long, long ago in a magical version of Britain. The extract explains why the Wizards and the Warriors in Britain began to hate each other.

Once there was Magic. It was a long, long time ago, in a British Isles so old it did not know it was the British Isles yet, and the Magic lived in the dark forests. Perhaps you feel that you know what a dark forest looks like.

Well, I can tell you right now that you don't. These were forests darker than you would believe possible, darker than inkspots, darker than midnight, darker than space itself, and as twisted and as tangled as a Witch's heart. They were what is now known as wildwoods, and they stretched as far in every direction as you can possibly imagine, only stopping when they reached a sea.

There were many types of humans living in the wildwoods. The Wizards, who were Magic. And the Warriors, who were not. The Wizards had lived in the wildwoods for as long as anyone could remember, and they were intending to live there forever, along with all the other Magic things.

Until the Warriors came. The Warriors invaded from across the seas, and though they had no Magic, they brought a new weapon that they called IRON, and *iron was the only thing that Magic could not work on*. The Warriors had *iron* swords, and *iron* shields, and *iron* armour, and even the horrifying Magic of the Witches was powerless against this metal.

First the Warriors fought the Witches, and drove them into extinction in a long and terrible battle. Nobody cried for the Witches, for Witches were bad Magic, the worst sort of Magic, the kind of Magic that tore wings from the larks and killed for fun and could end the world and everyone in it.

But the Warriors did not stop there. The Warriors thought that just because *some* Magic was bad, *that* meant that ALL Magic was bad.

So now the Warriors were trying to get rid of the Wizards too, and the ogres and the werewolves, and the untidy quarrelling mess of good sprites and bad sprites that burned like little stars through the darkness, casting spells on mischievous each other, and the giants who moved slow and careful through the undergrowth, larger than mammoths, and peaceable as babies.

The Warriors had sworn that they would not rest until they had destroyed EVERY LAST BIT OF MAGIC in the whole of that dark forest, which they were chopping down as fast as they could with their iron axes, to build their forts and their fields and their new modern world.

> You have now entered
> THE IRON WARRIOR EMPIRE
> **ALL MAGIC IS BANNED**
> in this territory.
>
> NO SPRITES, NO GIANTS,
> NO ROGREBREATHS,
> NO SNOWCATS, NO WEREWOLVES,
> NO GREENTEETHS
> (OR ANY OTHER MAGIC CREATURES).
> NO FLYING,
> NO ENCHANTED OBJECTS,
> NO SPELLING, CURSING OR CHARMING.
> NO MAGIC WHATSOEVER.
>
> And any Wizards entering these lands may most unfortunately have their heads removed.
>
> By Order of Her Majesty
>
> *Queen Sychorax*
>
> QUEEN SYCHORAX, IRON WARRIOR QUEEN

This is the story of a young boy Wizard and a young girl Warrior who have been taught since birth to hate each other like poison. The story begins with the discovery of A GIGANTIC BLACK FEATHER. Could it be that the Wizards and the Warriors have been so busy fighting *each other* that they have not noticed the return of an ancient evil? Could that feather really be the feather of a Witch?

From *The Wizards of Once*, by Cressida Cowell. Text and illustrations copyright © Cressida Cowell, 2017. Reproduced by permission of Hodder Children's Books, an imprint of Hachette Children's Books, Carmelite House, 50 Victoria Embankment, London imprint, EC4Y 0DZ.

Prediction

Name: _____

1 Look at the paragraph beginning *Until the Warriors came*. If the Witches return, do you think the Warriors will be able to defeat them again? Explain your answer using evidence from the text.

_____
_____
_____

2 marks

2 Do you think the Wizards will become extinct like the Witches? Explain your answer using evidence from the text.

_____
_____
_____

2 marks

3 Look at the poster. If the Wizard boy enters the Iron Warrior Empire, what is likely to happen to him?

_____
_____

1 mark

4 Which of the following would be the most effective title for the next chapter in the story? Tick **one**.

Feathers Flying ☐

Evil Returns ☐

A Fight with the Witches ☐

The Warriors Run ☐

1 mark

5 What do you think will happen after the Wizard boy and the Warrior girl meet?

_____
_____

1 mark

Photocopiable resource from *Complete Comprehension 5* © Schofield & Sims Ltd, 2020.

Mix it up!

Name: _____

1 *… darker than inkspots, darker than midnight, darker than space itself, …*
What effect does the author create with this choice of words?

_____
_____

1 mark

2 Look at the fourth paragraph. Find and copy **one** word that shows that the Witches' magic did not work on iron.

_____

1 mark

3 *… which they were chopping down as fast as they could with their iron axes, …*
How do you think the Wizards felt about this? Explain your answer using the text.

_____
_____
_____

2 marks

4 Look at the whole of Queen Sychorax's poster. Write a title for the poster to summarise what it tells us.

_____

1 mark

5 Draw lines to match each creature to its description. One has been done for you.

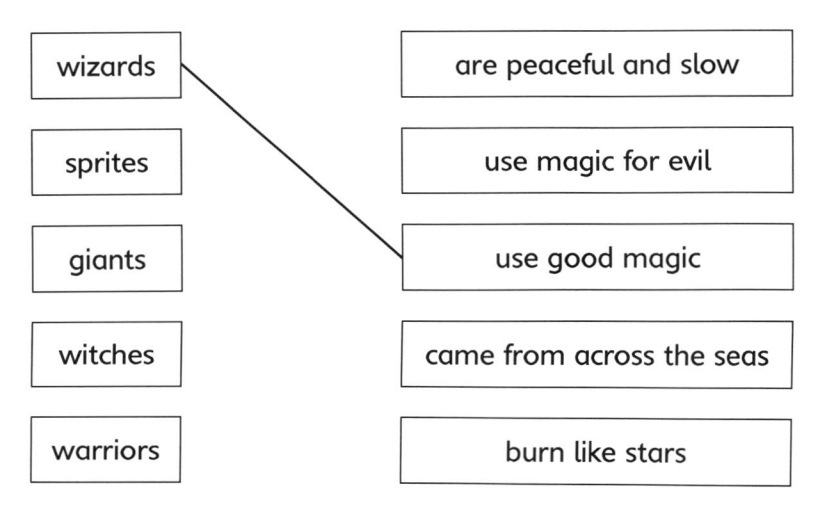

wizards		are peaceful and slow
sprites		use magic for evil
giants		use good magic
witches		came from across the seas
warriors		burn like stars

(wizards is connected to use good magic)

2 marks

Photocopiable resource from *Complete Comprehension 5* © Schofield & Sims Ltd, 2020.

Unit 6 — The Wizards of Once, by Cressida Cowell

The Polar Bear Explorers' Club
by Alex Bell

Unit 7 · Inference · Fiction

⬇ Printable text • Modelling slides   📖 Photocopiable text and questions • pages 82 to 85

Adventure and exploration are key themes in this story about Stella Starflake Pearl and her quest to become an explorer. This extract reveals Stella's innermost thoughts on the night before her birthday. Once Progress check 1 has been completed, you could discuss how the two extracts share a similar setting. You could also compare Stella's relationship with her pet polar bear, Gruff, to that of Marinka and Jack in the Unit 5 text, *The House with Chicken Legs*.

① Get ready

Discuss the **Key vocabulary** identified in the **Language toolkit** and then complete the vocabulary activities as desired. Please note that the selected vocabulary is a guide. Depending on the needs of your cohort, additional vocabulary discussion may be beneficial before, during and after reading. Next, display the text (pages 82 to 83) so the children can see the title and any illustrations, and encourage the children to discuss the following questions before reading.

1. **This text is an adventure story. What features do you think the story will have?**
   Answers will vary. You could make links to the Unit 2 text *How to Train Your Dragon* which, although set against a quasi-historical backdrop, is also an adventure story. Features discussed might include: an exciting event which sets off the action; a heroic main character; the characters going on a journey or quest.

2. **The main character in this story wants to be an explorer. What do you know about real-life explorers and exploration?**
   The children are likely to have encountered explorers in some form as part of the wider curriculum. You may also wish to discuss the wider definition of exploration in terms of how the children can explore the world. See the **Reading list** for some helpful resources.

3. **Have you ever read any other stories about exploration?**
   Whereas the previous question focuses on factual exploration, it is important to link the children's background knowledge to the reading of fiction. You may wish to refer back to the Unit 1 text *Dragonology*, which explains how a dragonologist can explore the world of dragons and their habitats.

Language toolkit

Key vocabulary

cajoled	deformed	destined
fond	navigator	orphaned
ought to	packed off	peculiar
solitary	tradition	turret

Vocabulary discussion questions

- Have you ever felt you **ought to** do something even though you didn't want to? What was it?
- When were you last **cajoled** by someone? What did they try to make you do?
- Can you think of some animals that are **solitary** and some that live in groups?
- What foods are you **fond** of eating and which do you dislike?
- What **traditions** do you have with your family and friends?

Vocabulary activities

- **Packed off** is an idiomatic phrase that means 'to send something to another location unceremoniously'. How many other words or groups of words can the children think of that mean something similar (e.g. 'send packing'; 'ship off'; 'oust'; 'turn out')?
- The word **solitary** comes from the Latin word *solus*, which means 'alone'. How many other words can the children think of that may derive from this word (e.g. 'solo'; 'solitaire'; 'soliloquy')?
- The word **navigator** has the suffix '–or', which shows that it is a condition or a property of a person or thing. How many other occupations can the children think of that end with '–or'?

2 First steps

Read the text together and then encourage the children to discuss the following questions.

1 **Who is the main character? What does she want to be?**
   Stella Starflake Pearl. She wants to be an explorer, specifically a navigator. The children may only focus on Stella's ambition to be an explorer. However, it is important to draw their attention to the fact that Stella actually wants to be a navigator.

2 **Who gave Stella her name? Why?**
   The fairies, because Felix, her adoptive father, could not think of a first name for her.

3 **Who is Gruff? What do we know about him?**
   Gruff is Stella's pet polar bear. He was an orphan with a deformed paw who Felix brought home one day. He likes to cuddle Stella and eat fish cookies.

3 Explore

- The children could research real polar explorers, such as Jade Hameister, who was just 16 years old when she reached the South Pole unassisted. Watch her TEDx talk to find out more about her journey and then vote on whether the children would want to travel to the South Pole like Jade. Discuss whether the hardships and dangers she faced were worth it.

- In the story, Felix has adopted a polar bear as a pet. The children could research real-life people who have kept wild animals as pets (e.g. Josephine Baker and her cheetah). Discuss how laws and regulations limit the type of animals people can keep as pets and whether the children think this is right or wrong.

- Stella Starflake Pearl is desperate to become an explorer, but in her world, girls are not allowed to have this occupation. Discuss the theme of gender equality, researching which roles have traditionally been seen as either male or female. You could also extend your discussion to today's debates on the gender pay gap, exploring how the children feel about this important issue. You could balance the discussion by talking about the positive changes that have taken place over recent decades, as well as what still needs to change.

4 Skills focus   See pages 80 to 81

Use the information from the **Skills guide** and the relevant **Skills graphic** to introduce the skill of inference.

1 Model the skill using the **Unit 7 Modelling slides** and the **Modelling inference** guidance on page 80.

2 The children can then attempt the **Inference** questions on page 84.

3 Finally, the **Mix it up!** questions on page 85 offer practice in a range of comprehension skills.

Answers and marking guidance for all questions are included on pages 80 to 81.

5 Where next?

- **Speaking and listening task:** In pairs, the children could predict and then role-play what happens next in the story, focusing on continuing the conversation that starts between Felix and Stella in the last paragraph of the extract.

- **Writing task:** In small groups, the children could discuss the possible reasons why Stella is not allowed to become an explorer. They could then write a letter to Felix, asking him to reconsider.

Reading list

Fiction
- *A Boy Called Christmas* by Matt Haig (Linked text: Progress check 1)
- *The Boy Who Sailed the Ocean in an Armchair* by Lara Williamson
- *The Eye of the North* by Sinéad O'Hart
- *Explorers on Witch Mountain* (*The Polar Bear Explorers' Club* Book 2) by Alex Bell
- *Race to the Frozen North: The Matthew Henson Story* by Catherine Johnson
- *To the Edge of the World* by Julia Green

Class reads
- *The Lost Book of Adventure* by Teddy Keen (ed)

Non-fiction
- *Alastair Humphreys' Great Adventurers* by Alastair Humphreys
- *Fantastic Female Adventurers* by Lily Dyu
- *The Incredible Ecosystems of Planet Earth* by Rachel Ignotofsky
- *Shackleton's Journey* by William Grill
- *Survivors* by David Long
- *Wild Girl: How to Have Incredible Outdoor Adventures* by Helen Skelton
- *You Wouldn't Want to be a Polar Explorer!* by Jen Green

Websites
- The British Antarctic Survey's Education page has some resources aimed at primary school learners.
- Jade Hameister's website is full of inspiring information about the young adventurer.

Modelling inference

See Unit 7 Modelling slides

Use the **Skills guide** (see pages 20 to 21) and the downloadable **Skills graphic** to support your modelling.

1. **Look at the first paragraph. How does Stella feel about going to stay with Aunt Agatha? Give <u>one</u> feeling and <u>one</u> piece of evidence from the text.**

   She feels unhappy/reluctant/she is dreading it because Aunt Agatha doesn't know how to look after children/she gave Stella a cabbage for her packed lunch.

   This question includes a locator. Model using this and remind the children that the question asks for two pieces of information. You could discuss possible feelings with them and then decide on the most apt word choice together. Model writing your answer in a table format (see **Modelling question 4** in **Unit 5**).

2. *But right now she was too angry and disappointed for presents, … .* **Why is Stella annoyed at this point in the story?**

   Because Felix wouldn't let her be an explorer and presents won't change this.

   Model scanning for the quote in the text and reading around the quote to gain a deeper understanding. The children may go back to the first paragraph and lift the text (e.g. 'Felix was still refusing to take her on his expedition'). If so, remind them that because we are making an inference, we need to use the text and our own knowledge, and ensure that our answer links directly to the inference we are being asked to make.

3. **Read from the paragraph beginning *Unfortunately, though,* … to the end of the text. How does Stella feel about Gruff? Give <u>one</u> feeling and <u>one</u> piece of evidence from the text.**

   She loves him. She gives him a treat of a fish cookie because she knows he will enjoy it.

   Model using the locator and remind the children that this question requires two pieces of information. Relate your discussion to the children's experiences of owning pets – how do they show they love and care for them? Model writing your answer in a table format (again, see **Modelling question 4** in **Unit 5**).

4. **Think about the whole text. Do you think Felix is caring? Explain your answer using the text.**

   Yes, because he says he has been searching everywhere to find her. Also, he saved her and Gruff from being snow orphans and dying out on the ice alone.

   Remind the children that the question refers to the whole text and explain that they will need to scan the text to find key information. Point out to them that this question requires us to do two things: give our opinion and give at least one piece of evidence to justify it. Model scanning the text for 'Felix' and discussing each point with the children to decide whether it shows he is caring or not. Some children may have differing opinions. This should be encouraged as long as they can justify their opinions using the text.

Inference questions mark scheme

See page 84

	Answer	Guidance
1	*Feeling*: uneasy *Evidence*: She doesn't want to go to Aunt Agatha's house because she hates it there.	The children may attribute various feelings to Stella. Any negative emotion should be accepted as long as it is linked to the text. Positive emotions based on a misreading of 'splendid' and 'cheerful' should not be accepted. **Award 1 mark for a plausible feeling. Award 2 marks for a plausible feeling with appropriate evidence from the text.**
2	Because only explorers have middle names and usually girls cannot be explorers.	The children may only give one point in their response (e.g. 'Only explorers have middle names'). This is acceptable but you could prompt them to verbally extend their answers. **Award 1 mark for a reference to explorers having middle names.**

	Answer	Guidance
3	She is avoiding Felix. ✓	The second option may prove tempting if the children remember Stella's thoughts from the first paragraph. Discuss that, while it is true that Stella does not want to go, she is actually hiding to avoid Felix. **Award 1 mark for the correct answer ticked.**
4	He was something else she had to look after and she might have thought it would be dangerous as polar bears are huge/aren't usually pets.	If the children find this challenging, discuss the prospect of bringing a polar bear to school. What might happen? How might this mirror Mrs Sap's thoughts? **Award 1 mark for one plausible reason linked to the text. Award 2 marks for two plausible reasons linked to the text.**
5	*Impression*: determined *Evidence*: She won't give up, even though Felix has told her lots of times that she can't go on the expedition and be an explorer.	The children may not yet feel confident with this style of question. Encourage them to find a piece of evidence first, before deciding what impression this gives them. **Award 1 mark for a plausible impression. Award 2 marks for a plausible impression with appropriate evidence from the text.**

Mix it up! questions mark scheme

See page 85

	Answer	Guidance
1	She never gets bored of looking at maps. She thinks a compass looks beautiful.	The children may lift their answers directly from the text. This should be accepted as long as the points are clear. **Award 1 mark for a reference to both points. Skill: Retrieval.**
2	peculiar	The children have encountered 'peculiar' in the **Key vocabulary**. If necessary, discuss the meaning of 'unusual' and gather some appropriate synonyms to support them. **Award 1 mark for the correct answer. Skill: Word meaning.**
3	The fairies gave Stella a middle name, so she must be an explorer.	The children may find this challenging as the paragraph includes references to a range of different things. Remind them that they are looking for the *main* point rather than *any* point and therefore it is likely to be mentioned more than once. **Award 1 mark for a reference to Stella having a middle name, meaning she must be an explorer. Skill: Summarising.**
4	He is moving slowly/heavily/awkwardly. OR His movements are slow/heavy.	Some children may say that Gruff is 'large'. As 'lumbering' is most often used to describe how large things move, this should be accepted as one point. **Award 1 mark for each correct answer, up to a maximum of 2 marks. Skill: Word choice.**
5	Yes, because the fairies gave her a middle name and only explorers have them/ because she lives with Felix who is an explorer so he'll show her how to be one.	The children will need to use the text and their background knowledge of similar stories to create their prediction. Due to the content of this text, there may be a wide range of reasons given for the prediction. Positive or negative responses should be accepted as long as appropriate evidence accompanies them. **Award 1 mark for a plausible prediction with one piece of evidence from the text. Award 2 marks for a plausible prediction with two pieces of evidence from the text. Skill: Prediction.**

The Polar Bear Explorers' Club, by Alex Bell

This is an extract from a story about Stella Starflake Pearl, a girl who is desperate to become an explorer, just like her adoptive father, Felix. There's just one problem: in Stella's world, girls are not allowed to become explorers.

Stella Starflake Pearl rubbed frost from the turret window and scowled out at the snow. She ought to be in the most splendid mood – it was her birthday tomorrow, and the only thing Stella loved more than birthdays was unicorns. But it was hard to be cheerful when Felix was still refusing to take her on his expedition. Even though she'd begged, pleaded, cajoled, threatened, and stormed – none of it had done any good at all. The thought of being packed off to stay with Aunt Agatha again made Stella feel positively sick. Aunt Agatha didn't know much about children, and sometimes she got things completely wrong, like the time she gave Stella a cabbage for her packed school lunch. No chocolate dinosaurs, or marshmallow cake, or treats of any kind – just a single, solitary, useless cabbage. Plus, Aunt Agatha had nostril hair. It was almost impossible not to sometimes stare at it.

Stella had wanted to be an explorer ever since she was old enough to know what the word meant. More specifically, she wanted to be a navigator. She never got tired of looking at maps and globes, and as far as she was concerned, a compass was just about the most beautiful thing in the whole entire world. After unicorns, obviously.

And if she wasn't meant to be an explorer, then why had the fairies given her a middle name? Everyone knew that only explorers had three names. Felix had given her his last name, Pearl, but then hadn't known what to do about a first name, so he'd asked the fairies to name her instead. This was probably a good thing, because Felix was fond of peculiar names like Mildred and Wilhelmina and Barbaretta. But the fairies had given her not one name, but two: Stella and Starflake. And surely that meant that she was absolutely destined to be an explorer.

Stella scrambled onto the turret window seat and pulled her legs up to rest her chin on her knees. It was getting dark outside, and she knew Felix would be looking for her to give her her twilight present. It was a tradition they had – Stella was always allowed to open one present the night before her birthday. But right now she was too angry and disappointed for presents, so she'd come up to the turret to hide. And if she tucked herself into the window seat she couldn't be seen from the end of the corridor.

Unfortunately, though, Gruff liked the turret too, and he had come lumbering over almost as soon as Stella had sat down, and was now poking his nose into her pockets in search of cookies. Mrs. Sap, their housekeeper, hadn't been very happy when Felix brought an orphaned polar bear cub home one day, but the bear would have died otherwise. Not only was he an orphan, he had a deformed paw as well, and would never have been able to survive in the wild. Stella thought it was the best thing ever to have a polar bear in the house, even if he did almost flatten her sometimes when he wanted to cuddle. Polar bears were quite startlingly huge.

She reached into her pocket for a fish cookie and held it out to Gruff, who took it from her with extreme gentleness and then crunched it up happily, covering her in crumbs and bear slobber. Stella was used to the bear slobber, so she didn't mind, but the downside of Gruff coming to see her was that he gave her presence away when Felix entered the corridor a few minutes later.

"Ah, there you are," he said, stopping by the window seat. "I've been searching high and low for you."

Stella looked up into his face – her favourite face in the whole world, the first one she could ever remember seeing. Stella had been a snow orphan, just like Gruff. If Felix hadn't found her when she was a baby, she would probably have died out there, alone on the ice.

From *The Polar Bears Explorers' Club* by Alex Bell, Faber and Faber Ltd, copyright © 2017 by Alex Bell. Reproduced by permission of the publishers.

Inference

Name: _____

1 Look at the first paragraph. How does Stella feel at this point in the story? Give **one** feeling and **one** piece of evidence from the text.

Feeling	Evidence

2 marks

2 Look at the third paragraph. Why is it important that Stella has a middle name?

_____
_____

1 mark

3 Look at the fourth paragraph. Why is Stella hiding in the turret? Tick **one**.

She is upset with Mrs Sap. ☐

She doesn't want to go to Aunt Agatha's house. ☐

She is avoiding Felix. ☐

She is playing hide and seek. ☐

1 mark

4 Why do you think Mrs Sap was not happy when Felix brought Gruff home?

_____
_____

2 marks

5 Think about the whole text. What impression do you get of Stella? Give **one** impression and **one** piece of evidence from the text.

Impression	Evidence

2 marks

The Polar Bear Explorers' Club, by Alex Bell

Unit 7

Photocopiable resource from *Complete Comprehension 5* © Schofield & Sims Ltd, 2020.

Mix it up!

Name: _____

1 *More specifically, she wanted to be a navigator.*
Give **two** reasons why Stella wanted to be a navigator.

1 _____

2 _____

1 mark

2 Look at the paragraph beginning *And if she wasn't meant to ...* . Find and copy **one** word that means 'unusual'.

_____

1 mark

3 Look at the paragraph beginning *And if she wasn't meant to ...* . What is the main point of this paragraph?

_____

_____

1 mark

4 *... and he had come lumbering over almost as soon as Stella had sat down, ...*
What does the word *lumbering* suggest about Gruff's movements? Give **two** points.

1 _____

2 _____

2 marks

5 Do you think Stella will become an explorer? Explain your prediction using evidence from the text.

_____

_____

_____

2 marks

Photocopiable resource from *Complete Comprehension 5* © Schofield & Sims Ltd, 2020.

A Boy Called Christmas
by Matt Haig

Printable text • Modelling slides • Photocopiable text and questions • pages 87 to 89

Matt Haig's wonderful children's books combine humour with important messages, emphasising the importance of being true to oneself and facing up to life's challenges. *A Boy Called Christmas* is the first in Haig's series about 'the true story of Father Christmas'. In this extract, we meet Nikolas, a young boy who leads a difficult life and receives very few Christmas presents, but who is destined to become someone extraordinary. This extract shares a similar setting to *The Polar Bear Explorers' Club* by Alex Bell (Unit 7). After completing this Progress check, you could compare how the authors have used language to set the scene and tone in the two texts. **For guidance on running this task, see page 11.**

Progress check questions mark scheme

#	Answer	Guidance
1	confuse	You could remind the children that a correct response should include one word only. **Award 1 mark for the correct answer.** **Skill: Word meaning.**
2	the pixies	Some children may use their extrinsic knowledge to answer (e.g. 'people in France'). Draw their attention to the question wording 'according to the text' and explain that they must answer using the information they can see in the text. **Award 1 mark for the correct answer. Skill: Retrieval.**
3	He feels frustrated because he wishes he could have a proper toy from the toyshop. OR He tried to be happy but it's hard because he doesn't have much to play with.	To achieve 2 marks, answers need to include an emotion and an appropriate explanation. Some children will lift the feeling from the text. This is acceptable as long as it shows an understanding of the text (e.g. accept 'He tried to be happy', but do not accept 'He was happy'). **Award 1 mark for a plausible emotion. Award 2 marks for a plausible emotion plus an explanation linked to the text. Skill: Inference.**
4	"I'm really sorry but we just can't afford it."	To answer correctly, the children need to infer that Nikolas's family are struggling financially. Some children may respond positively: this should only be accepted if the response includes a change in fortune (e.g. "Yes you can, as I've just been given a new job/we don't have to worry any more."). **Award 1 mark for a plausible response focusing on the answer to Nikolas's question (e.g. "I'm really sorry but you can't"). Award 2 marks for a plausible response that includes an explanation (e.g. "I'm really sorry but we just can't afford it"). Skill: Prediction.**
5	Impossible Things Can Happen OR Father Christmas/Nikolas Wishes for a Toy	This is quite a challenging question, as there are two main themes in this extract – Nikolas's destiny to become Father Christmas and his current life as a child. The children's answers need only refer to one of these themes. **Award 1 mark for a plausible title linked to the content of the text. Skill: Summarising.**

Progress check 1

Name: _____

1 Look at the paragraph beginning *Maybe you don't call him ...* . Find and copy **one** word that means the same as 'complicate'.

_____

1 mark

2 According to the text, who started calling Father Christmas by another name?

_____

1 mark

3 Read from *Now, Nikolas was a happy boy ...* to the end of the text. How do you think Nikolas feels about his life? Explain your answer using evidence from the text.

_____

_____

_____

2 marks

4 *"Can I have one?"*
Write a sentence to show what Nikolas's parents might say in response.

_____
_____
_____

2 marks

5 Think about the whole text. What would be an effective title for this extract?

_____

1 mark

Photocopiable resource from *Complete Comprehension 5* © Schofield & Sims Ltd, 2020.

A Boy Called Christmas, by Matt Haig

Have you ever wondered about the true story of Father Christmas? In this extract, we discover how a young boy named Nikolas began his journey to become a hero to children all over the planet.

You are about to read the true story of Father Christmas. Yes. Father Christmas. You may wonder how I know the true story of Father Christmas, and I will tell you that you shouldn't really question such things. It's rude, for one thing. All you need to understand is that I do know the story of Father Christmas, or else why would I be writing it?

Maybe you don't call him Father Christmas. Maybe you call him something else.

Santa or Saint Nick or Santa Claus or Sinterklaas or Kris Kringle or Pelznickel or Papa Noël or Strange Man With A Big Belly Who Talks to Reindeer And Gives Me Presents. Or maybe you have a name you've come up with yourself, just for fun. If you were an elf, though, you would always call him Father Christmas. It was the pixies who started calling him Santa Claus, and spread the word, just to confuse things, in their mischievous way.

But whatever you happen to call him, you know about him, and that's the main thing.

Can you believe there was a time when no one knew about him? A time when he was just an ordinary boy called Nikolas, living in the middle of nowhere, or the middle of Finland, doing nothing with magic except believing in it? A boy who knew very little about the world except the taste of mushroom soup, the feel of a cold north wind, and the stories he was told. And who only had a doll made out of a turnip to play with.

But life was going to change for Nikolas, in ways he could never have imagined. Things were going to happen to him. Good things. Bad things. *Impossible Things*. But if you are one of those people who believe that some things are impossible, you should put this book down right away. It is most certainly not for you. Because this book is full of *impossible things*.

Now, Nikolas was a happy boy. Well, actually, no. He would have told you he was happy, if you asked him, and he certainly *tried* to be happy, but sometimes being happy is quite tricky. I suppose, what I am saying is that Nikolas was a boy who believed in happiness, the way he believed in elves and trolls and pixies, but he had never actually seen an elf or a troll or a pixie, and he hadn't really seen proper happiness either. Take Christmas. This is the list of every present Nikolas had received for Christmas. In his entire life. 1. A wooden sleigh. 2. A doll carved out of a turnip. That's it.

The truth is that Nikolas's life was hard, but he made the best of it. He had no brothers or sisters to play with, and the nearest town – Kristiinankaupunki (Kris-tee-nan-cow-punky) – was a long way away. It took even longer to get to than it did to pronounce. And anyway there wasn't much to do in Kristiinankaupunki except go to church or look in the window of the toyshop.

"Papa! Look! A wooden reindeer!" Nikolas would gasp as he pressed his nose against the glass of that toyshop.

Or,

"Look! An elf doll!"

Or,

"Look! A cuddly doll of the king!"

And once he even asked,

"Can I have one?"

From *A Boy Called Christmas* by Matt Haig and Chris Mould, copyright © Matt Haig, 2015. Reproduced with permission of Canongate Books Ltd.

The Wolf Wilder
by Katherine Rundell

▽ Printable text • Modelling slides   📖 Photocopiable text and questions • pages 94 to 97

Wolves have long been feared. Despite dying out in many countries, they continue to play a part in our psyche through fairy tales like 'Little Red Riding Hood'. *The Wolf Wilder* transports us to an alternative Russia, where aristocrats keep wolves and feed them caviar. When a wolf attacks, superstition dictates that it must be sent to a wolf wilder rather than killed. The text in Unit 9 also features wolves: once both units have been completed, you could discuss the links between the two, focusing on their characterisation of wolves.

① Get ready

Discuss the **Key vocabulary** identified in the **Language toolkit** and then complete the vocabulary activities as desired. Please note that the selected vocabulary is a guide. Depending on the needs of your cohort, additional vocabulary discussion may be beneficial before, during and after reading. Next, display the text (pages 94 to 95) so the children can see the title and any illustrations, and encourage the children to discuss the following questions before reading.

1 **This story is set in an alternative universe Have you ever read other texts that are set in alternative versions of places or historical periods?**
   Although many children's books use this device, the children may not easily pick up on it. You could remind them of the settings in *How to Train Your Dragon* (Unit 2) and *The Wizards of Once* (Unit 6).

2 **This story is set in Russia. What do you know about Russia?**
   You could begin by asking or showing the children where Russia is on a map, then use resources from the **Reading list** to explore more about Russia.

3 **This story is about wolves. What do you know about wolves? Have you ever read any other texts about wolves?**
   The children should be able to discuss what wolves are or identify them from images. When discussing texts, many of the children may refer to fairy tales. You could share some of the texts given on the **Reading list** to explore this topic further.

4 **In the story, the wolves are in captivity. What does this mean? Have you ever seen a wild animal in captivity?**
   Answers will vary depending on the children's background knowledge and experiences. They are likely to mention zoos, as many will have visited one.

Language toolkit

Key vocabulary

arises	aristocrats	butlers
caviar	declared	elegant
insidious	merchants	ringmaster
roubles	tamed	unique

Vocabulary discussion questions

- Where would a **ringmaster** be employed?
- What job do **merchants** do?
- Can a lion ever be **tamed**? Explain why.
- If a problem **arises** when you are at school, what might you do to solve it?
- What is something **unique** about you?
- If somebody's behaviour is **insidious**, is it friendly and open or sly and cunning?

Vocabulary activities

- Discuss the fact that although **arises** and **aristocrat** look similar, they have different origins. **Arise** is from the Old English for 'rise away' and **aristocrat** is from the Ancient Greek *aristos* meaning 'best' and *kratos* meaning 'power'. Can the children think of any related words that use the suffixes '–crat' or '–cracy'?
- The word **declared** comes from the Latin *clarare*, meaning 'to make clear', and the prefix 'de–', meaning 'thoroughly'. Sometimes the prefix 'de–' can mean 'off' or 'from', as in 'depart'. Challenge the children to think of more words beginning 'de–' and to group them by meaning.
- The text includes some specialised vocabulary (e.g. **roubles**, **caviar** and **butlers**). You could use images to explore these words.

2 First steps

Read the text together and then encourage the children to discuss the following questions.

1 **Who hunts newborn wolves? Why?**
   Gangs of wolf merchants in the western wild parts of Russia. They sell them to aristocrats who think they are good luck.

2 **Why do aristocrats send their wolves to the wolf wilder?**
   If a wolf hurts somebody, it is bad luck to hurt or kill the wolf. The aristocrats send these wolves to the wolf wilder so that they can avoid the bad luck. Some children might say *so that they can be taught to be wild again and released*. If so, refer back to the text and discuss whether this is the motive for, rather than the result of, the aristocrats' actions.

3 **What is a wolf wilder?**
   A person whose job it is to teach captive wolves how to be wild again/to hunt and fight and howl/to distrust humans, so they can be released into the wild.

4 **Did you enjoy the story? Why? Why not?**
   Answers will vary. The children should be able to justify their responses.

3 Explore

- Wolves are much more fascinating creatures than their fictional depictions would have us believe. Continue your discussion from **Get ready** about the children's knowledge and opinions about wolves. The children could research wolves using the resources from the **Reading list**, finding out about their behaviour, habitats and what led to them dying out in some countries, including the United Kingdom.

- In the story, aristocratic Russians keep wolves as pets. Discuss whether wolves, being wild animals, would be happy to be kept as pets. You could talk about the fact that some real people keep wild animals as pets and status symbols.

- In some countries, conservationists are reintroducing animals into the environment. These are sometimes animals that have been kept captive like the wolves in this story, or sometimes species that used to live in the countryside but have died out. In the UK, beavers, which had died out in England by the 12th century, have been reintroduced. There are growing calls to reintroduce other animals, including wolves, to try to rewild the countryside and return it to its natural state. You could discuss the children's opinions of reintroduction and ask them to research some of the other reintroduction efforts that are taking place (see the website in the **Reading list**).

4 Skills focus   See pages 92 to 93

Use the information from the **Skills guide** and the relevant **Skills graphic** to introduce the skill of retrieval.

1 Model the skill using the **Unit 8 Modelling slides** and the **Modelling retrieval** guidance on page 92.

2 The children can then attempt the **Retrieval** questions on page 96.

3 Finally, the **Mix it up!** questions on page 97 offer practice in a range of comprehension skills.

Answers and marking guidance for all questions are included on pages 92 to 93.

5 Where next?

- **Speaking and listening task:** In groups, the children could create a presentation or video campaign persuading people that wolves are not the terrifying creatures portrayed by fairy tales and films. They could focus on the features of these majestic animals and their positive effects on the environment.

- **Writing task:** Continuing on from your discussions in **Explore**, the children could write letters to rewilding advocates, such as the organisation listed in the **Reading list**, asking them about their work.

Reading list

Fiction
- *Koshka's Tales: Stories from Russia* by James Mayhew
- *Nevertell* by Katharine Orton
- *The Tale of the Firebird* by Gennady Spirin
- *The Tzar's Curious Runaways* by Robin Scott-Elliot
- *A Wolf Called Wander* by Rosanne Parry
- *The Wolves of Willoughby Chase* by Joan Aiken (Linked text: **Unit 9**)

Class reads
- *The Ways of the Wolf* by Smriti Prasadam-Halls

Non-fiction
- *Journey Through Russia* by Anita Ganeri
- *Running with Wolves* by Jim Dutcher and Jamie Dutcher
- *Russia: The Land and the People* by Cath Senker
- *What If There Were No Gray Wolves?* by Suzanne Slade
- *When the Wolves Returned* by Dorothy Hinshaw Patent

Websites
- The 'Conservation' section of the Wildwood Trust's website has interesting information about reintroducing species to the countryside.

Schofield & Sims Complete Comprehension 5

Modelling retrieval

See Unit 8 Modelling slides

Use the **Skills guide** (see pages 16 to 17) and the downloadable **Skills graphic** to support your modelling.

1. **According to the text, what is a wolf wilder *not* like? Give two things.**

   1 lion tamer   2 circus ringmaster

   This question does not include a locator, so it is important to model identifying key words (e.g. 'wolf wilder'; '*not* like') and scanning the text to locate the appropriate section. You could also draw the children's attention to the expectations of the question: it asks for two points.

2. **How much do pure white wolf pups cost?**

   up to two thousand roubles

   Again, as there is no locator, model identifying the question's key words and scanning for them in the text. Model finding the sentence beginning 'A wolf pup can …'. Model noticing that there is some competing information here, as it mentions both ordinary wolf pups and pure white ones. Explain that you will take your time and think carefully about which information from the sentence is relevant for your question. Finally, model formulating an answer by calculating the cost of pure white pups compared to normal pups.

3. **Read from the paragraph beginning *But a wolf cannot …* to the end of the text. According to the text, what happens to wolves that bite people in Russia?**

   They are sent to the wolf wilder.

   Model using the locator to find the relevant part of the text, noting that it is quite lengthy. Explain that you will scan for the question's key words and their synonyms in this section. The target information straddles two paragraphs, and it is important to refer to this in your discussion, as some children would naturally stop reading at the end of the first paragraph. You could model referring back to the locator to check that you have used the whole of the specified section.

4. **Tick to show whether each statement is true or false.**

	T	F
Captured wolves wear golden chains.	✓	
A wolf can be tamed like a dog.		✓
Killing a wolf brings good luck.		✓
Wolves like caviar.		✓

   Although not stated explicitly, this question requires the children to think about the whole text. Model reading one statement at a time and identifying the key words. You could explain that a true statement will appear in the text, while a false statement may have a related statement in the text (perhaps including a negative), or not appear in the text at all. Model scanning the text to find the relevant information and then discuss whether each statement is true or false.

Retrieval questions mark scheme

See page 96

	Answer	Guidance
1	a piece of a finger OR the lobe of an ear/ an ear lobe OR a toe (or two)	Some children may provide a vague response (e.g. 'finger'). If so, ask them to refer back to the text and make sure they have retrieved the exact information given. **Award 1 mark for two correct answers.**
2	in the western wild areas of Russia	Some children may lift their answer directly from the text and others may paraphrase. Either is acceptable as long as the answer refers to west/western Russia. 'Russia' alone is insufficient. **Award 1 mark for the correct answer.**

	Answer	Guidance
3	when they (go mad and) bite someone	Some children may use only the second paragraph of the given section (e.g. 'when an aristocrat wants to get rid of them'). If so, prompt them to reread the preceding paragraph to find out why this might be. **Award 1 mark for reference to wolves biting, injuring or eating people.**
4	your toenails grow inwards OR your teeth will grow outwards OR your gums will bleed	If some children focus on other effects of the bad luck (e.g. life beginning to disappear), refocus them on the key word 'body'. **Award 1 mark for a correct answer.**
5	Peter the Great — had seven white wolves aristocrats — believe that killing a wolf is bad luck wolf wilders — smell of raw meat	The children need to use the whole extract to answer this question. If they find it challenging, you could provide them with a locator for each statement. **Award 1 mark for all three pairs correctly matched.**

Mix it up! questions mark scheme See page 97

	Answer	Guidance
1	Wolf wilders don't wear sequins but circus ringmasters often do.	This paragraph makes several comparisons between wolf wilders and other people. Some are obvious (e.g. remarks about appearance) while others require more inference (e.g. injuries). Both sides of the comparison need to be specified to gain the mark. If the children answer 'wolf wilders don't wear sequins', encourage them to extend their answer. **Award 1 mark for a reference to what wolf wilders wear, what they smell like or their injuries.** Skill: Comparison.
2	arises	Answers longer than one word should not be accepted. **Award 1 mark for the correct answer.** Skill: Word meaning.
3	It's about how killing a wolf brings bad luck. ✓	The distractors here are all plausible and closely linked to the content of the paragraph. You could discuss some strategies for finding the main point of a paragraph at this point (see page 19). **Award 1 mark for the correct answer ticked.** Skill: Summarising.
4	They are worried that the wolf will eat them.	The children must read around the locator quotation to find the necessary contextual information. Some may respond vaguely (e.g. 'the wolf'). If so, encourage them to explain what specifically about the wolf is making the butlers nervous. **Award 1 mark for a reference to the wolves eating them, injuring them or getting away.** Skill: Inference.
5	It makes the reader feel sorry for the captive wolves. OR It makes the reader happy that the wolf wilder can rewild the wolves.	This question requires deep understanding. To provide more support, you could discuss this question. Think aloud: *How do we feel about the idea of a human who can never laugh? Is this a good situation or something we would want to change to make that person's life better?* You could also provide the children with multiple choice options to choose from. **Award 1 mark for a reference to feeling sorry for the wolves in captivity/happy that the wolf wilder can rewild the wolves.** Skill: Relationship.

Schofield & Sims Complete Comprehension 5

The Wolf Wilder, by Katherine Rundell

This story introduces the mythical wolf wilders, people who rewild wolves in the snowy countryside of Russia. They believe that wolves should be set free and learn to howl, rather than being trapped in the homes of wealthy aristocrats who treat the wolves as playthings.

Wolf wilders are almost impossible to spot.

A wolf wilder is not like a lion tamer nor a circus ringmaster: wolf wilders can go their whole lives without laying eyes on a sequin. They look, more or less, like ordinary people. There are clues: more than half are missing a piece of a finger, the lobe of an ear, a toe or two. They go through clean bandages the way other people go through socks. They smell very faintly of raw meat.

In the western wild parts of Russia there are gangs of wolf merchants who hunt newborn pups. They snatch them, still wet and blind, and carry them away in boxes, selling them to men and women who live elegant lives in thick-carpeted houses in St Petersburg. A wolf pup can fetch a thousand roubles, a pure white one as much as twice that. A wolf in the house is said to bring good fortune: money and fame, boys with clean noses and girls without pimples. Peter the Great had seven wolves, all as white as the moon.

The captured wolves wear golden chains and are taught to sit still while people around them laugh and drink and blow cigar smoke into their eyes. They are fed caviar, which they find disgusting. Some grow so fat that the fur on their stomach sweeps the ground as they waddle up and down stairs, and collects fluff and ash.

But a wolf cannot be tamed in the way a dog can be tamed, and it cannot be kept indoors. Wolves, like children, are not born to lead calm lives. Always the wolf goes mad at the imprisonment, and eventually it bites off and eats a little piece of someone who was not expecting to be eaten. The question then arises: what to do with the wolf?

Aristocrats in Russia believe that the killing of a wolf brings a unique kind of bad luck. It is not the glamorous kind of bad luck, not runaway trains and lost fortunes, but something dark and insidious. If you kill a wolf, they say, your life begins to disappear. Your child will come of age on the morning that war is declared. Your toenails will grow inwards, and your teeth outwards, and your gums will bleed in the night and stain your pillow red. So the wolf must not be shot, nor starved; instead it is packed up like a parcel by nervous butlers, and sent away to the wolf wilder.

The wilder will teach the wolves how to be bold again, how to hunt and fight, and how to distrust humans. They teach them how to howl, because a wolf who cannot howl is like a human who cannot laugh. And the wolves are released back on to the land where they were born, which is as tough and alive as the animals themselves.

From *The Wolf Wilder* by Katherine Rundell. Published by Bloomsbury Children's Books, 2016. Copyright © Katherine Rundell. Reproduced by permission of the author c/o Rogers, Coleridge & White Ltd., 20 Powis Mews, London W11 1JN.

Retrieval

Name: _____

1 Look at the paragraph beginning *A wolf wilder is not ...* . Give **two** things a wolf wilder might be missing.

1 _____

2 _____

1 mark

2 According to the text, where are wolves hunted?

_____

1 mark

3 Read from the paragraph beginning *But a wolf ...* to *... sent away to the wolf wilder*. When do wolves get sent to the wolf wilder?

_____

_____

1 mark

4 Look at the paragraph beginning *Aristocrats in Russia ...* . Give **one** thing that might happen to your body if you kill a wolf.

_____

1 mark

5 Draw lines to match each person or group of people to the correct statement.

Peter the Great		believe that killing a wolf is bad luck
aristocrats		had seven white wolves
wolf wilders		smell of raw meat

1 mark

Photocopiable resource from *Complete Comprehension 5* © Schofield & Sims Ltd, 2020.

Unit 8 — The Wolf Wilder, by Katherine Rundell

Mix it up!

Name: _____

1 Look at the paragraph beginning *A wolf wilder ...* . Give **one** difference between a circus ringmaster and a wolf wilder.

_____

_____

1 mark

2 *Always the wolf goes mad at the imprisonment, and eventually it bites off and eats a little piece of someone who was not expecting to be eaten. The question then arises: what to do with the wolf?*
Find and copy **one** word that means 'comes up'.

_____

1 mark

3 Look at the paragraph beginning *Aristocrats in Russia ...* . What is the main point of this paragraph? Tick **one**.

It's about what the wolf wilders do. ☐

It's about killing wolves. ☐

It's about sending wolves to the wolf wilder. ☐

It's about how killing a wolf brings bad luck. ☐

1 mark

4 *... instead it is packed up like a parcel by nervous butlers, ...*
Why do you think the butlers are nervous at this point in the story?

_____

_____

1 mark

5 *They teach them how to howl, because a wolf who cannot howl is like a human who cannot laugh.*
What effect does this sentence have on the reader?

_____

_____

1 mark

Photocopiable resource from *Complete Comprehension 5* © Schofield & Sims Ltd, 2020.

Unit 9

The Wolves of Willoughby Chase
by Joan Aiken

▽ Printable text • Modelling slides 📖 Photocopiable text and questions • pages 102 to 105

Classic fiction is sometimes overlooked in a world where there is so much newer children's literature. *The Wolves of Willoughby Chase* is wonderful for exploring the meaning and in-context use of a wide range of vocabulary. The ever-present threat of the wolves provides a suspenseful atmosphere in this extract, in which the historical setting and the character of Miss Bonnie are also focal points. Wolves are also essential to the plot of the Unit 8 text, *The Wolf Wilder*, but there they are portrayed very differently. You could compare the presentation of wolves in both texts once both units have been completed.

1 Get ready

Discuss the **Key vocabulary** identified in the **Language toolkit** and then complete the vocabulary activities as desired. Please note that the selected vocabulary is a guide. Depending on the needs of your cohort, additional vocabulary discussion may be beneficial before, during and after reading. Next, display the text (pages 102 to 103) so the children can see the title and any illustrations, and encourage the children to discuss the following questions before reading.

1. **This text is an example of classic fiction. Classic texts were written a long time ago and are still popular today. Can you name any other classic stories?**
   You may have explored examples of classic children's literature during lessons. If so, you could prompt the children to recall the names and plots of these texts. If they cannot name any other examples, you could share some from the **Reading list**.

2. **This story is set during the Victorian era. What differences might you expect to find between a text set in the present day and this one?**
   You could ask the children to think about key topics such as housing and clothing, as they did in Unit 3 when discussing the Tudors. You could also choose to explore the Victorian era in more detail using the non-fiction resources listed in the **Reading list**.

3. **In this story, the main character has a maid. What is a maid? What do they do?**
   Unless the children have read other texts that feature servants, they may not be able to answer. As the children's understanding of this topic will be extended during **Explore**, at this point a basic understanding of what a maid is and does will be sufficient.

Language toolkit

Key vocabulary

commanded	corniced	eminence
hubbub	indignation	inevitable
obstinate	reckless	savage
sombre	survey	vigil

Vocabulary discussion questions

- What can be **savage**?
- When have you been **reckless**?
- What might you hear in a **hubbub**?
- Would you be likely to laugh and smile if you were in a **sombre** mood?
- If you **survey** the view outside your window, what are you doing?
- Why might you show **indignation** if someone was being **obstinate**?

Vocabulary activities

- **Savage, reckless, sombre** and **obstinate** are all powerful adjectives. Ask the children to find synonyms for their choice of one of these words and rank them in a 'Shades of meaning' scale (see page 15).

- **Inevitable** and **indignation** begin with the prefix 'in–'. What do the children think this prefix means? How many other words can they think of that share this prefix?

- This text contains some old-fashioned vocabulary with which the children may be unfamiliar (e.g. 'turrets'; 'battlements'; 'goffering'; 'porters'; 'stationmaster'; 'muskets'; 'fowling pieces'). You could discuss these terms to support their understanding.

Word meaning • Fiction

Schofield & Sims *Complete Comprehension 5*

98

2 First steps

Read the text together and then encourage the children to discuss the following questions.

1. **Where is the story set?**
   In a house called Willoughby Chase, in Willoughby Wold. The children may infer that the house is in England. However, as this is not referred to in the text, remind them to retrieve information they can see in the text only.

2. **Which characters appear in the extract? What are their roles?**
   A little girl called Miss Bonnie who lives in the house and her maid Pattern who looks after her.

3. **What is Miss Bonnie waiting for?**
   For someone to arrive on the train. The children may also note that the person who is arriving is female, as Miss Bonnie refers to her using the pronoun 'she'.

4. **Did you enjoy the story? Why? Why not?**
   Answers will vary. The children should be able to justify their responses (e.g. *I didn't like the idea of lots of wolves being near the train station*).

3 Explore

- Many of the texts that we think of as classic literature were written, and are set, in the Victorian and Edwardian eras (e.g. *The Secret Garden*). Discuss how Joan Aiken evokes the past in this extract. You might talk about the setting, the characters or other elements such as descriptions of clothing or interiors (e.g. petticoats; nursery). You could also encourage the children to compare the extract with life today – what is different?

- In the extract, Miss Bonnie is a child from a rich family who live in a large house. She is cared for by her maid, Pattern, and it is likely that her family employed many other servants to clean and cook for them. Discuss how in the past it was common for rich people to employ servants. The children could do some research to find out the differences between life 'below stairs' and upstairs.

- Throughout the extract, the pleasant description of Willoughby Chase is interspersed with comments about the ravenous wolves loose around the countryside. Joan Aiken builds up tension and atmosphere slowly through brief comments alluding to their presence. Discuss the language Aiken uses to do this and whether the children think she is successful in creating a tense atmosphere.

4 Skills focus   See pages 100 to 101

Use the information from the **Skills guide** and the relevant **Skills graphic** to introduce the skill of word meaning.

1. Model the skill using the **Unit 9 Modelling slides** and the **Modelling word meaning** guidance on page 100.

2. The children can then attempt the **Word meaning** questions on page 104.

3. Finally, the **Mix it up!** questions on page 105 offer practice in a range of comprehension skills.

Answers and marking guidance for all questions are included on pages 100 to 101.

5 Where next?

- **Speaking and listening task:** The children could work in pairs to role-play the extract, with one child acting as Miss Bonnie and one as Pattern. Challenge them to use clues from the reporting clauses (e.g. 'was her continual cry') to help them plan out what their characters' actions and expressions should be.

- **Writing task:** The children could rewrite the extract from the point of view of Miss Bonnie's maid Pattern. They could spend time discussing how Pattern might feel during her conversation with Miss Bonnie – is she frustrated at Miss Bonnie's impatience, or does she understand why she is so excited and eager?

Reading list

Fiction
- *The Lottie Project* by Jacqueline Wilson
- *Moondial* by Helen Cresswell
- *The Railway Children* by E. Nesbit
- *The Secret Diary of Jane Pinny: Victorian House Maid* by Philip Ardagh
- *The Secret Garden* by Frances Hodgson Burnett
- *The Wolf Wilder* by Katherine Rundell (Linked text: Unit 8)

Class reads
- *The Whispering Mountain* by Joan Aiken

Non-fiction
- *100 Facts on Victorian Britain* by Jeremy Smith
- *Vile Victorians (Horrible Histories)* by Terry Deary

Films
- *The Wolves of Willoughby Chase* (Atlantic Entertainment Group/Zenith Entertainment, 1989)

Modelling word meaning

See Unit 9 Modelling slides

Use the **Skills guide** (see pages 14 to 15) and the downloadable **Skills graphic** to support your modelling.

1 *There were hundreds of them at work, wrapped in sacking because of the bitter cold, and keeping together in groups for fear of the wolves, grown savage and reckless from hunger.* **Underline a group of words that tells you the weather was freezing.**

   bitter cold

   Although the quote is lengthy, it is still important to model locating it in the text. You should also draw the children's attention to the key words 'Underline' and 'group of words' in the question. You could discuss what the weather is like when it is freezing, to activate the children's background knowledge. Next, talk about words that are used to describe 'freezing' temperatures and model scanning the sentence for similar words. Remind them that they are looking for a group of words, so 'cold' alone would not be sufficient. Some may suggest 'wrapped in sacking'. Explain that the answer must describe the weather rather than what people are wearing as a result of the weather.

2 *… corniced with snow, … .* **Which word is closest in meaning to** *corniced*? **Tick one.**

   joined ☐ crowned ✓ covered ☐ decorated ☐

   The question includes a short quotation as its locator. Model finding it and reading the relevant paragraph. This will help the children to understand that the house's appearance is being described. Although they will have encountered 'corniced' in the **Key vocabulary**, you could recap its meaning before modelling substituting each option into the text and discussing whether it makes sense. Finally, model choosing the most effective synonym and ticking your chosen answer.

3 *"Will she be here soon, Pattern? Will she?" was her continual cry.* **What does** *continual* **tell you about how Miss Bonnie was speaking?**

   She asked the same thing again and again/lots of times/constantly.

   After modelling using the locator to find the correct section of text, draw the children's attention to the key word 'continual' and discuss its meaning. Remind them that they have to relate the meaning to the context. Discuss what 'continual' tells you about Miss Bonnie's speech and model writing a response that links the meaning and context together.

4 *Her square chin also gave promise of a powerful and obstinate temper, not always perfectly controlled.* **Find and copy one word that means the same as 'stubborn'.**

   obstinate

   Model finding the quote in the text. It is important to remind the children to always read around the target quote to learn more about the context. Discuss the meaning of 'stubborn' and gather synonyms for it. Next model searching the target sentence for a possible synonym. Model locating 'obstinate' and discuss whether it is a synonym. Finally, use substitution to see if 'stubborn' works in the target sentence.

Word meaning questions mark scheme

See page 104

	Answer	Guidance
1	fierce ✓	'Severe' can also be used as a synonym for 'savage' in a different context. If the children choose this option, you could recap the different meanings of 'savage'. **Award 1 mark for the correct answer ticked.**
2	hideous howling	As this question asks for a group of words, the children might include additional words in their answer. This is acceptable if the words are taken from the phrase 'the hideous howling of the wolves without'. **Award 1 mark for the correct answer.**

	Answer	Guidance
3	survey	You could discuss the meaning of 'observe' and in what contexts we might use this word, or a synonym for it, before the children attempt the question. **Award 1 mark for the correct answer.**
4	She could barely see them/couldn't see them very well. *OR* She almost couldn't see them.	Some children may overread and respond that Pattern 'couldn't see' the tongs (at all). If so, discuss whether 'hardly see' is the same as 'couldn't see' or whether it is less extreme. **Award 1 mark for a reference to not being able to see the tongs very well.**
5	completely	The children may focus on the sense of 'perfect' meaning 'to be without fault'. However, the adverbial form is used slightly differently here. If the children struggle, gather synonyms and encourage them to use substitution to decide which is most effective. **Award 1 mark for an appropriate synonym.**

Mix it up! questions mark scheme — See page 105

	Answer	Guidance
1	Willoughby Chase	Some children may provide only part of the name. This should not be accepted. You could prompt them to check that they have written the 'full name'. **Award 1 mark for the correct answer.** Skill: Retrieval.
2	She can quickly change moods.	Less precise answers such as 'sometimes she is cheerful and sometimes she is angry' should be accepted. Some children may say that Miss Bonnie is 'moody'. Do not accept this as it shows incomplete understanding. You could prompt the children to think about 'dance with laughter' and 'flash with indignation' as separate points. **Award 1 mark for a reference to Miss Bonnie's changing moods.** Skill: Word choice.
3	No, because Pattern says that the people who work at the station have been practising with their guns so they can stop the wolves if they attack the train. *OR* Yes, because there are lots of wolves around. Miss Bonnie is worried about the train so they must have delayed the train before.	The children's responses may be positive or negative; either is acceptable, as long as an appropriate explanation is given. **Award 1 mark for a plausible prediction with one piece of evidence from the text. Award 2 marks for a plausible prediction with two pieces of evidence from the text.** Skill: Prediction.
4	*Impression*: impatient *Evidence*: She won't stop asking Pattern when her visitor will arrive.	The children's own opinions are likely to influence their answers here. Accept any plausible impression linked to the text. **Award 1 mark for a plausible impression. Award 2 marks for a plausible impression with appropriate evidence from the text.** Skill: Inference.
5	Waiting for a Visitor ✓	Some children may choose 'Miss Bonnie' as much of the action revolves around her. You could remind them that titles should focus on the main points of the text – is the focus on telling us about Miss Bonnie, or telling us about Miss Bonnie's wait for her visitor? **Award 1 mark for the correct answer ticked.** Skill: Summarising.

The Wolves of Willoughby Chase, by Joan Aiken

This story is about a young girl called Bonnie who lives in a great house called Willoughby Chase. At this point in the story, Bonnie is waiting impatiently for someone's arrival.

It was dusk – winter dusk. Snow lay white and shining over the pleated hills, and icicles hung from the forest trees. Snow lay piled on the dark road across Willoughby Wold, but from dawn men had been clearing it with brooms and shovels. There were hundreds of them at work, wrapped in sacking because of the bitter cold, and keeping together in groups for fear of the wolves, grown savage and reckless from hunger.

Snow lay thick, too, upon the roof of Willoughby Chase, the great house that stood on an open eminence in the heart of the wold. But for all that, the Chase looked an inviting home – a warm and welcoming stronghold. Its rosy herring-bone brick was bright and well-cared-for, its numerous turrets and battlements stood up sharp against the sky, and the crenellated balconies, corniced with snow, each held a golden square of window. The house was all alight within, and the joyous hubbub of its activity contrasted with the sombre sighing of the wind and the hideous howling of the wolves without.

In the nursery a little girl was impatiently dancing up and down before the great window, fourteen feet high, which faced out over the park and commanded the long black expanse of road.

"Will she be here soon, Pattern? Will she?" was her continual cry.

"We shall hear soon enough, I dare say, Miss Bonnie," was the inevitable reply from her maid, who, on hands and knees in front of the fire, was folding and goffering the frills of twenty lace petticoats.

The little girl turned again to her impatient vigil. She had climbed up on to the window-seat, the better to survey the snowy park, and was jumping on its well-sprung cushions, covered in crimson satin. Each time she bounced, she nearly hit the ceiling.

"Give over, Miss Bonnie, do," said Pattern after a while. "Look at the dust you're raising. I can hardly see my tongs. Come and sit by the fire. We shall hear soon enough when the train's due."

Bonnie left her perch reluctantly enough and came to sit by the fire. She was a slender creature, small for her age, but rosy-cheeked, with a mass of tumbled black locks falling to her shoulders, and two brilliant blue eyes, equally ready to dance with laughter or flash with indignation. Her square chin also gave promise of a powerful and obstinate temper, not always perfectly controlled. But her mouth was sweet, and she could be very thoughtful on occasion – as now, when she sat gazing into the fire, piled high on its two carved alabaster wolfhounds.

"I hope the train hasn't been delayed by wolves," she said presently.

"*Nonsense*, Miss Bonnie dear – don't worry your pretty head with thoughts like that," replied Pattern. "You know the porters and stationmaster have been practising with their muskets and fowling pieces all the week."

From *The Wolves of Willoughby Chase* by Joan Aiken, Red Fox, 2004, copyright © 1962 by Joan Aiken. Reproduced by permission of The Random House Group Ltd.

Word meaning

Name: _____

1 *... the wolves, grown savage and reckless from hunger.*
Which word is closest in meaning to *savage*? Tick **one**.

severe ☐

fierce ☐

tame ☐

loud ☐

1 mark

2 Look at the second paragraph. Find and copy a group of words that describes the noises the wolves were making.

_____

1 mark

3 Look at the paragraph beginning *The little girl turned ...* . Find and copy **one** word that means the same as 'observe'.

_____

1 mark

4 *I can hardly see my tongs.*
What does the word *hardly* tell you about how well Pattern can see her tongs?

_____

_____

1 mark

5 *Her square chin also gave promise of a powerful and obstinate temper, not always perfectly controlled.*
What word could be used to replace *perfectly* in this sentence?

_____

1 mark

Photocopiable resource from *Complete Comprehension 5* © Schofield & Sims Ltd, 2020.

Mix it up!

Name: _____

1 What is the name of Miss Bonnie's home?

_____

1 mark

2 *... two brilliant blue eyes, equally ready to dance with laughter or flash with indignation.*
What does this group of words tell you about Miss Bonnie's personality?

_____

_____

1 mark

3 *"I hope the train hasn't been delayed by wolves, ..."*
Do you think the train will be delayed by the wolves? Explain your answer using evidence from the text.

_____

_____

_____

2 marks

4 Think about the whole text. What impression do you get of Miss Bonnie? Give **one** impression and **one** piece of evidence from the text.

Impression	Evidence
_____	_____
	_____
	_____

2 marks

5 Think about the whole text. Which of the following would be the most effective title for this extract? Tick **one**.

The Wolves Wait ☐   Winter and the Wolves ☐

Miss Bonnie ☐   Waiting for a Visitor ☐

1 mark

Photocopiable resource from *Complete Comprehension 5* © Schofield & Sims Ltd, 2020.

Unit 9 — The Wolves of Willoughby Chase, by Joan Aiken

Whale Boy
by Nicola Davies

▽ **Printable text** • **Modelling slides**   📖 **Photocopiable text and questions** • **pages 110 to 113**

Many children are thrilled by any encounter with animals. Although for most, interactions will be limited to pets and animals in captivity, some are lucky enough to observe wild animals in their own habitats. In this text, Michael and Eugenia come across a school of sperm whales while sailing near their Caribbean home. The wonderful description of the animals' behaviour is contrasted with that of a gathering storm, which provides an element of suspense and danger. You could discuss the links with the text in **Unit 11**, a newspaper article about orcas at SeaWorld, perhaps contrasting the experiences of the whales in this story with those in captivity.

---

① Get ready

Discuss the **Key vocabulary** identified in the **Language toolkit** and then complete the vocabulary activities as desired. Please note that the selected vocabulary is a guide. Depending on the needs of your cohort, additional vocabulary discussion may be beneficial before, during and after reading. Next, display the text (pages 110 to 111) so the children can see the title and any illustrations, and encourage the children to discuss the following questions before reading.

1. **The characters in this story are on a sailing trip together. Can you think of any other texts that you have read where the characters are on a journey?**
   As journeys are a common theme in children's literature, the children should be able to contribute some ideas. You could refer to traditional tales (e.g. 'Little Red Riding Hood') to discuss the theme of journeys from a familiar viewpoint.

2. **This story focuses on an encounter with whales. What do you know about whales?**
   In order to fully access this text, it is crucial that the children develop some knowledge of whales and their behaviour. See the **Reading list** for some helpful resources to explore this subject further.

3. **Have you ever seen an animal or bird in the wild? How did it make you feel?**
   Some children may be able to share anecdotes of their encounters with exotic animals, and some may even have seen a real whale. All of them should be able to contribute experiences with British wildlife.

4. **This extract is very descriptive. What types of language might you expect to find in a description?**
   All the children should be familiar with the key language features of a description. Challenge them to offer examples of these features to support their understanding.

Language toolkit

Key vocabulary

dimensions	flotsam	floundering
lolling	mesmerised	milling about
roughening	school	sluicing
squall	wallowed	wits

Vocabulary discussion questions

- What might you be doing if you **wallowed** in the bath? Can animals wallow?
- If a sailor was **sluicing** the deck of a ship, what would they be doing?
- **Flotsam** is often found floating on the sea or washed up on the beach. What is it made of?
- How many **dimensions** does a drawing of a cube have?
- If you use your **wits**, are you being clever or foolish?

Vocabulary activities

- A group of whales can be called a pod or a **school**. These are collective nouns. Investigate whether there are any other collective nouns for whales. Challenge the children to see how many other collective nouns for animals they can think of.
- The text includes a number of verbs that describe the whales' movement (e.g. **wallowed**; **milling about**; **lolling** around). How many synonymous verbs can the children think of?
- A **squall** describes a particular type of storm. How many other words can the children think of to describe stormy weather?

2 First steps

Read the text together and then encourage the children to discuss the following questions.

1. **Where is the story set?**
   On a boat in the middle of the sea.
2. **What type of whales are the children watching?**
   Sperm whales.
3. **What does Michael see that makes him get particularly excited?**
   Freedom, a whale he has swum with before.

3 Explore

- From the largest, the blue whale, to the smallest, the dwarf sperm whale, whale species are incredibly diverse. The children could research a whale of their choice, finding out about its main features and comparing it in size and appearance to the sperm whales from the text. You may wish to ask them not to choose orcas (killer whales), as they will be learning more about these whales in **Unit 11**.

- Sperm whales were the target of whaling ships during the 19th century. Whalers hunted the whales almost to extinction, killing them for their oil and for ambergris (a material used in perfume). Discuss the issue of hunting animals for food or other products, both in the past and present. Ask the children how they feel about this issue.

- The author, Nicola Davies, is known for her masterful use of description to evoke atmosphere. Discuss how the atmosphere changes over the course of the text, taking time to compare Davies' description of the whales with that of the impending storm.

4 Skills focus   See pages 108 to 109

Use the information from the **Skills guide** and the relevant **Skills graphic** to introduce the skill of word choice.

1. Model the skill using the **Unit 10 Modelling slides** and the **Modelling word choice** guidance on page 108.
2. The children can then attempt the **Word choice** questions on page 112.
3. Finally, the **Mix it up!** questions on page 113 offer practice in a range of comprehension skills.

Answers and marking guidance for all questions are included on pages 108 to 109.

5 Where next?

- **Speaking and listening task:** The children could discuss the verbs the author uses to show the whales' behaviour (e.g. 'wallowed'; 'rolled around'; 'clicked'; 'surfaced'; 'lolling'; 'milling about'; 'dived'). Which of them mean similar things and which are opposites? In small groups, they could then use the text to act out the movement and behaviour of the whales.

- **Writing task:** The children could watch a clip of whales swimming (see the **Reading list** for a resource suggestion) and then write a short description of the whales' movement, trying to write in a similar style to Nicola Davies.

Reading list

Fiction
- *The Longest Whale Song* by Jacqueline Wilson
- *Song for a Whale* by Lynne Kelly
- *A Symphony of Whales* by Steve Schuch
- *The Whale* by Vita Murrow and Ethan Murrow
- *The Whale Rider* by Witi Ihimaera
- *The Whales' Song* by Dyan Sheldon and Gary Blythe
- *Willa and the Whale* by Chad Morris and Shelly Brown

Class reads
- *Why the Whales Came* by Michael Morpurgo

Non-fiction
- *Extreme Weather (National Geographic Kids)* by Thomas M. Kostigen
- *How Long Is a Whale?* by Alison Limentani
- *The Incredible Ecosystems of Planet Earth* by Rachel Ignotofsky
- 'SeaWorld Decides to Stop Killer Whale Breeding Programme' by *The Guardian* (Linked text: **Unit 11**)
- *The Variety of Life* by Nicola Davies
- *Weather and Seasons* by Nancy Dickmann
- *When the Whales Walked* by Dougal Dixon
- *The World of the Whale* by Smriti Prasadam-Halls
- *The World of Whales* by Darcy Dobell

Films
- *Whale Rider* (South Pacific Pictures, 2002)

TV series
- *Blue Planet II* (Series 1, Episode 4, 'Big Blue', BBC, 2017) features sperm whales 7 minutes and 30 seconds into the episode.

Unit 10

Modelling word choice

▽ See Unit 10 Modelling slides

Use the **Skills guide** (see pages 26 to 27) and the downloadable **Skills graphic** to support your modelling.

1 Look at the paragraph beginning *Although it was hard …* . What does the group of words *crinkly expanses* tell you about the whales? Tick **two**.

   The whales were scarred. ☐
   The whales were wrinkly. ☑
   The whales were speckled. ☐
   The whales were large. ☑
   The whales were dark. ☐

   It is important to model using the locator to find the relevant part of the text. You should remind the children to read around any quotations from the question to gain an understanding of the context. You could also point out that the question requires two pieces of information. While 'crinkly' should be part of the children's vocabulary, you may need to discuss the meaning of 'expanses'.

2 *… making use of every bit of the three dimensions …* . What does this group of words tell you about how the whales moved?

   They moved every way that they could – up, down and side to side.

   Again, model using the locator to find the relevant part of the text. As it is a direct quote, model reading around the quote. After identifying the key words in the question and quote, discuss the meaning of 'three dimensions'. Demonstrate remembering to refer to the other part of the quotation ('making use of every bit') as well. Support the children to connect this with their knowledge of 'dimensions'.

3 Look at the paragraph beginning *The children were as mesmerised, …* . Find and copy **two** words that show that the whales had captured the children's attention.

   1 mesmerised   2 enchanted

   Model using the locator to find the relevant paragraph. You could discuss the meaning of 'captured the children's attention' and ask the children about the things that have captured *their* attention before and how this made them feel. Model thinking of synonyms for this state before scanning the text for words that answer the whole question.

4 *… the chaotic milling about ended, …* . What does the word *chaotic* tell you about the whales' activity?

   The whales were all moving haphazardly/in a frenzy.

   Model reading around the locator quotation for context. You could discuss the meaning of 'chaotic' and gather some appropriate synonyms before discussing how to answer this question. You should also model linking the discussion back to the whales' activity/movement. To help with this, discuss the whales' movement throughout the text, rather than just in this sentence.

Word choice questions mark scheme

☐ See page 112

	Answer	Guidance
1	She was very excited/surprised.	Some children may read this as a negative emotion. If so, prompt them to go back to the text and read around the quotation. **Award 1 mark for a correct answer.**
2	It was noisy. ☑ It was sudden. ☑	Some children may choose 'deep' as this is mentioned in the same paragraph. If so, refocus them on the word 'exploded'. Remind the children that even though only 1 mark is available, two words must be ticked to gain the mark. **Award 1 mark for both correct answers ticked.**

Whale Boy, by Nicola Davies

Schofield & Sims Complete Comprehension 5

Answer		Guidance
3	giants expanses	Do not accept reference to 'bigger' as this is comparative rather than a statement about the whales' large size. Although 'slab-like' and 'long' are vague, these responses are acceptable. As this is not a 'find and copy' question, also accept minor changes to the wording in the text (e.g. 'giant', 'expanse', 'slab'). **Award 1 mark for two correct answers.**
4	wild and frightening	There are a number of possible phrases that the children could focus on. All correct responses must be groups of words taken together from the text. Responses should be more than one word but less than a sentence in length. **Award 1 mark for an appropriate group of words taken from the last paragraph.**
5	a fierce storm was coming	Some children may respond vaguely (e.g. 'bad weather'). If so, prompt them to make their answer more specific: if they saw a really dark cloud in the sky, what would they expect to happen next? **Award 1 mark for reference to a storm/wet and windy weather.**

Mix it up! questions mark scheme   See page 113

Answer		Guidance
1	school	This question relies on the children's understanding of 'school' as a collective noun. You could do the activity in the **Language toolkit** if this knowledge is not yet secure. **Award 1 mark for the correct answer. Skill: Word meaning.**
2	his four white scars	As this question does not have a locator, the children need to identify 'Freedom' as a key word and scan the text for it. If necessary, provide them with a locator. **Award 1 mark for a reference to Freedom's scars. Skill: Retrieval.**
3	thrilled/excited/delighted because he cried out and told Eugenia that it was Freedom	The children may focus on the author's use of exclamation marks as their evidence. This is acceptable as long as it is linked to showing excitement or surprise. **Award 1 mark for a positive emotion. Award 2 marks for a positive emotion plus an explanation linked to the text. Skill: Inference.**
4	It has become dangerous and suspenseful.	Although some children may have already picked up on the way the tone changes across the course of the extract, the change is most marked in the last paragraph. This is a challenging question, but their work on **Word choice** question 4, should help them locate the relevant information. **Award 1 mark for a plausible atmosphere. Skill: Relationship.**
5	Yes ✓ I think the whales will help them because Michael knows Freedom and has swum with him before. No ✓ They have sailed too far out to sea and there is a storm coming. They are all alone because even the whales have gone.	Answers will vary as the children's inferences will be influenced by their personal reactions to the text. Accept negative or positive responses as long as their explanations are linked to the text. **Award 1 mark for an answer ticked plus one piece of appropriate evidence. Award 2 marks for an answer ticked plus two pieces of appropriate evidence. Skill: Prediction.**

Whale Boy, by Nicola Davies

In this extract, a boy called Michael and his friend Eugenia go on a sailing trip, where they encounter a pod of whales. Michael recognises one of the whales, Freedom, as one he has swum with before.

A dark, blocky head spurted a blow from its top corner, and a log-straight back wallowed in the waves: a sperm whale. Then another and another, their spouts making slightly different sounds as they popped through the dark blue surface.

PPPPFFFF!

Pppphhhhffff!

Pwwwafffff!

PPPPFFFWAAA!

Eugenia cried out in delight and surprise, and immediately began clicking away with her little camera. The whales were so close that even a tiny lens would show them clearly.

In amongst the hills and valleys of the roughening sea, more whales were surfacing! Their black snouts exploded with the first loud breath after a deep dive. The *Louisa May* was surrounded by more than ten sperm whales. Michael and Eugenia stared around in wonder, hardly able to believe that they were in the middle of a whole *school* of whales.

"I think you're a whale charmer!" Michael told Eugenia. She laughed and took some more pictures.

Although it was hard to judge the size of the whales, some were definitely bigger than Freedom, and one was much smaller. They gathered together, twenty metres in front of the boat, a mass of lolling giants, water sluicing over and between them. Slab-like noses appeared, crinkly expanses of dark grey flank and pale speckled undersides, with long u-shaped jaws showing under the surface. Pointed corners of tails, the flat paddles of flippers, a jumbled flotsam of dark shapes.

The whales rolled around each other, on their sides, on their backs, tail up, tail down, making use of every bit of the three dimensions that their watery world afforded them. They clicked so that the hull rang with the sounds.

Then two more whales surfaced on the edge of the group. One had a yellowish scar shaped like a target on its back, and its spout made a noise unlike the other whales', as if some musical instrument had got stuck inside the blowhole.

Weeeeepffffff!

The other whale swam very close beside it, and when they turned together, Michael saw Freedom's four white scars! This must be his family! This big flute-blowing whale could be his mother!

"That's my whale – Freedom!" he cried. "He's the one I swam with!"

The children were as mesmerised, as enchanted as if they had been whisked away by the angels who had stolen poor So-So's wits. For what might have been hours, they watched the whales lolling and rolling around together. There was no more room left on the camera. Eugenia rolled it up in a thick plastic bag and put it in her backpack to keep it dry.

Then, as if a signal had been given, the chaotic milling about ended, and the log-like backs and huge heads lined up side by side, blows all going in the same direction, right into the wind. Almost as quickly as they had surfaced, they dived again, Freedom next to the big squeaking whale that Michael assumed was his mother. Their tails rose out of the water long enough for him to see that some, like Freedom's, were perfect triangles, while others were scratched, torn, or misshapen. Big Squeaky's tail was so worn away that one side was like the prongs of a fork. It struck Michael that Freedom was being raised by an elderly lady, just as *he* was. One after another they slipped down under the surface with not even the tiniest splash, and were gone.

The children recovered their wits and looked around. They had followed the whales for quite a way, paying no attention to where they'd been headed. In front of them, far too close, were the white-capped waves of the channel, wild and frightening. When Michael turned back to see if he had at last reached a point where Peter hid the Devil, he saw that the island had disappeared behind a cloud like a huge purple bruise. A squall was racing towards them across the sea, and the little *Louisa May* was already floundering in the swell, a long, long way from a safe harbour.

From *Whale Boy* by Nicola Davies, Penguin Random House Children's, 2013. Reproduced by permission of David Higham Associates.

Word choice

Name: _____

1 *Eugenia cried out ...*
What does the group of words *cried out* tell you about Eugenia's emotions?

_____

_____

1 mark

2 *Their black snouts exploded ...*
What does this group of words tell us about the sound the whales made? Tick **two**.

It was quiet. ☐

It was noisy. ☐

It was sudden. ☐

It was slow. ☐

It was deep. ☐

1 mark

3 Look at the paragraph beginning *Although it was hard ...* . Give **two** words that show that the whales were large.

1 _____

2 _____

1 mark

4 Look at the last paragraph. Find and copy a group of words that show that the atmosphere has changed.

_____

1 mark

5 *... a cloud like a huge purple bruise.*
What does this group of words tell you about the weather?

_____

_____

1 mark

Photocopiable resource from *Complete Comprehension 5* © Schofield & Sims Ltd, 2020.

Mix it up!

Name: _____

1 Look at the paragraph beginning *In amongst ...* . Find and copy **one** word that means 'group'.

_____

1 mark

2 How did Michael recognise Freedom?

_____
_____

1 mark

3 *"That's my whale – Freedom!" he cried.*
How did Michael feel when he saw Freedom again? Explain your answer using evidence from the text.

_____
_____
_____

2 marks

4 Think about the last paragraph. How has the atmosphere changed?

_____
_____

1 mark

5 Think about the whole text. Do you think the *Louisa May* will get back to safety? Tick **one**.

Yes ☐   No ☐

Give **two** pieces of evidence from the text to support your opinion.

_____
_____
_____

2 marks

Photocopiable resource from *Complete Comprehension 5* © Schofield & Sims Ltd, 2020.

Unit 10 — Whale Boy, by Nicola Davies

SeaWorld Decides to Stop Killer Whale Breeding Program by *The Guardian*

Unit 11 · Relationship · Non-fiction

▽ Printable text • Modelling slides   📖 Photocopiable text and questions • pages 118 to 121

Orcas, or killer whales, are highly intelligent and social marine mammals. Marine parks around the world have been keeping orcas in captivity since the 1960s, despite fervent protests from animal rights activists. The text for this unit is a newspaper article from *The Guardian* that reports the decision by SeaWorld to stop breeding orcas in captivity. After completing this unit, you could make links to *Whale Boy* (Unit 10), and its description of sperm whales in the wild.

1 Get ready

Discuss the **Key vocabulary** identified in the **Language toolkit** and then complete the vocabulary activities as desired. Please note that the selected vocabulary is a guide. Depending on the needs of your cohort, additional vocabulary discussion may be beneficial before, during and after reading. Next, display the text (pages 118 to 119) so the children can see the title and any illustrations, and encourage the children to discuss the following questions before reading.

1 **This text is an extract from a newspaper article. What features would you expect to find in it?**
   The features you could discuss include: headline; byline showing the journalist's name; introductory paragraph with the '5 Ws' (what, where, when, who, why); columns; short paragraphs; quotations; pictures with captions.

2 **This text is about orcas, also known as killer whales. What do you know about these mammals?**
   Some children may be able to relate their understanding back to the discussion during the **Get ready** section of Unit 10. They will have further opportunities during the **Explore** section of this unit to research orcas, but you may wish to show them images or video clips of orcas before they read the text for the first time.

3 **This text tells the reader about the actions of SeaWorld, a theme park where people can interact with sea animals. Have you ever been to somewhere similar?**
   Answers will vary. If the children have little or no experience of this type of environment, show them images or a video clip of an orca show at SeaWorld to support their understanding.

Language toolkit

Key vocabulary

activists	applauded	captivity
defining moment	exhibition	extinction
humane	monumental	opposed
propelled	semblance	sentence

Vocabulary discussion questions

- Where might you see something held in **captivity**?
- If someone **applauded** you for doing something, would that mean they were happy or unhappy with what you did?
- Are all humans **humane**? Explain your opinion.
- Are you **opposed** to anything? What?
- Can you name some animals that have been driven to **extinction**?

Vocabulary activities

- The word **activists** is related to the word 'active'. Can the children think of a link between the two words? Can they think of other words in the same word family?
- **Monumental** and **defining moment** are both used to describe a significant event. Can the children think of significant events in their own lives? How else might they describe them?
- **Propelled** is a verb that describes something moving forward quickly. Gather synonyms together and encourage the children to use **propelled** in a sentence.

114   Schofield & Sims Complete Comprehension 5

2 First steps

Read the text together and then encourage the children to discuss the following questions.

1. **What has SeaWorld decided to do?**
   To stop breeding killer whales in captivity.
2. **What will happen to the orcas already at SeaWorld?**
   They will stay at SeaWorld under the care of vets.
3. **Which documentary made the public more aware of SeaWorld's treatment of orcas? What was the name of the orca in the documentary?**
   Blackfish. The orca's name was Tilikum.

3 Explore

- Orcas are known as 'killer whales' but they are actually a species of dolphin. The children could research orcas using the resources given in the **Reading list** and share some fascinating facts with the class. Did any of the things they thought were true about killer whales turn out to be false?
- Nowadays, many people feel outraged when they see animals being made to perform for public amusement and some disagree with zoos altogether. However, many zoos do treat their animals well and work hard to support conservation efforts. Discuss what the children's opinions are of zoos and keeping animals in captivity. You may wish to discuss the links between the orcas in this text and the captive wolves in **Unit 8**.
- Highlight the fact that a newspaper article will be influenced by the journalist's opinions, just like any text. You could discuss whether the children think the journalist agrees or disagrees with SeaWorld's treatment of orcas, based on her use of language. You could then look at other reporting of the same story, noting how each article has slightly different content (e.g. using articles from *The Independent* and *ScienceMag*).

4 Skills focus   See pages 116 to 117

Use the information from the **Skills guide** and the relevant **Skills graphic** to introduce the skill of relationship.

1. Model the skill using the **Unit 11 Modelling slides** and the **Modelling relationship** guidance on page 116.
2. The children can then attempt the **Relationship** questions on page 120.

3. Finally, the **Mix it up!** questions on page 121 offer practice in a range of comprehension skills.

Answers and marking guidance for all questions are included on pages 116 to 117.

5 Where next?

- **Speaking and listening task:** As a class or in small groups the children could work together to stage a debate about whether orcas that remain in captivity should be set free. One half should argue for their release and the other should argue against it. The children should use the points from the article and their own research to formulate their arguments.

- **Writing task:** In pairs, the children could write to their local zoo or animal park, asking about their conservation efforts and what they are doing to enrich their captive animals' lives.

Reading list

Fiction
- *The Dancing Bear* by Michael Morpurgo
- *The Emergency Zoo* by Miriam Halahmy
- *Seaside Sanctuary: Orca in Open Water* by Emma Carlson Berne
- *Whale Boy* by Nicola Davies (Linked text: **Unit 10**)
- *A World Full of Animal Stories* by Angela McAllister
- *Zoo* by Anthony Browne

Class reads
- *The One and Only Ivan* by Katherine Applegate

Non-fiction
- *An Anthology of Intriguing Animals* by Ben Hoare
- *Ivan: The Remarkable True Story of the Shopping Mall Gorilla* by Katherine Applegate
- *Killer Whales* by Kate Riggs
- *The Not Bad Animals* by Sophie Corrigan
- *Orcas of the Salish Sea* by Mark Leiren-Young
- *The Orca Scientists* by Kim Perez
- *The Spirit of Springer* by Amanda Abler
- *Tilikum's Dream* by Tracey Lynn Coryell

Films
- *Free Willy* (Warner Bros. Pictures, 1993)

TV series
- *The Secret Life of the Zoo* (Channel 4)

Websites
- The National Geographic website hosts an informative orca 'Factfile'.
- The SeaWorld website has links to its different Theme and Water Parks.

Schofield & Sims Complete Comprehension 5

Modelling relationship

See Unit 11 Modelling slides

Use the **Skills guide** (see pages 24 to 25) and the downloadable **Skills graphic** to support your modelling.

1 **Who do you think this article is written for?**

   People who are interested in animal rights.

   As this question does not include a locator, read aloud the headline and first sentences of the text, explaining that in a newspaper article these often offer a good summary of the article. Ask the children to think about what you have read, as well as their own reading of the whole article, and then discuss who might and might not read this article. Encourage them to justify their responses verbally to show deeper understanding.

2 *"Even the attempt to return the whale from* **Free Willy**, *Keiko, who was born in the wild, was a failure, ..."*. **Why do you think Joel Manby said this?**

   To emphasise that the people who are arguing for the whales to be released are wrong and to encourage people to take his side in the debate.

   As this question includes a quote as a locator, it is important to model using this to find the relevant sentence in the text. Next, model reading around the quote for context. After identifying the key words in the question and quote, discuss who Joel Manby is, why he has been included in the article and what his opinion of SeaWorld is. Finally, bring the discussion back to the quote and discuss why Manby said this. You could use a graphic organiser to help the children think through their responses.

3 **Look at the paragraph beginning** *The 2013 documentary ...* . **Why do you think this paragraph has been included?**

   To remind people about the negative effects of SeaWorld's breeding of orcas.

   Model using the locator to find the relevant paragraph. Next, identify the key words in the question. Discuss what this paragraph tells us: why do the children think the reference to Tilikum was included? What effect does it have on them when they read it? What effect might it have on others?

4 *Now the company is attempting to reverse its fortunes.* **What does this sentence tell you about the journalist's viewpoint?**

   She thinks SeaWorld is stopping breeding killer whales because they want to make money, not because they want to help orcas.

   Again, model reading around the locator quotation for context: in this case, the previous sentence. This is a challenging question as it requires the children to link the idea of SeaWorld wanting to make money to their motivations for announcing the ban on breeding. Discuss what it means to 'reverse one's fortunes', as well as the meaning of 'viewpoint'. Ask them to discuss what opinion the journalist has about SeaWorld. Does she write about them in a positive or negative way? Finally, link the quoted sentence to the journalist's overall viewpoint, discussing what it tells us about her thoughts.

Relationship questions mark scheme

See page 120

	Answer	Guidance
1	So that both sides of the argument are explained – SeaWorld's and those of animal rights activists.	If the children do not know what Peta is, discuss this briefly, so that they understand that Mimi Bekhechi is on the opposite side of the argument to Joel Manby. **Award 1 mark for a reference to including another point of view.**
2	breeding should continue ✓	Some children may struggle because this question requires them to use information from the previous two paragraphs. If necessary, provide them with a prompt. **Award 1 mark for the correct answer ticked.**

	Answer	Guidance
3	I think the journalist agrees with their decision to ban breeding because she says that SeaWorld have been criticised for how they treat orcas, like Tilikum who ended up killing people.	The children may disagree over the journalist's viewpoint depending on their depth of understanding. Some may refer to her trying to remain unbiased: this should also be accepted. **Award 1 mark for a plausible opinion. Award 2 marks for a plausible opinion plus an explanation linked to the text.**
4	to tell readers about SeaWorld's decision to stop breeding orcas in captivity OR to tell people about the reasons behind SeaWorld's decision OR to share different people's opinions about SeaWorld's decision	Some children may provide a vague response (e.g. 'to inform people'). If so, encourage them to make their response more specific to the text. **Award 1 mark for one reason linked to the text. Award 2 marks for two reasons linked to the text.**
5	It mentions lots of surprising aspects briefly, so you want to find out more. For example, it talks about Tilikum being involved in the deaths of people and the fact that no captive orcas have survived after being released into the wild.	If some children respond vaguely, (e.g. 'It gives lots of different opinions'), remind them to be specific and to refer to the text in their answer. Prompt them to think carefully about whether any details from the text surprised or shocked them. You could even supply them with a locator. **Award 1 mark for a plausible reason for wanting to find out more. Award 2 marks for a plausible reason with appropriate evidence from the text.**

Mix it up! questions mark scheme

See page 121

	Answer	Guidance
1	Joel Manby	If some children answer Jon Reilly, point out that he was only in charge of the San Diego branch of SeaWorld. Some may provide only part of the name. If so, prompt them to give the president's full name. **Award 1 mark for the correct answer.** Skill: Retrieval.
2	Looking after the remaining whales	The children may provide a range of responses. Accept any answer that refers to the orcas that will remain at SeaWorld. **Award 1 mark for a plausible subheading that relates to the content of the paragraphs.** Skill: Summarising.
3	That it was very significant/meaningful. OR That it was a really big change/a defining moment.	If some children use 'important' to explain the meaning of 'monumental', do not accept this, as this word appears in the locator quotation. Refer back to any synonyms for 'monumental' that you may have discussed in the Key vocabulary. **Award 1 mark for a reference to the significance of the decision.** Skill: Word choice.
4	pushed ✓	Although they will already have encountered 'propelled' in the Key vocabulary, you could revisit the definition in context before the children attempt this question. **Award 1 mark for the correct answer ticked.** Skill: Word meaning.
5	I am happy that they are stopping breeding but I think it's because they want to make money, not because they care.	It is likely that many of the children will feel pleased with the decision. However, as this question asks for their opinion, any is valid. **Award 1 mark for an opinion. Award 2 marks for an opinion plus an explanation linked to the text.** Skill: Inference.

Schofield & Sims Complete Comprehension 5

SeaWorld Decides to Stop Killer Whale Breeding Program, by *The Guardian*

This is an extract from a newspaper article that was written for *The Guardian*. The author of the article reports on a theme park called SeaWorld and its decision to stop breeding orcas, which are also known as killer whales.

SeaWorld will stop breeding orca whales in captivity, the company announced on Thursday, a move applauded by animal rights activists who have been calling for an end to the public exhibition of the animals altogether for years.

"By making this the last generation of orcas in our care and reimagining how guests will experience these beautiful animals, we are fulfilling our mission of providing visitors to our parks with experiences that matter," said Joel Manby, president and CEO of SeaWorld Entertainment Inc.

The breeding program will end immediately, and the killer whales currently at its parks will be the last, Manby said.

The Orlando-based theme park operator has faced falling visitor numbers and years of criticism over its treatment of the captive marine mammals as well as pressure from animal rights activists.

The director of People for the Ethical Treatment of Animals (Peta), Mimi Bekhechi, welcomed the news, but called for those still in captivity to be allowed ocean access.

"SeaWorld must open its tanks to the oceans to allow the orcas it now holds captive to have some semblance of a life outside these prison tanks," said Bekhechi in a statement.

But SeaWorld said the remaining whales – including a pregnant whale, Takara – will live out the rest of their lives under the care of their veterinary staff, as releasing them into the wild will likely kill them.

"These orcas have never lived in the wild and could not survive in oceans that include environmental concerns such as pollution and other manmade threats," said the company on its site. Although a few of SeaWorld's orcas were born in the wild, the majority were bred in captivity by the company.

"In fact, no orca or dolphin born under human care has ever survived release into the wild. Even the attempt to return the whale from *Free Willy*, Keiko, who was born in the wild, was a failure," said Manby in an op-ed published in the Los Angeles Times.

"The decision to end its orca breeding program globally and to commit to ending the collection of exhibit animals from the wild, as well as to a 'no orca' policy should SeaWorld expand its brand into new international markets, is a monumental and important first step forward in achieving a more humane business model for the company," said the Animal Welfare Institute.

In October 2015, the California Coastal Commission, which has authority over coastal building projects, said it would only approve SeaWorld's renovation plans if the company ended its controversial breeding program.

Jon Reilly, then president of SeaWorld San Diego, opposed the decision, declaring "a ban on breeding would sentence these animals to a slow extinction in our care".

The 2013 documentary *Blackfish*, which told the story of Tilikum, a SeaWorld whale kept in captivity and involved in the deaths of several people, propelled the theme park's treatment of orcas into the public eye.

Gabriela Cowperthwaite, the director of *Blackfish*, called the end of the breeding program "a defining moment".

"The fact that SeaWorld is doing away with orca breeding marks truly meaningful change," she said in a joint statement with SeaWorld and the Humane Society.

The film's effect on the park was staggering: profits dropped 84% between 2014 and 2015 as sales and attendance collapsed. Now the company is attempting to reverse its fortunes.

From 'SeaWorld Decides to Stop Killer Whale Breeding Program': www.theguardian.com/us-news/2016/mar/17/seaworld-to-stop-breeding-killer-whales-orcas-blackfish. Copyright © Guardian News and Media Limited.

Relationship

Name: _____

1 *The director of ... (Peta), Mimi Bekhechi, welcomed the news, but called for those still in captivity to be allowed ocean access.*
Why do you think Mimi Bekhechi's opinion has been included?

_____

_____

1 mark

2 Look at the paragraph beginning *Jon Reilly, then president of SeaWorld San Diego, ...* .
What was the viewpoint of Jon Reilly? Tick **one**.

breeding should be suspended ☐

breeding should be banned ☐

breeding should be reduced ☐

breeding should continue ☐

1 mark

3 What do you think the journalist's opinion is of SeaWorld's decision? Explain your answer using evidence from the text.

_____

_____

_____

2 marks

4 Why do you think this article was written? Give **two** reasons, using the text.

_____

_____

_____

2 marks

5 How has the article been designed to make you want to find out more? Give **one** point and **one** piece of evidence from the text to support your answer.

_____

_____

_____

2 marks

Mix it up!

Name: _____

1 What is the name of the president of SeaWorld Entertainment Inc.?

_____

1 mark

2 Read from the paragraph beginning *"SeaWorld must open its tanks ..."* to *"... the majority were bred in captivity by the company"*. What would be an effective subheading for these paragraphs?

_____

1 mark

3 *"The decision to end its orca breeding program globally ... is a monumental and important first step forward ..."*
What does the word *monumental* tell you about SeaWorld's decision?

_____

1 mark

4 *... propelled the theme park's treatment of orcas into the public eye ... .*
Which word is closest in meaning to *propelled*? Tick **one**.

pushed ☐

motivated ☐

turned ☐

inspired ☐

1 mark

5 How do you feel about SeaWorld's ban on orca breeding? Explain your opinion using evidence from the text.

_____

2 marks

Unit 12

Beetle Boy
by M.G. Leonard

Printable text • Modelling slides • Photocopiable text and questions • pages 126 to 129

Children tend to develop a fascination with or an aversion to insects. Those who become interested are often most enthusiastic about beetles, because of their varied colours and features. This unit's extract is about a beetle enthusiast, Darkus Cuttle. Darkus' father is an entomologist at the Natural History Museum and one day he mysteriously disappears. This text touches on some difficult themes (bereavement and depression) so be sensitive to the children's experiences. It is linked with Unit 13, *Beetle Boy: The Beetle Collector's Handbook* which gives factual information about Goliath beetles.

1 Get ready

Discuss the **Key vocabulary** identified in the **Language toolkit** and then complete the vocabulary activities as desired. Please note that the selected vocabulary is a guide. Depending on the needs of your cohort, additional vocabulary discussion may be beneficial before, during and after reading. Next, display the text (pages 126 to 127) so the children can see the title and any illustrations, and encourage the children to discuss the following questions before reading.

1. **This text is from a mystery story. What features might you expect to find in it?**
   Answers will vary depending on the children's prior reading. Possible answers include: something or someone going missing; problems to solve; good characters and bad characters. If some children comment on the type of atmosphere in mystery stories, encourage them to explain how this atmosphere is created (e.g. through off-page action, noises or unusual happenings).

2. **Mystery stories often feature the disappearance of someone or something. Have you read any other texts about a disappearance?**
   You may wish to share some texts from the fiction section of the **Reading list** that focus on a disappearance. The Unit 21 text, *The London Eye Mystery*, shares this theme, so you could choose to read this text to the children in advance to help build up their understanding of the mystery genre.

3. **In this story, the main character and his father are interested in insects. What do you know about insects?**
   Answers will vary, but the children should be able to comment on the insects that they see in their daily lives. You could use texts from the **Reading list** to boost the children's background knowledge.

Language toolkit

Key vocabulary

archaeologist	controlled atmosphere	entomology
ex-colleague	grief	outfoxed
pleasantries	retreated	specimen
unremarkable	vaults	widower

Vocabulary discussion questions

- Is there anything **unremarkable** about the town or city you live in?
- What sort of things might be stored in the **vaults** of a building?
- When might you exchange **pleasantries** with someone? What might you say?
- What type of job might you have if you were looking at a **specimen** of something?
- What things does an **archaeologist** look for?

Vocabulary activities

- People often use the prefix 'ex-' to hyphenate other words (e.g. **ex-colleague**; 'ex-classmate'). When else have the children seen this wording used?
- **Entomology** is the study of insects. Give the children some other words which end in the suffix '–ology' and describe the study of something (e.g. 'biology'; 'criminology'; 'pharmacology'). Can they decipher what these words mean?
- The text includes a number of scientific terms, including **specimen** and **controlled atmosphere**. Discuss these terms in more detail with the children, relating them to Dr Cuttle's occupation as an entomologist.

2 First steps

Read the text together and then encourage the children to discuss the following questions.

1. When did Dr Bartholomew Cuttle disappear?
   During the afternoon of Tuesday 27th September.
   Encourage the children to give a full answer.

2. What had been left open in the vault that Dr Cuttle was in when he disappeared?
   Several (Coleoptera) specimen drawers.

3. Who is Darkus' only living relative, apart from his father? Where is he currently?
   Maximilian Cuttle, a famous archaeologist. He is lost in the Sinai desert.

3 Explore

- The children could use the school library or online resources to research the wonderful world of insects and the benefits they bring to our environment. You could provide them with some question prompts, focusing on superlative adjectives (e.g. What is the *biggest* type of insect? What is the *smallest* kind? What is the *most venomous*/the *heaviest*/the *most colourful*?). Give them time to carry out their research and build up an understanding of why Dr Cuttle would want to study them. There are some useful resources in the **Reading list** to support this activity.

- Discuss how the author, M.G. Leonard, uses language to build mystery and atmosphere throughout the text. You could begin by discussing some of the details that the author includes in her description of Dr Cuttle's disappearance to make it seem mysterious (e.g. the fact that the office was locked from the inside, or that she says that Dr Cuttle would never abandon his son). You could also discuss how the author uses newspaper headlines to push the story forward, building momentum and making the reader go through multiple emotions, just like Darkus.

4 Skills focus   See pages 124 to 125

Use the information from the **Skills guide** and the relevant **Skills graphic** to introduce the skill of summarising.

1. Model the skill using the **Unit 12 Modelling slides** and the **Modelling summarising** guidance on page 124.

2. The children can then attempt the **Summarising** questions on page 128.

3. Finally, the **Mix it up!** questions on page 129 offer practice in a range of comprehension skills.

Answers and marking guidance for all questions are included on pages 124 to 125.

5 Where next?

- **Speaking and listening task:** Many people do not like insects, and some are even scared of them. The children could work in small groups to devise and deliver a speech to persuade people to love and care for insects. They should draw on the research they did in the **Explore** section to fill their speech with facts about insects and the role they play in keeping ecosystems healthy.

- **Writing task:** The children could use the first half of the text (up to 'It was a sealed chamber with a controlled atmosphere.') to write a brief police report of Dr Cuttle's disappearance. Their reports could note the key details of the case, including time, place, location and a description of the crime itself.

Reading list

Fiction
- *Beetle Queen* by M.G. Leonard
- *The Highland Falcon Thief* by M.G. Leonard and Sam Sedgman
- *The Mysteries of Harris Burdick* by Chris Van Allsburg
- *Nancy Parker's Diary of Detection* by Julia Lee
- *The Secret of the Night Train* by Sylvia Bishop

Class reads
- *The Battle for Perfect* by Helena Duggan

Non-fiction
- *The Bee Book* by Charlotte Milner
- *Beetle Boy: The Beetle Collector's Handbook* by M.G. Leonard (Linked text: **Unit 13**)
- *The Big Book of Bugs* by Yuval Zommer
- *Insect Detective* by Steve Voake
- *Sensational Butterflies* by Ben Rothery
- *Ultimate Bugopedia (National Geographic Kids)* by Darlyne Murawski and Nancy Honovich

Poetry
- *Insectlopedia* by Douglas Florian
- *UnBEElievables* by Douglas Florian

Websites
- National Insect Week is a website from the Royal Entomological Society and has some useful resources.
- The Natural History Museum in London has a virtual tour of the museum on its website.

Unit 12

Modelling summarising

See Unit 12 Modelling slides

Use the **Skills guide** (see pages 18 to 19) and the downloadable **Skills graphic** to support your modelling.

1. **Look at the first paragraph. Which statement best summarises the main point of this paragraph? Tick one.**

   Dr Cuttle has disappeared. ☐   Dr Cuttle would not leave his son. ✓
   Dr Cuttle was forgetful. ☐   Dr Cuttle worked at the museum. ☐

   Model using the locator to find the relevant part of the text. Next, model identifying the key words from the question (e.g. 'main point'). Explain that this shows that the question wants you to focus on summing up the whole of the first paragraph. Model rereading the paragraph and discuss its content with the children, before considering each of the options and choosing the best one.

2. **Look at the second paragraph. What is the main topic of this paragraph?**
   Dr Cuttle's movements on the 27th September.

   Model using the locator to find the relevant section of text and identify 'main topic' as the question's key words. As before, this question focuses on summarising the content of a paragraph: you should emphasise this by modelling rereading the whole of the paragraph, discussing its content as you go. Point out that this question is different from the previous one: this time, you will need to decide on your own wording. Discuss what the main point is and model refining the children's suggestions until you have reached the most effective response.

3. **What would be an effective title for the first half of this extract?**
   Dr Cuttle Disappears!

   Although this question does not have a traditional locator, it does talk about the 'first half' of the text. Model locating and reading aloud the first half, from 'Dr Bartholomew Cuttle …' to '… out of that vault.'. Discuss the purpose of a title with the children. Then, ask for the children's suggestions for a title, encouraging them to challenge each other's suggestions, and give ideas for refinement.

4. **Look at the paragraph beginning *Five years earlier, …* . Write one sentence to summarise the content of this paragraph.**
   It is about how Darkus and his dad coped when Darkus' mum died.

   As with the first two questions, model locating and rereading the relevant paragraph, as well as identifying the question's key words. The wording of this question is different because it asks the children to summarise the content in a sentence. Discuss what makes a good summary before taking suggestions of possible answers. Finally, model refining their suggestions until you have the best response.

Summarising questions mark scheme

See page 128

	Answer		Guidance
1	Dr Cuttle wouldn't just disappear.		Some children may focus on the other points we are told about Dr Cuttle. If so, discuss the paragraph and how the author contrasts Dr Cuttle's other behaviour with multiple references to him always being there for Darkus. **Award 1 mark for a reference to Dr Cuttle not being likely to abandon his son.**
2	Dr Cuttle's disappearance was mysterious. Dr Cuttle's disappearance was unexplained.	✓ ✓	Some children will focus on the fact of Dr Cuttle's disappearance. If so, remind them that we already know about this at this point in the story. You could focus their attention on details such as the room being locked from the inside and the lack of windows or doors. **Award 1 mark for both correct answers ticked.**

Beetle Boy, by M.G. Leonard

	Answer	Guidance
3	Because he disappeared in a mysterious way that no-one could understand, not even the police.	This is a complex question as it requires children to think about the journalists' points of view. Some children may overread the question and respond 'because they would sell a lot of papers'. In this case, ask them why that would happen. **Award 1 mark for a reference to the continuing mystery of Darkus' dad's disappearance.**
4	who is going to look after Darkus	Some children may focus on these sentences all being newspaper headlines. Although this is true, it should not be accepted as an answer as it does not refer to the content of the sentences. **Award 1 mark for a reference to what will happen to Darkus.**
5	Darkus' relationship with his dad OR life after Darkus' mum died	The theme of this part of the text is very different to that of the first part. However, some children may still focus on the disappearance. This should not be accepted unless it is written in conjunction with comments about Darkus and his dad, or their relationship. **Award 1 mark for a reference to Darkus and his dad or to what happened after Darkus' mum died.**

Mix it up! questions mark scheme

See page 129

	Answer	Guidance
1	to make it clear to the reader that Dr Cuttle didn't disappear because he wanted to	The children may phrase their responses in a variety of ways. As long as they imply that Dr Cuttle did not leave of his own volition, or that he was obliged to leave, they should be accepted. **Award 1 mark for a reference to Dr Cuttle not being likely to leave.** Skill: Relationship.
2	9.30 a.m.	The children may refer to the time in words or phrases, but the exact time must be given to gain the mark. However, accept answers that do not specify 'a.m.', as this information must be inferred from the text. **Award 1 mark for the correct answer.** Skill: Retrieval.
3	puzzle mystery	Some children may misread the rubric and think that they need to underline a group of words (e.g. 'unsolvable mystery'). If so, explain that they need to choose two separate words. **Award 1 mark for both correct answers underlined.** Skill: Word meaning.
4	*Impression*: caring *Evidence*: He takes tea and biscuits to his dad/stays with his dad when he's having a really bad day.	Many of the children are likely to focus on Darkus' kindness and care towards his dad. Others may focus on his reticence. Accept any impression that is taken from the text. **Award 1 mark for a plausible impression. Award 2 marks for a plausible impression with appropriate evidence from the text.** Skill: Inference.
5	He will start to look into his father's disappearance as it was very strange/ he doesn't believe that his father would leave him.	Opinions will vary, with some focusing on Darkus' daily life and others on his father's disappearance. As with all prediction questions, it is important to check the children's understanding by asking them to justify their responses. **Award 1 mark for a plausible prediction. Award 2 marks for a plausible prediction plus an explanation linked to the text.** Skill: Prediction.

Beetle Boy, by M.G. Leonard

This story introduces a boy called Darkus Cuttle. At this point in the story, Darkus' father, Dr Bartholomew Cuttle, has just mysteriously disappeared.

Dr Bartholomew Cuttle wasn't the kind of man who mysteriously disappeared. He was the kind of man who read enormous old books at the dinner table and got fried egg stuck in his beard. He was the kind of man who always lost his keys and never took an umbrella on rainy days. He was the kind of dad who might be five minutes later picking you up from school but he always came. More than anything else, Darkus knew his dad was not the kind of father who would abandon his twelve-year-old son.

The police report stated that September 27 had been an unremarkable Tuesday. Dr Bartholomew Cuttle, a forty-eight-year-old widower, had taken his son, Darkus Cuttle, to school and gone on to the Natural History Museum, where he was the Director of Science. He'd greeted his secretary, Margaret, at nine thirty, spent a morning in meetings discussing museum business, and eaten lunch at one o'clock with an ex-colleague, Professor Andrew Appleyard. In the afternoon, he'd gone down to the collection vaults, as he frequently would, via the coffee machine, where he'd filled his cup. He'd exchanged pleasantries with Eddie, the security guard on duty that day, walked down the corridor to the vaults, and locked himself in one of the entomology rooms.

That evening, when his father didn't come home, Darkus alerted the neighbours and they called the police.

When the police arrived at the museum, the room Dr Cuttle had entered was locked from the inside. Fearing he may have suffered a heart attack, or had an accident, they produced a steel battering ram and smashed the door open.

The room was empty.

A stone-cold cup of coffee sat with some papers on the table beside a microscope. Several Coleoptera specimen drawers were open, but there was no sign of Dr Bartholomew Cuttle.

He had vanished.

The vault had no windows or doors other than the one he had entered by. It was a sealed chamber with a controlled atmosphere.

The puzzle of the disappearing scientist made the front page of every newspaper. The unsolvable mystery drove journalists crazy, and not one of them could explain how Dr Cuttle had gotten out of that vault.

SCIENTIST DISAPPEARS! headlines screamed.

POLICE ARE OUTFOXED! newspapers cried.

ORPHANED BOY PLACED IN CARE! they reported. *HUNT IS ON FOR ONLY LIVING RELATIVE, FAMOUS ARCHAEOLOGIST MAXIMILIAN CUTTLE.*

And the next day: *ARCHAEOLOGIST LOST IN SINAI DESERT!*

BOY ALONE! they wailed.

Outside the foster home, journalists stopped Darkus in the street, taking pictures and shouting questions:

"Darkus, have you heard from your dad?"

"Darkus, is your father on the run?"

"Darkus, is your dad dead?"

Five years earlier, when his mother died, Darkus had retreated inside himself. He stopped playing outside with friends or inviting anyone over. His mum, Esme Cuttle, had been taken away suddenly by pneumonia. The shock was terrible. His dad was overcome with grief. Some days – blue days, Darkus called them – his father lay in bed and stared at the wall, unable to speak, tears rolling down his cheeks. On the bleakest blue days, Darkus would bring tea and biscuits and sit beside his dad, reading. It was doubly hard, losing Mum *and* Dad being so sad all the time. Darkus had to learn to take care of himself. At school, he got along with everyone, but he didn't have close friends. He kept to himself. The other children wouldn't understand and he wasn't sure he could explain it. The only thing that mattered was taking care of Dad and helping him get happy again.

Finally, four years after Mum's death, the blue days got fewer and farther apart, and Darkus watched with cautious joy as his father awoke from his long sleep of sadness. He became a proper dad again, playing soccer on Sundays, smiling at Darkus over the breakfast table, and teasing him about his unruly hair.

Beetle Boy © M.G. Leonard 2016. Reproduced with permission of Chicken House Ltd. All rights reserved.

Summarising

Name: _____

1 Look at the first paragraph. Write one sentence to summarise what this section of the story tells you.

_____
_____

1 mark

2 Read from the paragraph beginning *When the police arrived ...* to *... Dr Cuttle had gotten out of that vault*. What is the main point of this part of the story? Tick **two**.

Dr Cuttle's disappearance was mysterious. ☐

Darkus Cuttle had vanished. ☐

Dr Cuttle had disappeared. ☐

Dr Cuttle's disappearance was unexplained. ☐

1 mark

3 Read from the sentence beginning SCIENTIST DISAPPEARS! ... to ... *they wailed*. Summarise why the journalists were excited about Darkus' dad going missing.

_____
_____
_____

1 mark

4 Read from the sentence beginning ORPHANED BOY ... to ... *they wailed*. What is the main focus of these sentences?

_____
_____

1 mark

5 Look at the last two paragraphs. What is the main theme of this part of the story?

_____
_____

1 mark

Unit 12 — Beetle Boy, by M.G. Leonard

Mix it up!

Name: _____

1 Look at the first paragraph. Why do you think the story begins with this paragraph?

_____

_____

1 mark

2 Look at the second paragraph. At what time did Dr Cuttle speak to his secretary?

_____

1 mark

3 Look at the sentences below. Underline **two** words that mean the same as 'question'.

> The puzzle of the disappearing scientist made the front page of every newspaper. The unsolvable mystery drove journalists crazy, and not one of them could explain how Dr Cuttle had gotten out of that vault.

1 mark

4 Look at the paragraph beginning *Five years earlier, ...* . What impression do you get of Darkus? Give **one** impression and **one** piece of evidence from the text.

Impression	Evidence

2 marks

5 Think about the whole text. What do you think will happen to Darkus next? Explain your opinion using evidence from the text.

_____

_____

_____

2 marks

Unit 12 — Beetle Boy, by M.G. Leonard

Beetle Boy: The Beetle Collector's Handbook by M.G. Leonard

Printable text • Modelling slides • Photocopiable text and questions • pages 134 to 137

In this unit, the children will read another text by M.G. Leonard, author of *Beetle Boy* (Unit 12) and a passionate advocate for beetles. Leonard wrote this companion text with factual information as well as fictional anecdotes to further explore the wonderful world of beetles. It is written in the style of an old guide that the fictional character Darkus Cuttle is reading. This extract discusses the attributes of the Goliath beetle, one of the largest and heaviest insects on Earth. After this unit has been completed, you could discuss the similarities and differences between the two texts and consider why the author chose to handle her subject in two different ways.

1 Get ready

Discuss the **Key vocabulary** identified in the **Language toolkit** and then complete the vocabulary activities as desired. Please note that the selected vocabulary is a guide. Depending on the needs of your cohort, additional vocabulary discussion may be beneficial before, during and after reading. Next, display the text (pages 134 to 135) so the children can see the title and any illustrations, and encourage the children to discuss the following questions before reading.

1. **The text we are going to read is mainly non-fiction, but it has some fictional elements. Have you read any other books that mix fiction and non-fiction?**
   Answers will vary depending on the children's prior reading. However, they should be able to recall the Unit 1 text *Dragonology*, which was a fictional book written in the style of non-fiction. After the children have read the text in this unit, you may wish to discuss the similarities and differences between the two texts.

2. **This text explores the wonderful world of beetles. What do you know about beetles?**
   Answers will vary depending on the children's background knowledge. It is important that they understand that beetles are not just the small, black beetles they may find in their gardens or local park, but differ greatly across the world. Use the texts in the **Reading list** to support your discussion.

3. **The extract provides information on the Goliath beetle, named after the biblical character Goliath. What do you know about the story of David and Goliath?**
   If the children do not know the story of David and Goliath, briefly discuss the basic story with them and encourage them to speculate as to what the Goliath beetle's name may tell us about its attributes.

Language toolkit

Key vocabulary

aerobatic	antennae	biblical
canopy	coifed	iridescence
larvae	methodical	notoriously
protrude	replicates	sap

Vocabulary discussion questions

- Are **larvae** the same as insects? Why?
- Can you describe how you have **coifed** your hair today?
- How might you approach an experiment if you were being **methodical**?
- What releases **sap**?
- Whereabouts in a forest would you find the **canopy**? On the ground or high up?
- Peacock feathers have **iridescence**. Can you think of anything else that is iridescent?

Vocabulary activities

- **Replicates** begins with the prefix 're–' which means 'back'. Ask the children to think of other words beginning with 're–' and sort them according to whether they use 're–' meaning 'back' or 're–' meaning 'again'.
- Look at the word **aerobatic**. What do the children think it means? Can they think of any words that sound similar? If they break this word into two parts, does that help them to decide?
- The text includes a number of scientific and entomological terms (e.g. 'rearing'; **antennae**; 'exoskeleton'). Share the definitions of these terms, showing pictures where possible, before the children read the text.

2 First steps

Read the text together and then encourage the children to discuss the following questions.

1. **What is the Latin name for the Goliath beetle? What family does it belong to?**
   Golianthus goliatus. It belongs to the Scarabaeidae family. You could explain that 'the Latin name' means the scientific name for this species of beetle, and that scientific names are often given in the ancient language of Latin.

2. **What do Goliath beetle larvae eat?**
   Decaying wood.

3. **What can Goliath beetles be mistaken for? Why does this happen?**
   Birds, because of their size and the fact that they fly high up into the canopy of the forest.

4. **Did you enjoy the text? Why? Why not?**
   The children should be able to justify their responses.

3 Explore

- The children may be aware of some other types of beetle, such as the stag or scarab beetle. Encourage them to share what they know with the class and add your own suggestions to create a list of different types of beetle from around the world. The children could choose a particular beetle to find out more about and then collate their research to create the class's own beetle collecting handbook.

- This text discusses how people sometimes eat the larvae, or grubs, of the Goliath beetle. In many countries, insects are a good source of food and they are thought to taste delicious. Discuss with the children whether or not they would try/have tried insects and give them time to research what types of insect are eaten around the world.

- Scientists are allowed to name any species which they themselves discover and often name them after people. Another example of an insect that has been named after a person is *Scaptia beyonceae*, the Beyoncé horse fly, so named because of its golden hair! Ask the children to research other insects named after people, then discuss their findings.

4 Skills focus   See pages 132 to 133

Use the information from the **Skills guide** and the relevant **Skills graphic** to introduce the skill of word meaning.

1. Model the skill using the **Unit 13 Modelling slides** and the **Modelling word meaning** guidance on page 132.

2. The children can then attempt the **Word meaning** questions on page 136.

3. Finally, the **Mix it up!** questions on page 137 offer practice in a range of comprehension skills.

Answers and marking guidance for all questions are included on pages 132 to 133.

5 Where next?

- **Speaking and listening task:** Show the children the BBC documentary that is given in the **Reading list** or show them other videos of Goliath beetles. In pairs, they could record their own short documentary about these insects. They should use the knowledge they have learnt from the text alongside facts from the research they have done in the **Explore** activities.

- **Writing task:** The children could each write a letter to their local museum, enquiring about their collections and whether they have any intriguing specimens like the Goliath beetle.

Reading list

Fiction
- *Battle of the Beetles* by M.G. Leonard
- *Beetle Boy* by M.G. Leonard (Linked text: **Unit 12**)
- *Freda and the Blue Beetle* by Sophie Gilmore
- *Masterpiece* by Elise Broach

Class reads
- *The Evolution of Calpurnia Tate* by Jacqueline Kelly

Non-fiction
- *The Beetle Book* by Steve Jenkins
- *A Beetle Is Shy* by Dianna Hutts Aston
- *Bonkers about Beetles* by Owen Davey
- *Bugs in Danger* by Mark Kurlansky
- *Small Wonders* by Matthew Clark Smith
- *The Wonders of Nature* by Ben Hoare
- *A Year in Nature* by Hazel Maskell

Poetry
- *I Am the Seed That Grew the Tree* by Fiona Waters (ed)
- *Song of the Water Boatman and Other Pond Poems* by Joyce Sidman

Websites
- The Amateur Entomologists' Society's website has a section for young entomologists, The Bug Club.
- The BBC Earth Unplugged YouTube channel has an interesting video called 'Ultimate Fighting Champion: The Goliath Beetle'.
- The What's That Bug? website is a useful place to identify and research bugs.

Unit 13 — Word meaning — Non-fiction

Unit 13

❓ Modelling word meaning ▽ See Unit 13 Modelling slides

Use the **Skills guide** (see pages 14 to 15) and the downloadable **Skills graphic** to support your modelling.

1 *On one of my visits to Ghana, I witnessed Goliath grubs being prepared for supper.* **Which word is closest in meaning to** *witnessed*? **Tick one.**

   wondered ☐
   smelled ☐
   heard ☐
   observed ✓

   This question includes a locator, so you should model using the quotation to scan the text to find the relevant sentence. It is important to then model reading around the sentence to gain deeper understanding. Next, identify the key words in the question (e.g. 'closest in meaning' and 'witnessed'). Discuss what 'witnessed' means and gather synonyms. Use this knowledge to model thinking about each answer option in turn, discussing whether each word fits in the context of the quote.

2 **Look at the sentence beginning** *There is no finer way … .* **What does the word** *menagerie* **mean in this sentence? Tick one.**

   a collection ✓
   a swarm ☐
   a gathering ☐
   a family ☐

   Again, use the locator to model finding the relevant section of text. Demonstrate identifying the key word 'menagerie' in the question and locating this word in the text. Discuss what 'menagerie' means in this context, emphasising that the beetles did not gather themselves together but were brought together in captivity. Think aloud: *Which word could replace 'menagerie' here?* Finally, use this knowledge to model choosing the most effective option from the list.

3 **Look at the illustration label beginning** *Goliaths possess antennae … .* **Find and copy one word that means 'to stick out'.**

   protrude

   This is an unusual locator, so you could spend extra time modelling how to locate the relevant section of text. Read the label aloud, then model scanning it to identify what is described as 'sticking out'. Next, search for a single word that could be a synonym of 'stick out'. The children should recognise 'protrude' from the **Key vocabulary**.

4 **Look at the last sentence. What does** *mistaken for* **mean in this sentence?**

   The hunter thought that the Goliath beetle was something else (a bird).

   Model locating the last sentence and reading around it to gain understanding of the context. Identify the key words 'mistaken for' in the question and model locating them within the text. Discuss what the children think 'mistaken for' means. Point out that the question asks for its meaning in the context of this particular sentence and model relating your definition to the text when formulating your final answer.

Word meaning questions mark scheme ❓   📖 See page 136

	Answer	Guidance
1	decaying	If the children find this challenging, discuss what can rot (e.g. natural materials) as well as some possible synonyms to help give them an idea of what to look for in the paragraph. **Award 1 mark for the correct answer.**

	Answer	Guidance
2	You can eat the grub. ✓	Some children may choose 'you can drink the grub' as they may see eating and drinking as synonymous. If so, discuss what things we eat and what things we drink. Which group do they think a grub would fit into? **Award 1 mark for the correct answer ticked.**
3	The glasshouse has exactly the same conditions as the beetles' natural habitat.	If some children provide a straightforward definition of 'replicates' (e.g. 'copies'; 'same as'), encourage them to extend their answer and refer to the context of the whole sentence. **Award 1 mark for a reference to the conditions in the glasshouse being the same as tropical conditions.**
4	patterns	If the children find this challenging, provide them with some multiple choice options to stimulate discussion (e.g. 'plans'; 'patterns'; 'coverings'; 'disguises'). **Award 1 mark for the correct answer.**
5	curious puzzling	The children need to find two separate words from the paragraph, rather than a group of words. Although the use of the numbered response should support them to do this, you may wish to emphasise this. **Award 1 mark for each correct answer, up to a maximum of 2 marks.**

Mix it up! questions mark scheme

See page 137

	Answer	Guidance
1	The larvae can get very big.	Some children may use 'large' in their responses. As this is included in the quotation, it should not be accepted unless accompanied by another explanation. **Award 1 mark for a reference to the larvae being very big.** Skill: Word choice.
2	It makes you want to read on because you would probably not know that people ate them so you'd be intrigued to find out what was coming next.	The children's answers may reflect their personal opinions. Accept any plausible explanation. **Award 1 mark for a plausible reason why the paragraph was included. Award 2 marks for a plausible reason with appropriate evidence from the text.** Skill: Relationship.
3	Males have a Y-shaped horn but females have no horn. Males are bigger than females.	The children need to include both sides of the comparison for each point, either explicitly or through the use of a comparative or superlative adjective. **Award 1 mark for a reference to one of the following differences: horns, size, behaviour. Award 2 marks for a reference to two of the differences listed above.** Skill: Comparison.
4	defending sap flows	Some children may paraphrase the text (e.g. 'defend territory'). Where the intention is clear, accept paraphrasing. **Award 1 mark for a reference to defending sap flows.** Skill: Retrieval.
5	An unusual specimen ✓	As all the options appear in the paragraph, you could prompt the children to identify the main point of the paragraph before using that knowledge to choose the most effective subheading. **Award 1 mark for the correct answer ticked.** Skill: Summarising.

Beetle Boy: The Beetle Collector's Handbook, by M.G. Leonard

This text is a companion to the **Unit 12** story, *Beetle Boy*. It tells us wonderful facts about the Goliath beetle, which is one of the largest insects on the planet. Although a non-fiction text, it is written from the perspective of a fictional character called Dr Montgomery George Leonard.

GOLIATH BEETLE

(Golianthus goliatus) Family: Scarabaeidae

Goliath beetles are the most famous of the flower beetles. They are named after the biblical giant who was brought down by a boy, David, with a shot from his sling; and they are some of the largest and heaviest insects on Earth, ranging from five to eleven centimetres in size.

Delicious grub

Goliath larvae feed on decaying wood and can grow exceedingly large. A fully-grown larva would easily fill the palm of your hand. Despite looking as unappetising as uncooked haggis, this giant grub is edible and rich in protein. On one of my visits to Ghana, I witnessed Goliath grubs being prepared for supper. The contents of their guts were squeezed out, rather like a tube of toothpaste, and then they were smoked over a fire and dried out. Fried up with onions, tomatoes and spices they were quite delicious, although you must remember to remove the head before eating.

My oldest friend is an entomologist who I met at university; his name is Hector Dungworthy and he's known throughout Oxford for his love of the herringbone suit, and for sporting an excellently coifed moustache. He's a methodical scientist and wonderful company on field trips, but his passion is breeding and rearing beetles from all over the world. He has an extraordinary glasshouse where he replicates tropical conditions for his exotic beetles. There is no finer way to spend an evening than sat with a bottle of vintage port watching his beetle menagerie. Hector tells me that although the adult beetles live two or three months in the wild, where they have to deal with weather and predators, in captivity they can live for about a year.

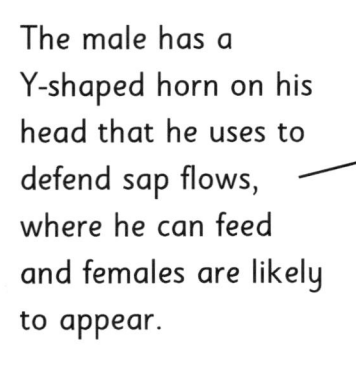

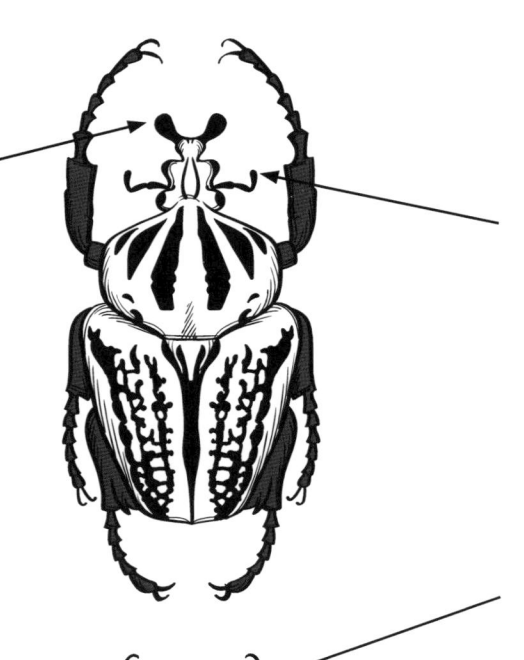

The male has a Y-shaped horn on his head that he uses to defend sap flows, where he can feed and females are likely to appear.

Goliaths possess antennae that protrude from their heads like handlebars and sharp claws for climbing trees.

Found in Africa's tropical forests, they are easy to recognise because of distinctive black-and-white, zebra-like markings on their exoskeletons.

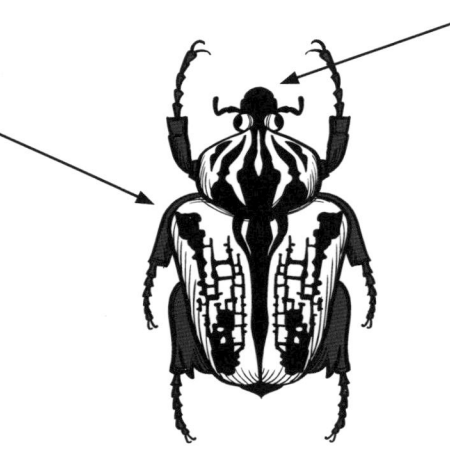

The female beetle is smaller than the male, and rather than having a horn, she has a spade-shaped head, which she uses for digging and burrowing down into the ground to lay her eggs.

Flights of fancy

Despite looking far too heavy to get off the ground, Goliath beetles do fly, high up in the canopy of the forest, and can be mistaken for birds. They launch themselves off branches, and the sight is extraordinary because their wings have a blueish purple iridescence, rather like oil on water.

One evening, when we were putting the world to rights in his glasshouse, Hector told me about a rather curious African Goliath beetle in the collection at the Natural History Museum in London, which has a series of puzzling holes in its exoskeleton. Upon investigation these holes were identified as the entry and exit wounds of gun shot; indeed, an X-ray revealed a shotgun pellet was still inside the unfortunate beetle's body! The position of the wounds showed that the beetle was shot in the back, and Hector believes the beetle must have been performing one of the high aerobatic displays that make Goliaths notoriously difficult to catch, when it was mistaken for a bird and brought down by gunfire.

The Beetle Collector's Handbook. Text © M.G. Leonard, 2018. Text reproduced with the permission of Scholastic Ltd. All rights reserved.

Unit 13

Word meaning

Name: _____

1 Look at the section **Delicious grub**. Find and copy **one** word that means 'rotting'.

_____

1 mark

2 *... this giant grub is edible ...*
What does the word *edible* mean in this sentence? Tick **one**.

You can play with the grub. ☐

You can drink the grub. ☐

You can eat the grub. ☐

You can squeeze the grub. ☐

1 mark

3 *He has an extraordinary glasshouse where he replicates tropical conditions for his exotic beetles.*
What does the word *replicates* mean in this sentence?

_____

_____

1 mark

4 Look at the illustration label beginning *Found in Africa's tropical ...* . What word could be used to replace *markings* in this sentence?

_____

1 mark

5 Look at the last paragraph. Find and copy **two** words that mean 'strange'.

1 _____

2 _____

2 marks

Beetle Boy: The Beetle Collector's Handbook, by M.G. Leonard

Photocopiable resource from *Complete Comprehension 5* © Schofield & Sims Ltd, 2020.

Mix it up!

Name: _____

1 *... can grow exceedingly large.*
What does this group of words tell you about the beetle larvae?

_____

_____

1 mark

2 Look at the paragraph beginning *Goliath larvae feed ...* . Why do you think this paragraph was included in the text?

_____

_____

_____

2 marks

3 Look at the illustration labels. Give **two** differences between male and female Goliath beetles.

_____

_____

_____

2 marks

4 What do male Goliath beetles use their horns for?

_____

_____

1 mark

5 Look at the last paragraph. What would be an effective subheading? Tick **one**.

Beetles at the Natural History Museum ☐

Hector's collection ☐

Aerobatic displays ☐

An unusual specimen ☐

1 mark

Photocopiable resource from *Complete Comprehension 5* © Schofield & Sims Ltd, 2020.

Unit 14

Inference | **Fiction**

The Boy at the Back of the Class
by Onjali Q. Raúf

▽ Printable text • Modelling slides   📖 Photocopiable text and questions • pages 142 to 145

Although an age-old issue, the challenges facing refugees and migrants have become far more visible recently. The text for this unit is taken from the award-winning book *The Boy at the Back of the Class*, by Onjali Q. Raúf, who has worked in refugee camps and seen people's struggles first-hand. It is a tale of a boy, Ahmet, and his new life in the UK. Once Progress Check 2, *Who are Refugees and Migrants?*, has been completed, you could discuss the thematic links between the two texts.

1 Get ready

Discuss the **Key vocabulary** identified in the **Language toolkit** and then complete the vocabulary activities as desired. Please note that the selected vocabulary is a guide. Depending on the needs of your cohort, additional vocabulary discussion may be beneficial before, during and after reading. Next, display the text (pages 142 to 143) so the children can see the title and any illustrations, and encourage the children to discuss the following questions before reading.

1. **This story is about a new boy joining a school. Can you remember your first day at school? How did you feel?**
   If none of the children can remember their first day at school, encourage them to share other 'firsts' (e.g. the first time they attended an after-school club). Discuss how the children felt and whether first days are generally positive or negative.

2. **This text uses a narrator who tells the story from their point of view. What is a narrator?**
   Most of the children should be able to explain what a narrator is and that many fiction books have narrators. You could discuss how the narrator in the text they will read is a character in the story, so the narration is written in the first person. Can the children think of any other texts they have read where the narrator is also a character in the story? You could refer back to the Unit 5 text, *The House with Chicken Legs*.

3. **In this story, the boy who joins the school is a refugee. What do you know about refugees?**
   It is likely that the children will have some knowledge of refugees from current affairs. In order to fully grasp the theme of the story, it is important that they understand why a refugee might leave their home for another country. You could use some titles from the **Reading list** to support your discussion.

Language toolkit

Key vocabulary

especially	every so often	glances
lemon sherbets	noticed	operator
period	scowl	serious
sneaking	specks	welcome

Vocabulary discussion questions

- When have you been made to feel **welcome**?
- If you are **especially** happy, how happy are you?
- If you **scowl**, how might you be feeling?
- What do you do **every so often** at school?
- What lesson do you usually have in first **period**?

Vocabulary activities

- 'Watch', 'staring' and **sneaking glances** all describe ways of looking at someone or something. How many similar words can the children think of?
- **Specks** of something are very small. Ask the children to collect synonyms for 'very small' and work together to set them out in a 'Shades of meaning' activity (see page 15).
- **Lemon sherbets** are a specific type of old-fashioned sweet that are still eaten today. Have any of the children ever tried one? Can they name any other old-fashioned sweets or foods that are still eaten today?

2 First steps

Read the text together and then encourage the children to discuss the following questions.

1. **What important event begins the story?**
   A new boy called Ahmet joins the class.

2. **What do we know about the narrator?**
   They are a child at the same school and in the same class as Ahmet. They are friends with Josie, Tom and Michael. They like lemon sherbets. Encourage the children to gather as many details as possible from the extract.

3. **What does the narrator keep trying to do throughout the extract? Why?**
   The narrator keeps looking at Ahmet and tries to wave at him in P.E. because they want to make friends with him.

3 Explore

- Discuss with the children how people are welcomed into their school. What is done to make visitors feel wanted? How does the school make sure new children feel safe and secure? Do the children think any areas could be improved? Challenge them to present their ideas to the head teacher or school council.

- After sharing some of the resources in the **Reading list** with the children, discuss how they feel about negative opinions about refugees (e.g. that they take jobs or use government money). What do they think could be done to persuade people to welcome refugees and migrants, and to educate them about the struggles people have faced before moving to another country? This is a sensitive topic and you should consider the backgrounds of the children in your class before starting the discussion.

- Refugees and migrants often become valued members of society, working hard to support their families and communities. The children could research a person who came to the country as a refugee or migrant, finding out about their birth country, their journey and their new life.

4 Skills focus   See pages 140 to 141

Use the information from the **Skills guide** and the relevant **Skills graphic** to introduce the skill of inference.

1. Model the skill using the **Unit 14 Modelling slides** and the **Modelling inference** guidance on page 140.

2. The children can then attempt the **Inference** questions on page 144.

3. Finally, the **Mix it up!** questions on page 145 offer practice in a range of comprehension skills.

Answers and marking guidance for all questions are included on pages 140 to 141.

5 Where next?

- **Speaking and listening task:** The children could work in small groups to create a welcome video for refugees and migrants. It could include specific links to a town or city, or be a general welcome to the country.

- **Writing task:** The children could work in pairs to compose a letter that welcomes a new person to school. They should think about what it would be helpful for the new child to know about and choose language that will create a welcoming and positive tone. These could then be given to new children on arrival to help them settle in.

Reading list

Fiction
- *The Arrival* by Shaun Tan
- *A Grain of Hope* by Nicola Philp
- *The Journey* by Francesca Sanna
- *My Name Is Not Refugee* by Kate Milner
- *The Other Side of Truth* by Beverley Naidoo
- *Saving Hanno: The Story of a Refugee Dog* by Miriam Halahmy
- *The Silver Sword* by Ian Serraillier
- *The Star Outside My Window* by Onjali Q. Raúf
- *When Hitler Stole Pink Rabbit* by Judith Kerr
- *Wisp: A Story of Hope* by Zana Fraillon

Class reads
- *No Ballet Shoes in Syria* by Catherine Bruton

Non-fiction
- *Refugees and Migrants* by Ceri Roberts
- *Seeking Refuge: Ali's Story* by Andy Glynne
- *What Is a Refugee?* by Elise Gravel
- *Who are Refugees and Migrants?* by Michael Rosen and Annemarie Young (Linked text: Progress check 2)
- *Yusra Mardini: Refugee Hero and Olympic Swimmer* by Kelly Spence

Poetry
- 'Lament for Syria' by Amineh Abou Kerech

Websites
- Amnesty International has a dedicated education section on their website which includes resources to teach children about refugee and asylum issues.

Unit 14

Modelling inference

▽ See Unit 14 Modelling slides

Use the **Skills guide** (see pages 20 to 21) and the downloadable **Skills graphic** to support your modelling.

1. **Read from the paragraph beginning** *We all watched …* **to** *… they would be his friends too.* **Why might Ahmet not enjoy sitting next to Clarissa? Give two reasons.**

   She doesn't like boys and she is scowling and staring at him.

   This question includes a locator, so it is important to model using this to find the relevant paragraphs. Next, model identifying key words in the question (e.g. 'not enjoy'; 'Clarissa') and show the children how to scan methodically through the text to find them. The two paragraphs contain multiple reasons why Ahmet might not like sitting next to Clarissa. Discuss these and model choosing the two strongest ones for your final answer. Some may attempt to use extrinsic knowledge; this should only be encouraged if it relates to the text.

2. **Look at the paragraph beginning** *Most of the time … .* **Why do you think Ahmet only stared back at the other children every so often?**

   Because he was curious about them/wanted to be friends with them but he was scared.

   Again, model using the locator to find the correct paragraph. Model identifying key words (e.g. 'stared') and scanning the text for them, before reading around them to gain an understanding of the context. You could discuss the children's experiences of similar situations, such as when they wanted to do something but hesitated to do so. What were they feeling to make them hesitant?

3. *We had geography in first period that morning, so we couldn't get up to say hello to the new boy.* **How might the narrator have felt at this point in the story? Explain your answer using the text.**

   Guilty because they wanted to say hello but couldn't, and they are worried that Ahmet feels like no-one wants to be his friend.

   Model using the locator to find the relevant paragraph. As the locator is a quotation, you should explain that reading around the quotation is important. Although you discussed the term 'narrator' in **Get ready**, you could check the children's understanding before continuing. With this type of question, it is useful to model asking how the children would feel if they were the narrator at this point. Discuss all the different things the narrator might be feeling before settling on a plausible option for the answer. Alternatives might include: 'Disappointed/frustrated because the boy wanted to say hello and make friends, but there wasn't time because their first lesson started'.

4. **What impression do you get of the narrator? Give one impression and one piece of evidence from the text.**

   The narrator is kind because they want to be Ahmet's friend.

   As there is no locator, it is important to point out to the children that this question is about the whole text. Model scanning the text for mentions of the narrator's thoughts about Ahmet. Find a piece of evidence and discuss what impression this gives you of the narrator. Model writing your answer in a table format (see **Modelling question 4** in **Unit 5**).

Inference questions mark scheme

See page 144

	Answer	Guidance
1	anxious because he doesn't know anybody in the class	Some children may benefit from putting themselves in Ahmet's shoes. How would they feel in the same situation? **Award 1 mark for a plausible emotion. Award 2 marks for a plausible emotion plus an explanation linked to the text.**
2	Because she didn't want Ahmet sitting next to her.	Some children will explain why Clarissa did not want Ahmet sitting next to her (e.g. 'Because she doesn't like boys/she misses Dena'). An explanation is not necessary to gain the mark. **Award 1 mark for a reference to her not wanting Ahmet to sit next to her.**

	Answer	Guidance
3	Because it might make Ahmet trust him/ feel welcome/be his friend.	Some children may answer that it is a nice thing to do. Although true, this does not show enough inferential understanding. If so, prompt them to explain how the act of kindness might change the situation. **Award 1 mark for a reference to it showing Ahmet that the narrator is kind/can be trusted/ can be a friend.**
4	frustrated because he keeps trying to make friends with the boy, but the boy doesn't want to be OR upset because he's trying to be friendly and it's not working	This is a challenging question as it requires a close inference. You may wish to encourage the children to think about similar experiences that have happened to them. **Award 1 mark for a plausible emotion. Award 2 marks for a plausible emotion plus an explanation linked to the text.**
5	*Impression*: shy *Evidence*: He keeps his head down most of the time and won't speak to anyone.	Many of the children are likely to focus on Ahmet's apparent shyness or anxiety. Any plausible feeling should be accepted, as long as it relates to the text. **Award 1 mark for a plausible impression. Award 2 marks for a plausible impression with appropriate evidence from the text.**

Mix it up! questions mark scheme

See page 145

	Answer	Guidance
1	predicting ✓	If the children find this question challenging, remind them to try substituting each option into the text to see which seems most plausible. **Award 1 mark for the correct answer ticked.** **Skill: Word meaning.**
2	Clarissa is mean and scowls, but the narrator is kind and tries to figure out ways to be Ahmet's friend.	The children need to refer to both Clarissa and the narrator's contrasting reactions in their answer. If only one side is given (e.g. 'Clarissa is mean and the narrator isn't'), encourage them to explain the other side of their comparison. **Award 1 mark for a reference to both Clarissa's negative reaction and the narrator's positive reaction. Skill: Comparison.**
3	They were like a lion's. OR They were the strangest colour that the narrator had ever seen.	Some children may lift their responses directly from the text and refer to the colour of Ahmet's eyes (e.g. 'like a bright ocean'). If so, prompt them to explain why the narrator thought this made Ahmet's eyes interesting. **Award 1 mark for a reference to Ahmet's eyes being an unusual colour or being lion-like. Skill: Retrieval.**
4	He might go over to him and give him a lemon sherbet.	The children are likely to have contrasting views on what might happen next in the story. As long as a prediction is informed by the text and is plausible, it should be accepted. **Award 1 mark for a plausible prediction linked to the text. Skill: Prediction.**
5	The New Boy	The children should be encouraged to think about the main point of the extract, i.e. Ahmet's arrival and the narrator's attempts to become his friend. This will then support them to think of an appropriate title linked closely to the content. **Award 1 mark for any plausible title. Skill: Summarising.**

The Boy at the Back of the Class, by Onjali Q. Raúf

In this story, Ahmet arrives at his new school and meets his new classmates. The narrator, another child, wants to become Ahmet's friend but doesn't quite know how.

After whispering for a few more seconds with Mrs Khan, Mrs Sanders left the classroom. We expected Mrs Khan to say something, but she seemed to be waiting, so we waited too. It was all very serious and exciting. But before we could start guessing about what was going on, Mrs Sanders came back, and this time she wasn't alone.

Standing behind her was a boy. A boy none of us had ever seen before. He had short dark hair and large eyes that hardly blinked and smooth pale skin.

"Everyone," said Mrs Khan, as the boy went and stood next to her. "This is Ahmet, and he'll be joining our class from today. He's just moved to London and is new to the school, so I hope you'll all do your very best to make him feel welcome."

We all watched in silence as Mrs Sanders led him to the empty chair. I felt sorry for him because I knew he wouldn't like sitting next to Clarissa very much. She still missed Dena, and everyone knew she hated boys – she says they're stupid and they smell.

I think it must be one of the worst things in the world to be new to a place and have to sit with people you don't know. Especially people that stare and scowl at you like Clarissa was doing. I made a secret promise to myself right there and then that I would be friends with the new boy. I happened to have some lemon sherbets in my bag that morning and I thought I would try and give him one at break-time. And I would ask Josie and Tom and Michael if they would be his friends too.

After all, having four new friends would be much better than having none. Especially for a boy who looked as scared and as sad as the one sitting at the back of our class. For the rest of the day I kept sneaking glances over my shoulder at the new boy and noticed that everyone else was doing the same.

Most of the time he kept his head down low but every so often I'd catch him staring right back at us. He had the strangest coloured eyes I'd ever seen – like a bright ocean but on a half-sunny, half-cloudy day. They were grey and silvery-blue with specks of golden-brown. They reminded me of a programme I saw about lions once. The camera operator had zoomed into a lion's face so much that its eyes had taken up the whole screen. The new boy's eyes were like those lion's eyes. They made you want to never stop staring.

When Tom joined our class last year I had stared at him a lot too. I didn't mean to, but I kept imagining that he came from an American spy family – like the ones you see in the movies. He told me later that he had thought there was something wrong with me. The new boy probably thought there was something wrong with me too, but it's hard to stop staring at new people – especially when they have eyes like a lion's.

We had geography in first period that morning, so we couldn't get up to say hello to the new boy. Then at break-time I looked around the playground for him but couldn't see him anywhere. In second period we had P.E. but the new boy didn't join in; he sat in the corner staring at his rucksack, which was red with a black stripe on it and looked very dirty. I thought he must have forgotten his P.E. kit because his bag looked empty and saggy. I tried waving at him, but he never looked up – not even once.

From *The Boy at the Back of the Class*, by Onjali Q. Raúf. Text copyright © Onjali Q. Raúf, 2018. Reproduced by permission of Orion Children's Books, an imprint of Hachette Children's Books, Carmelite House, 50 Victoria Embankment, London imprint, EC4Y 0DZ.

Inference

Name: _____

1 Look at the paragraph beginning *Standing behind her …* . How might Ahmet be feeling at this point in the story? Explain your answer using evidence from the text.

_____

_____

_____

2 marks

2 Look at the sentence beginning *Especially people that stare and scowl …* . Why was Clarissa scowling?

_____

_____

1 mark

3 *I happened to have some lemon sherbets in my bag that morning and I thought I would try and give him one at break-time.*
Why might it be a good idea for the narrator to do this?

_____

_____

1 mark

4 Read the last sentence. How might the narrator be feeling at this point in the story? Explain your answer using evidence from the text.

_____

_____

_____

2 marks

5 What impression do you get of Ahmet? Give **one** impression and **one** piece of evidence from the text.

Impression	Evidence
_____	_____
	_____
	_____

2 marks

Photocopiable resource from *Complete Comprehension 5* © Schofield & Sims Ltd, 2020.

Mix it up!

Name: _____

1 *But before we could start guessing about what was going on, ...*
Which word is closest in meaning to *guessing*? Tick **one**.

talking ☐

smiling ☐

predicting ☐

checking ☐

1 mark

2 Compare how Clarissa and the narrator react when Ahmet arrives. Give **one** difference.

_____

_____

1 mark

3 Look at the paragraph beginning *Most of the time ...* . What was interesting about Ahmet's eyes?

_____

1 mark

4 Think about the whole text. What do you think the narrator will do next to try to become Ahmet's friend?

_____

_____

1 mark

5 Think about the whole text. What would be an effective alternative title for this extract?

_____

1 mark

Unit 14

The Boy at the Back of the Class, by Onjali Q. Raúf

Photocopiable resource from *Complete Comprehension 5* © Schofield & Sims Ltd, 2020.

Progress check 2

Who are Refugees and Migrants? And Other Big Questions

by Michael Rosen and Annemarie Young

Printable text • Modelling slides   Photocopiable text and questions • pages 147 to 149

Every country is enriched by its people, whether they are born there or arrive later in life. Today more than ever, as we strive to win equality and justice for all people, it is important to celebrate every individual's contribution to our diverse society. This unit's text brings together the stories of a number of refugees and migrants to ask big questions about society. In this extract, the poet Benjamin Zephaniah discusses his experiences, from his parents' emigration to the racism he has suffered. After this Progress check is completed, you could discuss this text alongside that of Unit 14, comparing their presentation of refugees and migrants. **For guidance on running this task, see page 11.**

Progress check questions mark scheme

	Answer	Guidance
1	Jamaica and Barbados	Responses must include references to the nationalities of both of Zephaniah's parents to gain the mark. **Award 1 mark for a reference to both countries.** Skill: Retrieval.
2	He says that life in Jamaica is hard and that if his mum had not left, he might have died like his cousins.	A complete response to this question requires the children to link Zephaniah's thoughts about the difficult life some people lead in Jamaica with the effect this might have had on him if his mother had not left. You could provide some additional scaffolding if any of the children struggle to explain their answer. **Award 1 mark for a reason linked to the text. Award 2 marks for a reason linked to the text with a plausible explanation.** Skill: Inference.
3	diverse ✓	Although the children will be familiar with the target word 'different', this question is challenging as all the answer options sound plausible. You could remind them to look for the word closest in meaning in the context of this sentence. **Award 1 mark for the correct answer ticked.** Skill: Word meaning.
4	people from different backgrounds usually all live together happily	Some children may focus on the news as the key point. If so, discuss that news is mentioned to support the author's main point about people from different backgrounds usually living together with no problems. **Award 1 mark for the correct answer.** Skill: Summarising.
5	Because it makes it clear that even though people think refugees and migrants are from poor or war-torn countries, anyone can be one, even a middle-class person from the Lake District.	The children need to understand the overall theme of the text to respond fully – they must understand that many people would not expect refugees to come from England/the Lake District. If necessary, discuss the definition of 'refugee' and explore a range of views about where refugees might come from and why they might have come to England. **Award 1 mark for a plausible reason. Award 2 marks for a plausible reason with an explanation linked to the text or to the general definition of 'refugee'.** Skill: Relationship.

Non-fiction

Progress check 2

Name: _____

1 Where did Benjamin Zephaniah's parents come from?

_____

1 mark

2 Read from the paragraph beginning *My mum came from ...* to the paragraph ending *... have a difficult life.* How can you tell that Benjamin Zephaniah is glad his mother went to England?

_____

_____

_____

2 marks

3 *People of different backgrounds live together naturally, ...*
Which word is closest in meaning to *different*? Tick **one**.

diverse ☐

ordinary ☐

rare ☐

special ☐

1 mark

4 Look at the paragraph beginning *People of different backgrounds live together naturally, ...* What is the main point of this paragraph?

_____

_____

1 mark

5 Look at the section **It can happen to anyone**. Why do you think this section has been included in the text? Explain your answer using evidence from the text.

_____

_____

_____

2 marks

Who are Refugees and Migrants? And Other Big Questions, by Michael Rosen and Annemarie Young

Every country benefits from the experiences and ideas of all its people, whether they are born there or come there from another country. In this text, we hear about the experiences of the famous poet, Benjamin Zephaniah, whose parents came from the Caribbean to England in the 1950s.

My Experience: Benjamin Zephaniah

Benjamin Zephaniah is a poet, novelist, playwright, musician, performer and television and radio presenter. He's also patron of a number of charities and organisations.

If I talk to anybody for long enough I find that their family came here from somewhere. Everyone comes from somewhere.

My parents came from Jamaica and Barbados

My mum came from Jamaica and my dad came from Barbados, and they met in England. What happened with my mum was that she and her sister were looking at a poster where it said, 'Come to the Motherland … help build the Mother Country' – that was Britain – and Mum said to her sister, "Fancy going?" and her sister said, "I've heard it's really cold," and Mum said, "Give it a try!" so she did, but her sister stayed behind in Saint Elizabeth. Mum's uncle, who had brought her up, gave her £20 for the ticket and she came to Britain in 1957.

When I go to Jamaica I see how different people live. Their lives are hard. My cousins are always dying at sea, or in hurricanes, and my family live in poverty, so I'm aware that if my mum hadn't decided to come to England on that day in 1957, I too would have a difficult life.

My mum always tried to see the nice side of people

Mum said that this country gave her everything. When I took her back to visit Jamaica, she didn't like it, and she wasn't like some Jamaicans who want to go back there to be buried. She wanted to be buried in Witton, in Birmingham.

She was like that, but she knew that I was on the receiving end of racist attacks, like when someone slapped a brick on the back of my head. She just didn't like anyone making a fuss about that sort of thing. She'd say, "We're guests." And she believed that it would all be all right in the end when we get to heaven. She always tried to see the nice side of people.

People of different backgrounds live together naturally, but when a small thing goes wrong it becomes big news. No one reports it when it goes well, it's not news then. I love our differences. It teaches me that I am a citizen of Britain, but it also teaches me to be a citizen of the world.

Think about

> People sometimes talk about 'integration' as though it's only the minority group that integrates with the majority, but have you ever noticed whether people who live, work or go to school with migrants pick up aspects of their culture?

It can happen to anyone

When I think about refugees, I think that what they're going through could happen to anyone. It could happen because of war, or the weather.

I took in some refugees. They were middle class white people from the Lake District in England. They had to grab what they could when the floods came. I think to start off with, they weren't particularly sympathetic to refugees, but they soon changed their mind, because now they know it can happen to anyone.

From 'My Experience', by Benjamin Zephaniah, taken from *Who Are Refugees and Migrants? What Makes People Leave Their Homes? And Other Big Questions* (Wayland, 2016). Extract text copyright © 2016, Benjamin Zephaniah. Reproduced by permission of the author c/o United Agents LLP, 12 – 26 Lexington Street, London W1F 0LE.

The Jamie Drake Equation
by Christopher Edge

Unit 15 — Retrieval — Fiction

▽ Printable text • Modelling slides   📖 Photocopiable text and questions • pages 154 to 157

Space is known by some as the final frontier. Although human beings have explored most corners of the Earth, our interactions with space have been much more limited. Perhaps that is why the universe intrigues children and adults alike. The extract for this unit focuses on a boy, Jamie Drake, whose dad is an astronaut. Jamie is an expert on the solar system, and the text is a great way to introduce the children to the wonders of space. The text *Once Upon a Star* in Unit 16 discusses some of the same information but in a different format. You may wish to compare the two texts once both units have been completed.

1 Get ready

Discuss the **Key vocabulary** identified in the **Language toolkit** and then complete the vocabulary activities as desired. Please note that the selected vocabulary is a guide. Depending on the needs of your cohort, additional vocabulary discussion may be beneficial before, during and after reading. Next, display the text (pages 154 to 155) so the children can see the title and any illustrations, and encourage the children to discuss the following questions before reading.

1. **The main character in this story loves to tell people facts about space. What do you like finding out facts about?**
   Although not every child enjoys reading non-fiction texts, most are likely to have heard an interesting fact at some point. You could take a few minutes to allow them to share interesting facts about their favourite topics with each other.

2. **This story is about space and the wider universe. What do you know about space?**
   The children should study some elements of space as part of the science curriculum in Key Stage 2 and some will have also read factual texts on the subject independently. If the children struggle to contribute, you could spend some time exploring one of the non-fiction titles on the **Reading list**.

3. **Have you ever read any other fictional texts about space? What did they have in common?**
   There are many examples of children's literature which link to the topic of space, but some of the children may only be able to contribute non-fiction texts or film and TV content. In this case, you may wish to share fictional texts from the **Reading list** to support the children to make thematic links.

Language toolkit

Key vocabulary

balanced	depths	exists
human race	interdimensional	launches
orbit	phantom	scorching
solar system	supposed	tons

Vocabulary discussion questions

- What are you **supposed** to do before you go to bed?
- What might you wear on a **scorching** summer's day?
- When you have **tons** of something, do you have a little or a lot?
- When something is in **orbit**, what does it do?

Vocabulary activities

- **Interdimensional** begins with the prefix 'inter–'. What do the children think this prefix means? Can they find other examples of words which share the prefix (e.g. 'international')?
- If something is a **phantom**, this can mean it is a ghost or something unreal. What other words and groups of words can the children suggest to describe things that are not real (e.g. 'vision'; 'apparition'; 'spirit'; 'wraith'; 'illusion'; 'spook')? As a class, explore how different words might be used for different situations.
- Although this text is a story, it refers to a number of scientific concepts. You could discuss this subject-specific terminology (e.g. 'planet'; 'Venus'; 'star'; 'International Space Station') in addition to the vocabulary terms above.

Schofield & Sims Complete Comprehension 5

2 First steps

Read the text together and then encourage the children to discuss the following questions.

1. **What is the main character's name?**
   Jamie Drake. This information can be found in the fifth paragraph as well as in the extract title. This is a good opportunity to remind the children to read all the text provided, including the title.

2. **Give one fact that Jamie tells the reader about the universe.**
   Answers will vary but may focus on the formation of the universe, our solar system, or the Goldilocks zone.

3. **What is Jamie's dad's job? Where is he during this part of the story?**
   He is an astronaut. He is currently in space on the International Space Station.

3 Explore

- In the extract, Jamie's dad is an astronaut who is working on the International Space Station. Discuss with the children what they know about astronauts and their work in space. You could discuss the work of famous astronauts such as Chris Hadfield, Helen Sharman and Tim Peake. You could also explore the events of the 'space race' of the 1960s. See the **Reading list** for some helpful resources.

- Jamie relays some facts about planets in the extract. Discuss with the children what they know about the planets in our solar system. Are they similar to or different from Earth? Are there planets outside our solar system? The children could research the conditions on a planet of their choice, deciding whether it would be wise to send astronauts to explore their chosen planet.

- Jamie's dad is on a mission to find alien life. Although Earth is the only planet in the Goldilocks zone, many people believe that it cannot be the only planet that has life on it. Discuss with the children whether they believe in aliens, and what they think aliens might look like, perhaps using some images as inspiration. You could encourage them to think back to stories they have read about aliens to help them.

4 Skills focus   See pages 152 to 153

Use the information from the **Skills guide** and the relevant **Skills graphic** to introduce the skill of retrieval.

1. Model the skill using the **Unit 15 Modelling slides** and the **Modelling retrieval** guidance on page 152.

2. The children can then attempt the **Retrieval** questions on page 156.

3. Finally, the **Mix it up!** questions on page 157 offer practice in a range of comprehension skills.

Answers and marking guidance for all questions are included on pages 152 to 153.

5 Where next?

- **Speaking and listening task:** Jamie enjoys telling people the facts he has learnt about the universe. Working in small groups, the children could choose an aspect of the universe to research and produce a short video which explains key facts about their chosen topic to other children.

- **Writing task:** Astronauts spend a long time away on the International Space Station. The children could write letters or emails to an astronaut at NASA (the US space agency) or ESA (European Space Agency), asking questions about their life in space, their training schedule and how it feels to go in a space shuttle. They could then use the website resources in the **Reading list** to try to find answers to their questions.

Reading list

Fiction
- *The Girl with Space in Her Heart* by Lara Williamson
- *The Kid Who Came from Space* by Ross Welford
- *The Many Worlds of Albie Bright* by Christopher Edge

Class reads
- *The Infinite Lives of Maisie Day* by Christopher Edge

Non-fiction
- *100 Things to Know about Space* by Alex Frith et al.
- *Knowledge Encyclopedia: Space!* by DK
- *Professor Astro Cat's Frontiers of Space* by Dr. Dominic Walliman and Ben Newman
- *Science for Exploring Outer Space* by Mark Thompson
- *Space Encyclopedia* by David A. Aguilar
- *The Space Race* by Sarah Cruddas

Poetry
- 'Once Upon a Star' by James Carter (Linked text: Unit 16)
- *The World's Greatest Space Cadet* by James Carter

Websites
- The ESA website has a kids' area which features interesting articles and a fascinating video called 'Fun Facts about the ISS' presented by American astronaut Anne McClain.

Unit 15

Modelling retrieval
See Unit 15 Modelling slides

Use the **Skills guide** (see pages 16 to 17) and the downloadable **Skills graphic** to support your modelling.

1. **Look at the first paragraph. What two things turn into stars?**
   gas and dust
   This question includes a locator, so it is important to model using this to find the correct paragraph in the text. Model identifying the key words from the question and locating the information needed in the paragraph. Although 'turn' is not directly taken from the text, the verb 'turned' is used. You could use this as an opportunity to remind the children to look for related words for each key word.

2. **Look at the third paragraph. What is special about Earth?**
   It is the only planet where life is known to exist.
   Again, model using the locator to find the relevant paragraph. Next, model identifying the question's key words (e.g. 'Earth') to help narrow down the amount of text you will use to retrieve the information. This question requires some inference, as the children need to decide which fact shows that Earth is special. You could discuss the meaning of 'special', including the fact that often something special is one of a kind.

3. **Read from *Our family's solar system is …* to *… start to wobble*. Give one thing that would happen if you moved any part of the real solar system.**
   Planets would crash into each other/fly off into space.
   As before, model using the locator to find the relevant paragraphs. Model identifying the key words and scanning the relevant part of the text for appropriate information. There are two possible answers, so you could discuss both before selecting one to be your final response. It is important to model checking it against the question, which asks for '*one* thing'.

4. **Think about the whole text. Number the events to show the order in which they happen in the text.**

The solar system was created.	1
Dad flew into orbit.	4
Mum and Dad argued a lot.	3
Charlie was born.	2

   Although this question involves sequencing statements, it is a retrieval question because no summarising is needed. It is important to point out that this question is about the whole text and that it means that you are going to need to scan the text to find key information. Model identifying key words from the first event and scanning the text to find the corresponding information. Repeat this with the other events, then model numbering the events in the text. Finally, model numbering each event in your answer.

Retrieval questions mark scheme
See page 156

	Answer	Guidance
1	(about) 4.5 billion years ago	Responses must include both '4.5' (in words or figures), 'years' and 'ago' to gain the mark. Although the inclusion of 'about' is not required, you could encourage the children to be specific. **Award 1 mark for the correct answer.**
2	the Goldilocks zone	As this question has no locator, you could direct the children towards the fourth paragraph if necessary. **Award 1 mark for the correct answer.**

Answer				Guidance
3	number of days …	10		If the children find this challenging, you could explain that the key word 'number' shows that they need to scan the text for numbers, both in figures and words. **Award 1 mark for all three sections completed correctly.**
	number of kilometres …	400		
	number of years …	4		
4	It's Jamie's birthday and his dad is doing a spacewalk.			This question requires two pieces of information from two different paragraphs. You could give more specific locators for each one if necessary. **Award 1 mark for a reference to both Jamie's birthday and the spacewalk.**
5		F	O	You may wish to discuss the difference between fact and opinion with the children before they attempt this question. **Award 1 mark for at least two statements correctly ticked. Award 2 marks for all four statements correctly ticked.**
	Earth is in the Goldilocks zone.	✓		
	Mum is a star.		✓	
	The temperature on Venus is 400 degrees.	✓		
	Dad is an astronaut.		✓	

Mix it up! questions mark scheme

See page 157

	Answer	Guidance
1	transformed ✓	The children may tick 'rotated' as it is a synonym of 'turned' in another context. If they struggle, discuss the different meanings of 'turned'. **Award 1 mark for the correct answer ticked.** Skill: Word meaning.
2	*Similarity*: They are both planets. *Difference*: Saturn is much colder than Earth. OR Life exists on Earth but it doesn't on Saturn.	The paragraph discusses the differences between the planets, but it does not talk about similarities. Prompt the children to use inference to come up with a similarity: do they know what Earth and Saturn have in common? **Award 1 mark for one similarity or difference. Award 2 marks for one similarity and one difference.** Skill: Comparison.
3	to tell us about the Goldilocks zone	You may wish to prompt the children to think about a suitable subheading for this paragraph, to support them to identify the main point. **Award 1 mark for a reference to the Goldilocks zone.** Skill: Summarising.
4	*Feeling*: proud *Evidence*: He talks about his dad's spacewalk and how he's part of the mission to find alien life.	There are a number of possible responses. Some children may assign more general feelings to Jamie (e.g. 'He cares about him'). These are valid responses and should be accepted. **Award 1 mark for a plausible feeling. Award 2 marks for a plausible feeling with appropriate evidence from the text.** Skill: Inference.
5	No, because I think Jamie's dad's spacewalk will go wrong. I think Jamie will have to save him because the title is *The Jamie Drake Equation*.	The children's predictions will vary depending on their personal opinions and background knowledge. Accept any plausible prediction as long as it is linked to the text. **Award 1 mark for a plausible prediction. Award 2 marks for a plausible prediction plus an explanation linked to the text.** Skill: Prediction.

The Jamie Drake Equation, by Christopher Edge

This is an extract from a story about a boy called Jamie who is obsessed with the solar system and space in general. In this part of the story, he introduces his family and his knowledge of space to the reader.

You're supposed to start a story at the beginning, right? The thing is, knowing exactly *when* that is can be kind of difficult. I mean, I could start this story with how the solar system was formed about four and a half billion years ago. That was when the centre of a huge cloud of gas and dust that was spinning in space got super-hot and turned into a star, but *this* story really got started way before that.

It's all about putting things in the right order. That's how the solar system got going after all. Once the Sun was formed all the rest of the dust and stuff got stuck together to make all the planets and moons, and since then they've just kept spinning round the Sun, year after year.

Some are a bit too close, like Venus where it's a scorching four hundred degrees in the shade, while others are too far out and freezing cold, like Saturn and Neptune. But out of all of those planets, all those worlds, there's only one where we know that life exists. And that's our world – the planet Earth.

That's because it's right in the middle of the Goldilocks zone. Now, this isn't like the Phantom Zone in Superman – some kind of interdimensional prison where the three bears have locked up Goldilocks for crimes against porridge. The Goldilocks zone is the name for the region of space around a star where life has a chance of existing. Somewhere not too hot and not too cold, but just right. And in our solar system, Earth has got this spot all to itself.

It's a bit like my family, really. There's Mum, Dad, Charlie and me, Jamie Drake. Dad's the star in our family's solar system because he's an astronaut. Everyone at school knows his name and he's been on TV loads of times talking about his latest space mission. He's kind of like Captain Kirk crossed with Han Solo, but cooler because he's a real person.

To be fair, I reckon Mum's the star too because she keeps everything running smoothly when Dad's not around, so that just leaves Charlie and me in the Goldilocks zone.

It used to be that I had this spot all to myself, but then four years ago Mum and Dad told me that I was going to have a baby sister. At first I wasn't too sure, but then Mum explained that tons of people think that the perfect family has four people in it, so by adding a little sister our family was going to be just the right size, and when baby Charlotte was born I kind of had to agree.

Our family's solar system is now perfectly balanced. Mum + Dad = Me + Charlie.

Now, if you move any part of the real solar system, then the whole thing goes to pieces with planets crashing into each other or flying off into the depths of space. Everything has to be in just the right place for the Earth to keep spinning safely around the Sun. So with Dad now four hundred kilometres above our heads on the International Space Station, I'm keeping a close eye on things at home in case any bits of the Drake family solar system start to wobble.

So far, everything's OK. In fact, Mum and Dad were arguing a lot before he blasted off into orbit and I think having this break has just made them realise how much they love each other after all. And in ten days' time, Dad will land safely back on Earth and our family can get back to normal. It's just a shame he's going to miss my birthday on Friday.

That's the day of his spacewalk. The day the human race launches its first mission to the stars in search of alien life. I just hope he hasn't forgotten to get me a present.

From *The Jamie Drake Equation* by Christopher Edge, Nosy Crow, copyright © Christopher Edge 2017. Reproduced by permission of Nosy Crow Ltd.

Retrieval

Name: _____

1 Look at the first paragraph. When was our solar system created?

_____

1 mark

2 What is the name of the part of the solar system where life can exist?

_____

1 mark

3 Read from the paragraph beginning *It used to be ...* to the end of the text. Complete the table using information from the text.

number of days until Dad gets back	
number of kilometres Dad is above the Earth	
number of years since Charlotte was born	

1 mark

4 Read from the paragraph beginning *So far, everything's ...* to the end of the text. Give **two** things that are happening on Friday.

_____

_____

1 mark

5 Think about the whole text. Tick to show whether each statement is fact or opinion.

	Fact	Opinion
Earth is in the Goldilocks zone.		
Mum is a star.		
The temperature on Venus is 400 degrees.		
Dad is an astronaut.		

2 marks

Mix it up!

Name: _____

1 *... got super-hot and turned into a star, ...*
Which word is closest in meaning to *turned*? Tick **one**.

transformed ☐   rotated ☐   exploded ☐   flew ☐

1 mark

2 Look at the third paragraph. Give **one** similarity and **one** difference between Saturn and Earth.

Similarity	
Difference	

2 marks

3 Look at the fourth paragraph. What is the main point of this paragraph?

_____

1 mark

4 Think about the whole text. How does Jamie feel about his dad? Give **one** feeling and **one** piece of evidence from the text.

Feeling	Evidence

2 marks

5 Do you think Jamie's dad will return home on time? Explain your prediction using evidence from the text.

_____
_____
_____

2 marks

Unit 15

The Jamie Drake Equation, by Christopher Edge

Photocopiable resource from *Complete Comprehension 5* © Schofield & Sims Ltd, 2020.

Once Upon a Star
by James Carter

▽ **Printable text** • **Modelling slides**   📖 **Photocopiable text and questions** • **pages 162 to 165**

Throughout history, human beings have used religion and science to try to explain the creation of the universe and our existence within it. Scientists now believe that all life can be traced back to a singular point: the Big Bang. The text for this unit tells the story of this complex event through poetry. James Carter's lyrical poem is a wonderful way to bring the Big Bang theory to life. You may wish to discuss the links between this text and the Unit 15 text, *The Jamie Drake Equation*. Both units discuss the creation of the universe, but in different ways.

1 Get ready

Discuss the **Key vocabulary** identified in the **Language toolkit** and then complete the vocabulary activities as desired. Please note that the selected vocabulary is a guide. Depending on the needs of your cohort, additional vocabulary discussion may be beneficial before, during and after reading. Next, display the text (pages 162 to 163) so the children can see the title and any illustrations, and encourage the children to discuss the following questions before reading.

1. **This text is a narrative poem. What features would you expect to find in it?**
   It is likely that the children will have encountered narrative poetry during their time at school, but they may not know to identify it as such. A simple definition of a narrative poem is one that tells the reader a story or describes a process. Possible features to discuss include: figurative language; repetition; use of chronological order; alliteration; verses.

2. **This poem tells the story of the creation of the universe. What do you know about the Big Bang?**
   You could encourage the children to think back to the Unit 15 text, *The Jamie Drake Equation*. See **Reading list** for additional resources.

3. **What do you know about stars?**
   Discuss what stars actually are, including what they are made of and the fact that the Sun is a star. You could delve deeper by reading some of the texts on the **Reading list** together.

4. **The poem is unusual because it teaches the reader facts through poetry. Have you ever read any other poems or songs that do the same?**
   You could start by discussing which other poems the children have read in general, before working together to identify which of these were narrative poems and which of the poems told the reader facts about something.

Language toolkit

Key vocabulary

delight	explosion	fired
galaxy	gradually	kerrang
mass	nor	shore
stardust	trillion	universe

Vocabulary discussion questions

- What might you see, hear and smell if you were walking along a **shore**?
- If you are doing something **gradually**, are you rushing it or taking your time?
- What would a huge **explosion** sound like?
- When a pot is **fired** in a kiln, what happens?
- What is something that brings you **delight**?

Vocabulary activities

- **Universe** begins with the prefix 'uni–', as do the words 'universal' and 'university'. Discuss what the children think the prefix means. Can they work out the links between these three words?

- Explain that **kerrang** refers to the loud noise made by striking a chord on an electric guitar, and that it is an example of onomatopoeia. Ask the children to think of other examples of onomatopoeia, perhaps thinking about the sounds that other musical instruments make for inspiration.

- **Stardust** is a scientific term and it is also a compound word, made up of 'star' and 'dust'. Discuss how many other compound words the children know (e.g. spaceship), including any other scientific terms.

2 First steps

Read the text together and then encourage the children to discuss the following questions.

1. According to the poem, how many stars are there?
   'A billion trillion (maybe more)'.
2. What do scientists call the event that created the universe?
   The Big Bang.
3. What is at the heart of everything in our solar system?
   The Sun.
4. Did you enjoy the poem? Why? Why not?
   The children should be able to justify their responses (e.g. *I liked learning facts from a poem*).

3 Explore

- The main focus of the poem is the creation of the universe and the phenomenon known as the Big Bang. Remaining respectful of the children's religious beliefs, discuss in more detail what the Big Bang is and why it is important. You could refer to some of the resources on the **Reading list**.
- The poem ends by saying that everyone is made of stardust and is a star. This is factually true, but this verse also expresses a particular sentiment about people. Discuss the poet's play on words and how he is being both literal and figurative. You could ask the children why they think the poet calls everyone stars and discuss reasons why they might use the word 'star' to describe someone.
- Discuss the types of language used in this poem, such as onomatopoeia ('a mighty BOOM'; 'a huge KERRANG'), alliteration ('lights like lanterns'; 'sea of stars'; 'fired and formed'), personification ('fire blew'; 'our Sun gives us delight'), and precise word choices ('the lid is lifted off our world'). The children could gather examples of these features and think of their own examples to add to the list.

4 Skills focus   See pages 160 to 161

Use the information from the **Skills guide** and the relevant **Skills graphic** to introduce the skill of word meaning.

1. Model the skill using the **Unit 16 Modelling slides** and the **Modelling word meaning** guidance on page 160.
2. The children can then attempt the **Word meaning** questions on page 164.

3. Finally, the **Mix it up!** questions on page 165 offer practice in a range of comprehension skills.

Answers and marking guidance for all questions are included on pages 160 to 161.

5 Where next?

- **Speaking and listening task:** The children could work together as a class to act out the Big Bang and the creation of the universe. You could show a video clip of the Notre Dame Science's cosmological dance for inspiration (see **Reading list**).
- **Writing task:** The children could write their own factual poems about a particular element of the universe (e.g. stars; galaxies; other planets; the Sun). Encourage them to use the language features identified during the **Explore** section.

Reading list

Fiction
- *George's Secret Key to the Universe* by Lucy Hawking and Stephen Hawking
- *The Jamie Drake Equation* by Christopher Edge (Linked text: **Unit 15**)
- *Sputnik's Guide to Life on Earth* by Frank Cottrell Boyce
- *What Stars Are Made Of* by Sarah Allen

Class reads
- *Cosmic* by Frank Cottrell Boyce

Non-fiction
- *Balloon to the Moon* by Gill Arbuthnott
- *Curiosity: The Story of a Mars Rover* by Markus Motum
- *Dr Maggie's Grand Tour of the Solar System* by Dr Maggie Aderin-Pocock
- *A Hundred Billion Trillion Stars* by Seth Fishman
- *Older Than the Stars* by Karen C. Fox
- *Path to the Stars* by Sylvia Acevedo
- *Shooting for the Stars* by Norah Patten
- *Star Seeker* by Theresa Heine
- *The Sun and Stars* by Ellen Labrecque
- *When the Stars Come Out* by Nicola Edwards

Poetry
- *Spaced Out* by Brian Moses and James Carter

Websites
- The British Interplanetary Society website contains resources about space exploration, including information tailored for children.
- The YouTube channel of the College of Science at University of Notre Dame (Indiana, USA) hosts a video of the 'The Real Big Bang Theory – A Cosmological Dance'.

Unit 16

❓ Modelling word meaning ▽ See Unit 16 Modelling slides

Use the **Skills guide** (see pages 14 to 15) and the downloadable **Skills graphic** to support your modelling.

1 **Look at the second verse. Find and copy <u>two</u> words that mean the same as 'lamps'.**

   1 lights   2 lanterns

   Model using the locator to find the second verse. If necessary, discuss the meaning of 'verse' before continuing. Point out that this question asks the children to find and copy two separate words, as some of them may assume they are being asked to find a group of two words. The word 'lamps' should be familiar to the children, but you could discuss possible synonyms before locating the two correct words in the text and writing down your answers.

2 **Look at the fourth verse. Find and copy <u>one</u> word that means the same as 'went off'.**

   burst

   Again, model using the locator to find the correct verse. You could discuss the varied meanings of 'went off' with the children, both in terms of someone leaving and something blowing up. Discuss which meaning is more likely to be used in a poem about the creation of the universe. You could then talk about possible synonyms before modelling how to scan the verse for plausible words. If the children suggest 'explosion' as an answer, explain that 'went off' is a verb, so you need to look for another verb; 'explosion' cannot be correct because it is a noun.

3 **… *gradually they fired and formed* … . What does the word *gradually* mean in this line?**

   That the stars formed slowly over time.

   This question has a quotation as the locator, so it is important to model using this to find the relevant line of the poem, and to model reading around the quotation for context. Model identifying the key words in the question and focus on the word 'gradually'. Discuss its general meaning and then model relating this to the context of the poem (i.e. the formation of stars). You could explain why an answer such as 'it means slowly', which does not refer back to the context, is not specific enough to gain the mark.

4 **… *each a mighty sparky mass* … . Which word is closest in meaning to *mass* in this line? Tick <u>one</u>.**

   weight ☐   mess ☐   clump ✓   group ☐

   As before, model using the locator to find the correct line and make sure to model reading around the quotation. Discuss the meaning of 'mass', pointing out that it can mean slightly different things depending on the context. Some children may assume that 'weight' is the correct answer, as this is one of the meanings of 'mass'. Discuss each option in turn, replacing 'mass' with each option in the text and talking about which word is most effective and why. You could draw attention to the preceding description 'clouds of dust and gas' and ask the children which answer best describes the shape of a group of clouds.

Word meaning questions mark scheme ❓ See page 164

Answer		Guidance
1	shine	Although the target word 'shine' is simple, the use of 'illuminate' in the question increases the challenge. You may wish to discuss the meaning of 'illuminate' with the children before they attempt this question. **Award 1 mark for the correct answer.**
2	chill ✓	The answer options are all associated with cooler temperatures. If the children find this challenging, you could work together to complete a 'Shades of meaning' activity (see page 15) to support their understanding. **Award 1 mark for the correct answer ticked.**

Once Upon a Star, by James Carter

	Answer	Guidance
3	formed	The use of 'assembled' in the question increases the challenge. Again, you could discuss the meaning of this word with the children before they attempt the question. **Award 1 mark for the correct answer.**
4	The Sun gives us pleasure/makes us happy.	If the children answer only with the meaning of 'delight', without relating this to the context of the Sun, prompt them to extend their answer. **Award 1 mark for a reference to the Sun giving a positive feeling.**
5	centre	Accept responses that include more than one word, as this is not a 'find and copy' question. **Award 1 mark for an appropriate synonym.**

Mix it up! questions mark scheme

See page 165

	Answer	Guidance
1	the Big Bang ✓	You could provide the children with a more specific locator if needed. **Award 1 mark for the correct answer ticked. Skill: Retrieval.**
2	That there are lots and lots/millions of/countless stars.	The children must relate their answer to the context of the poem for it to be accepted. Encourage those who give only the meaning (e.g. 'lots') to extend their answer and link it back to the context given in the question. **Award 1 mark for a reference to a large number of stars. Skill: Word choice.**
3	How the planets formed	The children may give a range of responses. As long as they refer to the formation of the planets or Earth in particular, different subheadings should be accepted. However, you could discuss how 'How the planets formed' is more specific than 'Planets', for example. **Award 1 mark for a plausible subheading that relates to the content of the verse. Skill: Summarising.**
4	It keeps Earth warm and means that we can grow food.	This question is unusual as it almost seems like a retrieval question. Consequently, some children may copy words from the poem to answer it. This should not be accepted. The children may also bring in ideas from their extrinsic knowledge (e.g. 'It keeps us healthy'). These should not be accepted unless they are clearly linked to the information in the text. **Award 1 mark for a reference to two of the following: temperature, food, light, pleasure. Skill: Inference.**
5	So that the reader understands that everything, including them, came from stars/the Big Bang.	This is a challenging question as it requires the children to think about the effect of the line on themselves as the reader. If they struggle, prompt them to read the whole verse carefully and think about the connection the poet is making between stars and humans. You could refer back to your discussions in the Explore session to remind them that this line contains a play on words: can they say which meaning is more relevant here? **Award 1 mark for a plausible reason. Skill: Relationship.**

Once Upon a Star, by James Carter

This is a poem about the creation of the universe. It describes how the universe began and how the solar system, and our planet Earth, were created.

As the lid is lifted off our world
the day goes quiet, dark and cold
then down comes night and if cloud free
look up – you'll find the galaxy

A billion trillion (maybe more)
lights like lanterns on a shore
GIANTS they are and from so far
they just seem small
we call them STARS

And we have one – it's called THE SUN
but did you know it's where we're from?
There's more of that, as you'll soon see
now let's head back through history

Once upon a star
there were no stars to shine
no Sun to rise, no Sun to set
no day, no night, nor any time
there was no Earth, nor universe
until a great explosion burst…

A mighty BOOM
a huge KERRANG
that scientists call…
THE BIG BANG!

So then what?
EVERYTHING!
As all of space and time begin
very slowly, first of all
the universe would have to cool

A sea of stars at last were born
gradually they fired and formed
out of clouds of dust and gas
each a mighty sparky mass
and one of these became our Sun
our solar system had begun!

Giant rocks and fire blew
and so in time our planets grew
and right down here our Earth did too!
With skies so wide and oceans blue
then life swam – crawled – flew

And still our Sun gives us delight
our warmth, our food, our daily light
it's at the heart of everything
for round the Sun the planets spin

We're from that star that seems so far
we're made of stardust, yes we are
So what are YOU?

YOU'RE A STAR!

From *Once Upon a Star: A Poetic Journey Through Space* by James Carter and Mar Hernandez, Caterpillar Books, 2018. Reproduced by permission.

Word meaning

Name: _____

1 Look at the fourth verse. Find and copy **one** word that means the same as 'illuminate'.

_____

1 mark

2 *... the universe would have to cool*
Which word is closest in meaning to *cool* in this line? Tick **one**.

freeze ☐

chill ☐

thaw ☐

ice ☐

1 mark

3 Look at the seventh verse. Find and copy **one** word that means 'assembled'.

_____

1 mark

4 *And still our Sun gives us delight ...*
What does the word *delight* mean in this line?

_____
_____

1 mark

5 *... it's at the heart of everything ...*
What word could be used to replace *heart* in this line?

_____

1 mark

Mix it up!

Name: _____

1 Look at the whole text. According to the poem, which came first? Tick **one**.

the Big Bang ☐

the Earth ☐

the universe ☐

the Sun ☐

1 mark

2 *A sea of stars ...*
What does this group of words tell you about the stars?

_____

_____

1 mark

3 Look at the verse beginning *Giant rocks ... .* What would be an effective subheading for this verse?

_____

1 mark

4 Read from *Giant rocks and fire blew ...* to the end of the poem. Why is the Sun so important to Earth? Give **two** points.

_____

_____

1 mark

5 *... so what are YOU?*
YOU'RE A STAR!
Why do you think the poem ends with these lines?

_____

_____

1 mark

Photocopiable resource from *Complete Comprehension 5* © Schofield & Sims Ltd, 2020.

Unit 17

Retrieval

Harry Houdini
by Laura Lodge

▽ Printable text • Modelling slides   📖 Photocopiable text and questions • pages 170 to 173

No magician has provoked more interest than the great Harry Houdini. Although most famous for his daring escapes and stunts, Houdini started out with simple magic tricks. This short biography traces his life from childhood to the end of his career, and describes some of his most memorable tricks, such as his escape from a straightjacket while hanging upside down! You could make links with the Unit 18 text once both units have been completed.

1 Get ready

Discuss the **Key vocabulary** identified in the **Language toolkit** and then complete the vocabulary activities as desired. Please note that the selected vocabulary is a guide. Depending on the needs of your cohort, additional vocabulary discussion may be beneficial before, during and after reading. Next, display the text (pages 170 to 171) so the children can see the title and any illustrations, and encourage the children to discuss the following questions before reading.

1   **This text is a biography. What is a biography? What features might you find in one?**
    Answers will vary depending on the children's prior reading. A simple definition of a biography is a text that tells the story of a person's life. Possible features to discuss include: factual content, usually in chronological order; subheadings; written in the third person.

2   **The text is about a magician, illusionist and escapologist called Harry Houdini. What do you know about these professions? Have you ever heard of Harry Houdini?**
    The children are likely to be familiar with the term 'magician' but may need to discuss the differences between a magician and an illusionist or escapologist (the **Reading list** contains some useful resources). It is a good idea to gauge what, if anything, they know about Houdini. You could discuss possible questions they have about him that they hope will be answered by the text.

3   **Harry Houdini was famous for doing magic tricks. Have you ever seen a magic trick being performed? Have you ever done a magic trick yourself?**
    It is likely that the children will have seen a friend or professional do a magic trick at some point, or they may have watched a magic show on television. To support their understanding, you could share some video clip examples, such as those from *Help! My School Trip Is Magic* (see **Reading list**).

Language toolkit

Key vocabulary

destitute	errands	escapades
escapologists	fraudulent	freight
illusionists	optical illusion	quelled
signature	sleight of hand	tonne

Vocabulary discussion questions

- Can people who are not **escapologists** still have **escapades**? Why?
- If someone is **destitute**, what things do they not have?
- What **errands** might someone need to run each week?
- Which animals might weigh a **tonne**?
- If someone is **fraudulent**, what are they doing?

Vocabulary activities

- **Escapades** and **escapologists** both come from the Latin *ex*, meaning 'out of' and *cappa*, meaning 'cloak'. Discuss the links between the Latin origins and the modern words.
- Discuss the difference between an illusion and an **optical illusion**. **Optical** comes from the Greek *optos* meaning 'seen' and relates to vision or sight. Challenge the children to think of an associated word (e.g. 'optician').
- Nouns that denote a person who practises a certain custom, occupation or belief often end with the suffix '–ist' (e.g. **illusionist**). How many similar nouns can the children find that end in '–ist'?

Non-fiction

166   Schofield & Sims Complete Comprehension 5

2 First steps

Read the text together and then encourage the children to discuss the following questions.

1. **What was Harry Houdini's real name?**
   Erik Weisz. For much of the text, Houdini is named using the Americanised form of his name, so some children may answer 'Ehrich Weiss'. Explain that this is a changed form of Houdini's original name that he adopted because it was easier for English speakers to pronounce.

2. **Why did Ehrich start performing in the circus?**
   To support his family because they were destitute/poor. This meant that even the children in the family needed to work so that they had enough money to live.

3. **What were three of Houdini's most famous tricks?**
   Jennie the vanishing elephant; escaping from a straightjacket upside down; breaking free from a locked box underwater. If the children struggle, direct them to the panel on the second page of the text, which describes Houdini's tricks.

3 Explore

- When Houdini was a child, he had to do odd jobs to support his family. Explain that during the late 19th century, many children had to work and earn money for their families rather than go to school. In Britain, education was only made compulsory in 1880 and, even then, children only had to attend school between the ages of 5 and 10. Discuss the children's opinions on this issue with reference to Houdini's experiences. Would they prefer to work or go to school? Do they think today's education system is better or worse than that of 1880?

- The children could research simple magic tricks, such as those using cards and coins, which Houdini himself enjoyed before he moved on to more dangerous stunts. They could learn their favourite trick to perform in front of another class.

- The text mentions Houdini's influence on magicians today. You could discuss the work of some modern magicians (e.g. David Blaine and Derren Brown), although be mindful that some tricks may not be suitable for a young audience. The children might also enjoy learning about the high-wire artist Philippe Petit in the film *Man on Wire* (see **Reading list**).

4 Skills focus

See pages 168 to 169

Use the information from the **Skills guide** and the relevant **Skills graphic** to introduce the skill of retrieval.

1. Model the skill using the **Unit 17 Modelling slides** and the **Modelling retrieval** guidance on page 168.

2. The children can then attempt the **Retrieval** questions on page 172.

3. Finally, the **Mix it up!** questions on page 173 offer practice in a range of comprehension skills.

Answers and marking guidance for all questions are included on pages 168 to 169.

5 Where next?

- **Speaking and listening task:** The children could work in small groups to create a presentation about Houdini. This could be done using PowerPoint® or they could even create a short biographical film. They could use photographs, drawings and puppetry alongside narration to depict the key events from Houdini's life.

- **Writing task:** Although Houdini's tricks were thrilling to watch, many of them were incredibly dangerous. Ask the children to each write an argument for or against Houdini's stunts. Half the class could write in favour and half against.

Reading list

Fiction
- *The Magic Misfits* by Neil Patrick Harris
- *The Nowhere Emporium* by Ross MacKenzie (Linked text: **Unit 18**)
- *Young Houdini: The Magician's Fire* by Simon Nicholson
- *The Young Magicians and the Thieves' Almanac* by Nick Mohammed

Class reads
- *The Houdini Box* by Brian Selznick

Non-fiction
- *Escape! The Story of the Great Houdini* by Sid Fleischman
- *Illusionology* by Albert Schafer

Films
- You could show clips from *Man on Wire* (Magnolia Pictures, 2008).

Websites
- The CBBC YouTube channel offers some video clips from the TV series *Help! My School Trip Is Magic*.

Unit 17

Modelling retrieval

See Unit 17 Modelling slides

Use the **Skills guide** (see pages 16 to 17) and the downloadable **Skills graphic** to support your modelling.

1 Look at the paragraph beginning *Harry Houdini was born … .* Where did Erik emigrate from? Tick **one**.

Budapest ✓   Wisconsin ☐   New York City ☐   United States of America ☐

Model using the locator to find the correct paragraph. You could discuss the meaning of 'emigrate' before scanning the text for it. Demonstrate reading around this word, as the pertinent information is in the previous sentence. If the children suggest 'United States of America', discuss the difference between immigration and emigration, and draw attention to the wording of the question ('emigrate *from*').

2 Look at the paragraph beginning *Harry Houdini was born … .* Give **two** things Ehrich did because he loved the stage.

1 practising gymnastics/acrobatics   2 reading about magic at the library

Again, model using the locator and scanning for the question's key words (e.g. 'loved the stage') in the text. Establish that the question refers to 'Ehrich' because this is the name Erik took when he got to the United States. Find the relevant sentence and model reading around it to look for clues. If the children suggest Ehrich's performance in the circus troupe, explain that this *caused* his love of the stage, rather than resulting from it.

3 Look at the paragraph beginning *After spending a year … .* Why was Houdini given the nickname 'The Handcuff King'?

Because he escaped from handcuffs in a locked cell in Scotland Yard.

The nickname given to Harry is reproduced exactly in the text, but it is still important to model scanning carefully for these key words. You could also model reading around them in the text, explaining that you need to use the text rather than making an inference based only on the nickname.

4 Think about the whole text. Draw lines to match each trick to the relevant fact.

Jennie the vanishing elephant	was inspired by a boy called Randolph
Escaping from a straightjacket	weighed 5 tonnes
Escaping from handcuffs	happened at Scotland Yard

Draw attention to the fact that this question is about the whole text and explain that you will need to scan the entire text to find the information that you need to correctly match the tricks and facts. Model identifying key words from the first trick and scanning the text to find the corresponding information. It is a good idea to physically model drawing a clear matching line between the trick and relevant fact. Repeat this process for the remaining tricks.

Retrieval questions mark scheme

See page 172

	Answer	Guidance
1	for a better life	The children may use a direct quotation to answer or paraphrase the text (e.g. 'They wanted to get better jobs'). Either is acceptable. **Award 1 mark for a reference to the family moving for a better life.**
2	He bought and resold newspapers. OR He polished shoes. OR He ran errands. OR He joined a circus troupe.	Some may respond vaguely (e.g. 'He worked lots of jobs.'). If so, encourage them to make their answer more specific. **Award 1 mark for two correct answers.**

Harry Houdini, by Laura Lodge

Schofield & Sims Complete Comprehension 5

	Answer	Guidance
3	(an agent called) Martin Beck	This is a challenging question as the children need to use some vocabulary as well as retrieval knowledge. You could discuss synonyms for 'noticed' and 'gifted' before the children attempt this question. **Award 1 mark for a reference to Martin Beck. Partial names should not be accepted.**
4	It was nailed shut. ✓ He had to wear leg irons. ✓	Although all the options are plausible, the incorrect options are only found within other sections of the text. If necessary, prompt the children to draw their answer from the panel on the second page of the text. **Award 1 mark for both correct answers ticked.**
5	Harry's name when he was born — Erik Weisz his age when he changed his name to Harry Houdini — 17 his age when he died — 52	This question requires the children to retrieve information from across the whole text. Some of them may benefit from being given locators for each statement. **Award 1 mark for two sections completed correctly. Award 2 marks for all sections completed correctly.**

Mix it up! questions mark scheme

See page 173

	Answer	Guidance
1	daring	The children may not have encountered the word 'bold' to describe a character or event. If necessary, discuss the meaning of this word before they attempt this question. **Award 1 mark for the correct answer. Skill: Word meaning.**
2	(Childhood)	Remind the children that they need to find the main point of the whole section. The answer options are all mentioned in the named paragraph, but only the correct answer is a summary of the entire paragraph. **Award 1 mark for the correct answer circled. Skill: Summarising.**
3	At the start of his career his tricks were a lot safer but later in his career they got much more dangerous.	Some children may benefit from a locator for Houdini's early career (the paragraph beginning *After spending a year …*). Remind them to refer to both sides of the comparison in their response. **Award 1 mark for a reference to Houdini's tricks becoming more dangerous. Skill: Comparison.**
4	to make you think about how Harry is still important today	This question requires the children to think about themselves as readers of the text. You could discuss their reactions to the last sentence before they attempt this question. Does the sentence make them want to find out more? Does it make them want to read on? Does it make the subject more relevant to their lives today? **Award 1 mark for a plausible opinion linked to the text. Skill: Relationship.**
5	Yes ✓ Because he had a love of the stage from childhood so he enjoyed performing. Also, he kept thinking of more interesting stunts – you wouldn't do this if you didn't enjoy it.	The children's responses will depend on their personal opinions. Although it is more plausible to infer that Houdini enjoyed his job, accept negative answers as long as appropriate evidence is given to justify the opinion. **Award 1 mark for an answer ticked plus one piece of appropriate evidence. Award 2 marks for an answer ticked plus two pieces of appropriate evidence. Skill: Inference.**

Harry Houdini, by Laura Lodge

This is a short biography of the famous magician and escapologist Harry Houdini, who lived from 1874 to 1926.

Harry Houdini's daring escapades made him one of the most famous escape artists to have ever lived, and his name is still recognised all over the world today.

Harry Houdini was born Erik Weisz in Budapest, Hungary, on 24th March 1874. At the age of four, Erik and his family emigrated to the United States of America, looking for a better life. The family changed their names to make them easier to pronounce: 'Weisz' became 'Weiss' and 'Erik' became 'Ehrich'. The Weiss family were almost destitute, relying on charity and the odd jobs the children took to make a little money. Ehrich bought and resold newspapers, polished shoes and ran errands – anything to support his family. Eventually, Ehrich's willingness to help his family out by doing anything and everything led to his first performance, when he joined his friend's circus troupe. Performing as 'Ehrich, Prince of the Air', nine-year-old Ehrich showed skill on the trapeze and a love of the stage was born. For a few years, Ehrich's urge to perform was quelled by practising gymnastics, acrobatics and reading up on the art of magic at the public library. But at the age of 12, Ehrich suddenly left home, riding off on a freight train in search of adventure.

After spending a year away from home, Ehrich returned to help his family, working in various jobs while still trying to make money from his true passion, magic. Around the age of 17, Ehrich Weiss became Harry Houdini. Harry and his brother Dash became 'The Brothers Houdini', performing magic tricks and sleight of hand, but when they were not very successful, Harry started to experiment as an escape artist. Eventually, an agent called Martin Beck recognised Harry's talent and arranged for him to tour Europe with his escape act. When Harry successfully escaped from handcuffs in a locked cell at Scotland Yard during a stay in London, his fame was secured, and he gained a new nickname: 'The Handcuff King'.

Jennie the vanishing elephant

One of Harry's most famous tricks involved the apparent disappearance of a 5-tonne elephant called Jennie. The audience was amazed when Jennie disappeared right in front of their eyes. In reality, the cabinet Jennie disappeared into was huge and this, coupled with the fact that the stage was the largest on Earth, produced an optical illusion. Jennie never left the stage; instead, she just walked to the other end of the cabinet!

Escaping from a straightjacket upside down

Many pictures of Harry show him being hung upside down locked in a straightjacket. This trick was inspired by a young boy Harry met while touring in Sheffield, Randolph Osborne Douglas. The 'suspended straightjacket escape' became his signature trick and involved him being locked in a straightjacket and hung upside down from a building or a crane.

Breaking free from a locked box underwater

In 1912, having been put in handcuffs and leg irons, Harry climbed into a box which was nailed shut, weighed down and thrown into a river. He managed to achieve what looked impossible, by escaping in just 57 seconds without even breaking the box!

Harry continued to perform in his later life. He kept busy, acting in movies, learning to fly aeroplanes and even working to expose fraudulent psychics, before dying in 1926 at the age of 52. His work inspired some of the most famous magicians, escapologists and illusionists today, such as David Blaine and Derren Brown.

Retrieval

Name: _____

1 Look at the paragraph beginning *Harry Houdini was born ...* . Why did the Weisz family move to the United States of America?

_____

1 mark

2 Give **two** ways in which Ehrich helped to support his family.

1 _____

2 _____

1 mark

3 Look at the paragraph beginning *After spending a year ...* . Who first noticed how gifted Harry was?

_____

1 mark

4 What made Houdini's locked box trick so dangerous? Tick **two**.

It was nailed shut. ☐

He had to wear a straightjacket. ☐

He had to wear leg irons. ☐

It was put in a cage. ☐

He was tied up with ropes. ☐

1 mark

5 Complete the table using information from the text.

Harry's name when he was born	
his age when he changed his name to Harry Houdini	
his age when he died	

2 marks

Mix it up!

Name: _____

1 Look at the first paragraph. Find and copy **one** word that shows that Houdini's tricks were bold.

_____

1 mark

2 Look at the paragraph beginning *Harry Houdini was born ...* . Which of the following would be the most effective subheading for this section of the text? Circle **one**.

| Changing names | Childhood | Moving to America | Joining the circus |

1 mark

3 Compare Harry's tricks at the start of his career with those later in his career. Give **one** difference.

_____

_____

1 mark

4 *His work inspired some of the most famous magicians, escapologists and illusionists today, such as David Blaine and Derren Brown.*
Why do you think the biography ends in this way?

_____

_____

1 mark

5 Think about the whole text. Do you think Harry enjoyed his work? Tick **one**.

Yes ☐   No ☐

Give **two** pieces of evidence from the text to support your opinion.

_____

_____

_____

2 marks

Photocopiable resource from *Complete Comprehension 5* © Schofield & Sims Ltd, 2020.

Unit 18 — Inference — Fiction

The Nowhere Emporium
by Ross MacKenzie

▽ Printable text • Modelling slides   📖 Photocopiable text and questions • pages 178 to 181

Magic is at the heart of much of children's fiction. These stories defy the rules of reality, as in the text for this unit, which relates the mysterious appearance of the Nowhere Emporium, a shop full of dreams and imagination. Ross MacKenzie's evocation of people's wonder and amazement in response to the shop will spark the children's curiosity. As a magical atmosphere also pervades in our Unit 17 text, *Harry Houdini*, you could choose to discuss the links between the two once this unit has been completed.

① Get ready

Discuss the **Key vocabulary** identified in the **Language toolkit** and then complete the vocabulary activities as desired. Please note that the selected vocabulary is a guide. Depending on the needs of your cohort, additional vocabulary discussion may be beneficial before, during and after reading. Next, display the text (pages 178 to 179) so the children can see the title and any illustrations, and encourage the children to discuss the following questions before reading.

1. **This story features a magical plot and setting. What features might you expect to find when reading it?**
   Answers will vary. However, all children should be able to contribute basic features, such as: witches and wizards; magical creatures; potions and spells; fantastical or unexplained events.

2. **Have you read any stories about magical things we cannot explain?**
   Many children's texts share this theme and some of the children may refer to the Unit 5 and 6 texts. You could share some other examples from the **Reading list** to broaden their understanding.

3. **In this story, a magical shop, or emporium, appears. Have you read other stories about magical shops?**
   A popular response may be the *Harry Potter* series, in which the shops of Diagon Alley are a key setting. You could also refer to texts from the **Reading list** in your discussion, as many have been chosen for their links to shops.

4. **This story also discusses imagination. What is imagination? What do you use it for?**
   Some children may find imagination challenging to define. However, all should be able to remember times when they have been asked to use it, and articulate what they use it for. Broach the subject of what it might be like to have no imagination, in preparation for reading the end of the text.

Language toolkit

Key vocabulary

abuzz	emerged	entranced
fine	hearsay	intricate
jostled	recall	rumour
spectacle	startling	theories

Vocabulary discussion questions

- What is the difference between a **rumour** and a report?
- When have you **jostled** or been **jostled**?
- How are **theories** different from facts?
- What has **entranced** you? What was so wonderful about it?
- How might you react to some **startling** news?
- Can you **recall** something that happened to you yesterday? What was it?

Vocabulary activities

- **Rumour** and **hearsay** are synonymous. Can the children think of other ways to describe talk that might be untrue or unfounded?
- **Fine** can be used to describe something that is **intricate** or well crafted. However, it can also be used to describe something that is 'just okay'. Can the children think of other words, including slang words, that can have a positive and more negative meaning depending on the context (e.g. 'smart'; 'sick'; 'terrific').
- Look at the word **spectacle** together. Can the children think of any words that come from the same word family (e.g. 'spectator'; 'spectacular'; 'spectacles')?

Schofield & Sims Complete Comprehension 5

2 First steps

Read the text together and then encourage the children to discuss the following questions.

1. **When did the Nowhere Emporium appear?**
   At dawn on a crisp morning in November. Encourage the children to extend their response to include all the details from the text.

2. **What does the Nowhere Emporium look like?**
   It has bricks the colour of midnight that shimmer and sparkle, a fine golden gate blocking the doorway and writing that reads 'The Nowhere Emporium' over the windows.

3. **What did the tall, polite stranger want?**
   He wanted to know about the Nowhere Emporium.

3 Explore

- Ask the children to imagine a magical shop where dreams can come true. Then, discuss some amazing and strange shops from around the world, such as Hamleys, The Time Travel Mart and Hoxton Street Monster Supplies. What would the children have in their own magical emporium? What would they sell and what would be the price of admission?

- In the story, people pay with their imaginations to enter the Nowhere Emporium. Discuss with the children whether they would give up their imagination in order to visit somewhere such as the Nowhere Emporium. What would life be like without any imagination – would it be worth it?

- Talk about the ways in which the Nowhere Emporium tempts and persuades people inside. For example, the outside of the emporium shimmers and glitters. The emporium also smells of a hundred scents, all carefully designed to draw you in. You could explore these features in relation to real shops, such as bakeries or florists that rely on smells and displays to entice customers in.

4 Skills focus   See pages 176 to 177

Use the information from the **Skills guide** and the relevant **Skills graphic** to introduce the skill of inference.

1. Model the skill using the **Unit 18 Modelling slides** and the **Modelling inference** guidance on page 176.

2. The children can then attempt the **Inference** questions on page 180.

3. Finally, the **Mix it up!** questions on page 181 offer practice in a range of comprehension skills.

Answers and marking guidance for all questions are included on pages 176 to 177.

5 Where next?

- **Speaking and listening task:** Following on from their discussion in **Explore**, the children could work in pairs to role-play shopkeepers and advertise their own magical shop. Thinking about using persuasive language, they should try to entrance the listener and entice them to step inside. You could then allow the pairs to perform to the class and allow each child to choose the three shops they would most like to visit.

- **Writing task:** The children could create an advertising poster to persuade people to visit the Nowhere Emporium. They could use some of the same devices Ross MacKenzie uses to entice visitors into the shop.

Reading list

Fiction
- *A Boy Called Hope* by Lara Williamson
- *The Elsewhere Emporium* by Ross MacKenzie
- *Harry Potter: A Journey Through a History of Magic* by the British Library
- *The House of Madame M* by Clotilde Perrin
- *Howl's Moving Castle* by Diana Wynne Jones
- *The Imagination Box* by Martyn Ford
- *The Magic Hat Shop* by Sonja Wimmer
- *The Magic Nation Gift Shop* by Judy McCarty Kuhn
- *Ned's Circus of Marvels* by Justin Fisher
- *Nevermoor: The Trials of Morrigan Crow* by Jessica Townsend
- *Nightlights* by Lorena Alvarez
- *Pages & Co: Tilly and the Bookwanderers* by Anna James
- *Peter Pan* by J.M. Barrie
- *The Secrets of Hexbridge Castle* by Gabrielle Kent
- *A Series of Unfortunate Events* by Lemony Snicket
- *The Train to Impossible Places* by P.G. Bell

Class reads
- *The Land of Neverendings* by Kate Saunders

Non-fiction
- *Harry Houdini* by Laura Lodge (Linked text: Unit 17)
- *Strange but True* by Kathryn Hulick
- *Unlock Your Imagination* by DK

Poetry
- *The Magic Box* by Kit Wright
- *Lost Magic* by Brian Moses

Schofield & Sims Complete Comprehension 5

Unit 18

Modelling inference

See Unit 18 Modelling slides

Use the **Skills guide** (see pages 20 to 21) and the downloadable **Skills graphic** to support your modelling.

1 *… by midday the place was abuzz with rumour and hearsay.* **Why was this?**

   People had heard about the strange new shop and were excited but didn't quite believe it.

   Model using the locator to find the correct part of the text. Next, model reading around the quotation, especially the preceding sentence, which is crucial to answering this question. Recap the meaning of the target words 'abuzz', 'rumour' and 'hearsay' before continuing. Discuss what has happened in the text – why has the emporium's arrival resulted in rumour and hearsay?

2 **What impressions do you get of the emporium? Give two impressions, using evidence from the text to support your answer.**

   It is mysterious because it appears and disappears randomly.
   It is magical because the gate suddenly turns to dust.

   Model identifying key words in the question and scanning for this information in the text. You should also model reading around the relevant information when you find it in order to get a sense of the context. Although the children should be familiar with this question format, they are used to being asked for only one impression. Draw their attention to the fact this time you need to give two impressions as well as evidence from the text. You could model writing your answer in a table format (see **Modelling question 4** in **Unit 5**).

3 *He asked questions … .* **Do you think the stranger has visited the Nowhere Emporium before? Explain your answer using evidence from the text.**

   No, because he does not know its name, only that it is a shop built from midnight bricks.

   Again, model using the locator to find the relevant part of the text. As the quotation provided is short, it is crucial to model reading around it. Identify the key word 'stranger' and work together to find mentions of him in the text. Model using a graphic organiser to note down what you know from the text about the stranger's knowledge of the emporium, and what you think, to help you formulate your opinion. Finally, model writing a response, including evidence from the text to justify your answer.

4 *But the tall man couldn't find a single person in the village who could recall the Emporium.* **Why do you think this was?**

   When the people entered the emporium, their imaginations were taken, which affected their memory.

   Again, model using the locator and reading around it for more information. Explain that this question requires you to think about the overall themes of the text. Discuss this with the children before exploring why they think the villagers did not recall the emporium. Talk about a range of responses and model choosing the most effective as your final answer. Other possible reasons include the villagers lying to avoid telling the stranger, or their memories having been wiped to prevent them telling others about the emporium.

Inference questions mark scheme

See page 180

	Answer	Guidance
1	They were intrigued and wanted to know what it was.	Ask the children to put themselves in the villagers' shoes. How would they feel if a mysterious shop suddenly appeared from nowhere, overnight? **Award 1 mark for a reference to people wanting to know more about the new shop.**
2	to entice people inside	This question relies on the children understanding that the shop's appearance is designed to persuade people to visit. Ask them to imagine being in front of two shops – a normal-looking one and one with shimmering midnight bricks. Which would they visit? **Award 1 mark for a reference to encouraging people to visit or the shop looking exciting/intriguing.**

The Nowhere Emporium, by Ross MacKenzie

Schofield & Sims Complete Comprehension 5

	Answer	Guidance
3	They were desperate to find out what was happening.	The children need to read around the quotation. You could prompt them to do this to ensure understanding. **Award 1 mark for a reference to the crowd's excitement or anticipation.**
4	*Impression*: inquisitive *Evidence*: He asks all the villagers questions about the emporium.	Some children may use a word from the text (e.g. 'polite'). If so, remind them that they need to give *their* impression, not the impression of the villagers. **Award 1 mark for a plausible impression. Award 2 marks for a plausible impression with appropriate evidence from the text.**
5	They had given their imagination away/paid with their imagination.	Some children may refer to memory, rather than imagination, in their answer. As long as they can justify their response appropriately, this is acceptable. **Award 1 mark for a reference to their imagination or memory.**

Mix it up! questions mark scheme

See page 181

	Answer	Guidance
1	They all started telling each other straight away.	This question requires the children to understand the meaning of 'word travelled'. You could discuss the meaning of this phrase before the children attempt the question, perhaps by demonstrating how word can travel around the classroom. **Award 1 mark for a reference to the villagers telling each other.** Skill: Word choice.
2	intricate	Some children may assume that 'fine' is also a possible synonym. If so, discuss the meaning of 'fine' – can something that is simple in design also be finely wrought? **Award 1 mark for the correct word underlined.** Skill: Word meaning.
3	walked forward OR touched the brickwork OR examined their fingers	Some children will refer to the crowd in the preceding sentences. Remind them that the question is asking what people did just before they entered the emporium. **Award 1 mark for two correct answers.** Skill: Retrieval.
4	A stranger arrives	The children may refer to other points from these sentences. If so, remind them that subheadings and titles usually refer to the main content – what is the most important event in these sentences? **Award 1 mark for a plausible subheading that relates to the stranger or the villagers' lack of memory.** Skill: Summarising.
5	I think the emporium will go to another village and take their imagination too. I think this because the stranger was asking questions, so the emporium has obviously been to other places before.	The children's predictions will be extremely varied. They may focus on the emporium's next target or the stranger's next steps. Accept any prediction that is plausible and linked to the text. **Award 1 mark for a plausible prediction. Award 2 marks for a plausible prediction plus an explanation linked to the text.** Skill: Prediction.

The Nowhere Emporium, by Ross MacKenzie

This extract tells the story of the Nowhere Emporium, a secret and mysterious shop which arrives from nowhere. What will it sell? What will entry cost?

The shop from nowhere arrived with the dawn on a crisp November morning.

Word travelled quickly around the village, and by midday the place was abuzz with rumour and hearsay.

"There were four shops in the row yesterday. Today there are five!"

"Did you hear! It sits between the butcher's and the ironmonger's..."

"The brickwork is black as midnight, and it sparkles strangely in the light!"

By evening time, a curious crowd had begun to gather around the mysterious building. They jostled for position and traded strange and wonderful theories about where the shop had come from and what it might sell, all the while hoping to catch a glimpse of movement through the darkened windows.

The shop was indeed built from bricks the colour of midnight, bricks that shimmered and sparkled under the glow of the gas streetlamps. Blocking the doorway was a golden gate so fine and intricate that some wondrous spider might have spun it. Over the windows, curling letters spelled out a name:

THE NOWHERE EMPORIUM

There was a glimmer of movement in the entranceway, and a ripple of excitement passed through the crowd. And then silence fell – a silence so deep and heavy that it seemed to hang in the atmosphere like mist.

The shop's door swung open. The fine golden gate turned to dust, scattering in the wind.

The air was suddenly alive with a hundred scents: the perfume of toasted coconut and baking bread; of salty sea air and freshly fallen rain; of bonfires and melting ice.

A dove emerged from the darkness of the shop and soared through the air, wings flashing white in the blackness. The enchanted crowd watched as it climbed until it was lost to the night. And then, as one, they gasped. The black sky exploded with light and colour, and a message in dazzling firework sparks and shimmers spelled out:

THE NOWHERE EMPORIUM IS OPEN FOR BUSINESS. BRING YOUR IMAGINATION...

The writing hung in the air just long enough for everyone to read it, and then the words began falling to the ground, a rain of golden light. The crowd laughed in delight, reaching out to catch the sparks as they fell.

Everybody who'd gathered outside the Emporium was entranced. No one had ever seen a spectacle such as this. One by one they walked forward, touched the sparkling black brickwork, examined the tips of their fingers. And then they stepped through the door to find out what was waiting.

Two days later, when the shop had vanished, a stranger arrived in the village. He was polite, and he paid for his room with stiff new banknotes. But something about him — his startling height perhaps, or the hungry look in his cold blue eyes — troubled the villagers.

He asked questions about a shop built from midnight bricks.

But the tall man couldn't find a single person in the village who could recall the Emporium.

Within a day he too was gone, and all trace of these strange events faded from the history of the place.

Those who'd walked through the Emporium's doors had no memory of anything they might have seen inside. More importantly, none of them recalled the price of admission — the little piece of themselves they'd given for a glimpse at the Emporium's hidden secrets and wonders.

Bring your imagination, the sign in the sky had requested.

From *The Nowhere Emporium* by Ross Mackenzie © 2015. Published by Floris Books. Reproduced with permission.

Inference

Name: _____

1 *By evening time, a curious crowd had begun to gather around the mysterious building.* Why do you think this happened?

_____

_____

1 mark

2 Look at the paragraph beginning *The shop was indeed ... .* Why do you think the emporium looked like this?

_____

_____

1 mark

3 *And then silence fell ...*
Why did the crowd go quiet?

_____

_____

1 mark

4 Read from the sentence beginning *Two days later, ...* to the end of the story. What impression do you get of the stranger? Give **one** impression and **one** piece of evidence from the text.

Impression	Evidence
_____	_____
	_____
	_____

2 marks

5 Think about the end of the extract. What was the price that the people paid to go into the emporium?

_____

_____

1 mark

Photocopiable resource from *Complete Comprehension 5* © Schofield & Sims Ltd, 2020.

Unit 18 — The Nowhere Emporium, by Ross MacKenzie

Mix it up!

Name: _____

1 Look at the second sentence. What does the group of words *word travelled quickly* tell you about how the villagers reacted?

_____

_____

1 mark

2 Look at the sentence below. Underline **one** word that means 'detailed'.

> Blocking the doorway was a golden gate so fine and intricate that some wondrous spider might have spun it.

1 mark

3 Give **two** things the people who entered the emporium did just before stepping through the door.

1 _____

2 _____

1 mark

4 Read from the sentence beginning *Two days later, ...* to *... history of the place*. What would be an effective subheading for this part of the story?

_____

1 mark

5 Think about the whole text. What do you think will happen next? Explain your answer using evidence from the text.

_____

_____

_____

2 marks

Photocopiable resource from *Complete Comprehension 5* © Schofield & Sims Ltd, 2020.

Unit 18

The Nowhere Emporium, by Ross MacKenzie

Plague!
by John Farndon

Printable text • Modelling slides • Photocopiable text and questions • pages 186 to 189

Pandemics and epidemics were more common in the past, with the Black Death (plague) being the worst pandemic in human history. This unit's text discusses the impact of diseases like the bubonic plague and smallpox on people in the past. The author, John Farndon, tells the gruesome truth about people's symptoms, using humour to sustain children's interest. The theme of this text links to the Unit 20 text, *The Island at the End of Everything*, which introduces Culion Island, a former leper colony. You could discuss the links between the two texts once both units have been completed.

1 Get ready

Discuss the **Key vocabulary** identified in the **Language toolkit** and then complete the vocabulary activities as desired. Please note that the selected vocabulary is a guide. Depending on the needs of your cohort, additional vocabulary discussion may be beneficial before, during and after reading. Next, display the text (pages 186 to 187) so the children can see the title and any illustrations, and encourage the children to discuss the following questions before reading.

1. **This text is from an information book written for children. What features might you find in it?**
   Answers will vary, but all the children should be able to name basic features of an information text (e.g. organisational devices such as a title and subheadings; factual content; technical language; statistics). You could explain that authors often use humour and gruesome facts to engage younger readers. You may also wish to discuss what we would *not* expect to find (e.g. we would not expect the language to be too formal or scientific).

2. **This text is all about diseases. What other books have you read that discuss diseases or illnesses?**
   The children may suggest fiction texts, and they should all be able to refer to texts that discuss the human body as this is a key part of the science curriculum. The **Reading list** has a selection of texts to support your discussion.

3. **The main focus of this text is the plague. What is the plague? What do you know about plagues?**
   If the children are unable to contribute, discuss the topics of disease and medicine, perhaps focusing on the concept of germs. You could tell them about the most famous outbreaks of plague in the UK – the Black Death in the Middle Ages and the Great Plague of 1665.

Language toolkit

Key vocabulary

apocalypse	bacteria and viruses	culprit
engulfing	erupt	outbreaks
pandemics	pesky	pestilence
utterly	vaccination	vengeance

Vocabulary discussion questions

- Apart from volcanoes, what other things can **erupt**?
- Can you name a **vaccination** you have had?
- Are **outbreaks** the same as breaking out of somewhere? Why or why not?
- What might happen in an **apocalypse**?
- How would a **pesky** person act?
- What would it look like if something was **engulfing** something else?

Vocabulary activities

- The word **pandemics** begins with the prefix 'pan–', which means 'all'. Encourage the children to use dictionaries to explore some other words that share this prefix (e.g. 'panorama'; 'pandemonium').
- Many abstract nouns, such as **vengeance** and **pestilence**, end in the suffixes '–ence' or '–ance'. How many other abstract nouns can the children think of for each suffix? They could also try to find some related words for each abstract noun (e.g. 'avenge'; 'pest').

2 First steps

Read the text together and then encourage the children to discuss the following questions.

1 How many children under the age of 3 survived smallpox during the 1700s?
   1 in 3.

2 According to the text, what was one of the worst pandemics?
   The Black Death.

3 Where was the first outbreak of the Justinian plague?
   Constantinople (Istanbul). You could challenge the children to find all the places that were affected by the Justinian plague.

3 Explore

- The children could research historical cures for the plague and the work of plague doctors by reading some of the texts from the **Reading list** and discussing which they think might work and which would not. Would drinking vinegar help? How about rubbing onions on boils?

- The village of Eyam in Derbyshire is famous for its role during the 1665 plague. When the plague hit the village, the residents decided to quarantine themselves so that the disease would not spread to the surrounding villages. This act required great bravery and helped to stop the outbreak spreading. The children could research Eyam, or another place in their locality, finding out what happened there during the Black Death or later during the Great Plague. The **Reading list** has some useful resources.

- Although its origins remain in dispute, many people believe that the nursery rhyme 'Ring a Ring o' Roses' refers to the plague. Recite the rhyme for the children and ask them whether they think it is about the plague. Discussion points could include: what the 'roses' refer to; why people might have 'posies' in their pockets; whether 'a-tishoo' (i.e. sneezing) is a symptom of the plague; and the more sinister meaning behind 'they all fall down'. You could extend the discussion to talk about the origins and meanings of some other popular nursery rhymes. See the **Reading list** for suggested resources.

4 Skills focus   See pages 184 to 185

Use the information from the **Skills guide** and the relevant **Skills graphic** to introduce the skill of retrieval.

1 Model the skill using the **Unit 19 Modelling slides** and the **Modelling retrieval** guidance on page 184.

2 The children can then attempt the **Retrieval** questions on page 188.

3 Finally, the **Mix it up!** questions on page 189 offer practice in a range of comprehension skills.

Answers and marking guidance for all questions are included on pages 184 to 185.

5 Where next?

- **Speaking and listening task:** The children could work in groups to research the Black Death in more detail. They could then create a presentation to communicate the key facts they have learnt.

- **Writing task:** The children could build on what they found out about historical cures for the plague during the first **Explore** activity by each writing a plague doctor's manual. The short manuals should advise plague doctors how to treat their patients using the historical practices the children have read about (e.g. smelling herbs).

Reading list

Fiction
- *The Great Plague* by Pamela Oldfield
- *The Island at the End of Everything* by Kiran Millwood Hargrave (Linked text: **Unit 20**)
- *Plague: A Cross on the Door* by Ann Turnbull
- *Plague Dogs* by Richard Adams
- *Plague: Outbreak in London* by Tony Bradman

Class reads
- *Children of Winter* by Berlie Doherty

Non-fiction
- *The Bacteria Book* by Steve Mould
- *Bubonic Plague* by Barbara Krasner
- *Killer Bugs* by Catherine Chambers
- *Medical Milestones and Crazy Cures* by Dr Chris van Tulleken
- *Pop Goes the Weasel: The Secret Meanings of Nursery Rhymes* by Albert Jack
- *The Science of Medical Technology* by Cath Senker

Websites
- The BBC School Radio website has a series of episodes about Eyam as part of their Primary Drama: Key Stage 2 resources.
- The Eyam Museum website has a number of useful teaching resources about the village of Eyam and the plague in general.

Modelling retrieval

See Unit 19 Modelling slides

Use the **Skills guide** (see pages 16 to 17) and the downloadable **Skills graphic** to support your modelling.

1 Which invention made smallpox disappear?

vaccination

As this question does not include a locator, model identifying the key word 'smallpox' and scanning the text to find it. Although 'smallpox' appears in the text, other key words, such as 'invention' and 'disappear', do not. Remind the children that sometimes synonyms of the key words in the question are used in the text. You could discuss synonyms for 'invention' and 'disappear' before modelling scanning for these in the text.

2 When was the Justinian plague?

541–542 CE

Model identifying the key words 'Justinian plague', scanning the text and then finding the first mention in the seventh paragraph. You should also model reading around the key words to get a sense of context. As this question asks when the plague was (rather than when it started or ended), ensure that you model locating the date range, rather than a single date. You could also discuss why it is important to add 'CE' to the date range for specificity. If the children do not understand the terms 'BCE'/'BC' and 'CE'/'AD', briefly discuss these.

3 Look at the section 'Deadly Blisters'. According to the text, how did scientists find out what caused the Justinian plague?

They dug up some bodies from the time and tested them.

Model using the locator to find the correct section in the text. The locator is for a large section, so you should model how to identify key words from the question and scan for them within this section. Draw the children's attention to 'According to the text'. This is an important signpost as it reminds them that they should take their answer directly from the text.

4 Think about the whole text. Tick to show whether each statement is fact or opinion.

	F	O
Smallpox has vanished.	✓	
It's not nice when you get sick.		✓
Smallpox made life dreadful.		✓
There have been many pandemics.	✓	

It is important to point out that this question is about the text as a whole. It may also be helpful to discuss the difference between fact and opinion before answering the question. When ready, model identifying key words from the first statement and scanning the entire text to find the corresponding information. Discuss whether each statement is a fact or opinion before modelling writing your answer.

Retrieval questions mark scheme

See page 188

	Answer	Guidance
1	angry gods	Some children may respond with 'gods' alone. This should be accepted, but it is advisable to ask the children to make their answers more specific. **Award 1 mark for a reference to (angry) gods.**
2	plague pestilence	Some children may answer 'Justinian plague' and 'Black Death'. If so, explain that they should look for names that people gave to outbreaks, rather than historical names. Encourage them to think of synonyms for 'scary' and prompt them to scan for the key word 'names' in the text, or provide a locator (the 'Deadly Rider' subheading). **Award 1 mark for two correct answers.**

	Answer	Guidance
3	1353	The locator makes this question relatively straightforward, although the children must give the end date rather than the range to gain the mark. **Award 1 mark for the correct answer.**
4	Justinian plague OR the Black Death OR 1800s plague in Asia	The locator for this question requires the children to read multiple sections of the text. You could discuss the locator and the key words 'Yersinia pestis' to support them to answer this tricky question. **Award 1 mark for two correct answers.**
5	<table><tr><th></th><th>T</th><th>F</th></tr><tr><td>The Justinian plague killed 2 million people.</td><td></td><td>✓</td></tr><tr><td>The Justinian plague was caused by Yersinia pestis.</td><td>✓</td><td></td></tr><tr><td>Flu is as bad as the plague.</td><td></td><td>✓</td></tr><tr><td>Rats brought the plague to Constantinople.</td><td>✓</td><td></td></tr></table>	This question requires understanding from across the whole text. Some children may benefit from being given locators for each statement to support their retrieval. **Award 1 mark for at least two statements correctly ticked. Award 2 marks for all four statements correctly ticked.**

Mix it up! questions mark scheme

See page 189

	Answer	Guidance
1	It helps the reader to connect their experiences to the information in the text.	Some children may provide an answer focused on making the reader want to read the text. Although this is partially correct, encourage them to expand their answer to explain why this happens. **Award 1 mark for a reference to connecting children's background knowledge to the text. Skill: Relationship.**
2	It has completely vanished/been completely cured.	The children need to read the next sentence in the relevant paragraph to fully understand this group of words in context. Prompt them to read around the quote if necessary. **Award 1 mark for a reference to having been able to cure/prevent smallpox. Skill: Word choice.**
3	If they don't know what caused it, they can't find out how to stop it.	This is a challenging question for the children. You could explore the idea by discussing other phenomena that were not well understood by people in the past. **Award 1 mark for a reference to being unable to stop the disease. Skill: Inference.**
4	to explain what would happen if you got the plague	Some children may focus too much on the existing subheading for this section and answer that the main point is about how someone with the plague would look. In this case, encourage them to reread the paragraph – is it only about appearance or does it refer to other symptoms? **Award 1 mark for a reference to the signs, effects or symptoms of the plague. Skill: Summarising.**
5	offender ✓	The children will have discussed 'culprit' in the **Key vocabulary**. However, if they find this question challenging, you could recap your earlier discussion and encourage them to use substitution to choose the most appropriate answer option. **Award 1 mark for the correct answer ticked. Skill: Word meaning.**

Plague!, by John Farndon

This extract is from an information text about plagues and other diseases that have affected people throughout history. It is full of gruesome details about different types of diseases from around the world.

Introduction

It's not nice when you get sick. But if you ever feel sorry for yourself, then this book might just make you feel a little better. In the past, people were battered again and again by horrible diseases that made their skin rot, their hair fall out, their hands turn black, their lungs collapse, and their faces erupt with boils – and that's if they were lucky…

A Happy Ending

Smallpox made life utterly dreadful for English children in the 1700s. Only one out of every three children under the age of three survived it. But smallpox is one of the success stories of modern medicine. Thanks to the discovery of vaccination, it has vanished from the world entirely.

God's Vengeance

One of the frightening things about diseases is that people once had no idea what caused them. Now we know diseases are spread by germs (tiny bacteria and viruses), so we can look for ways to fight them. But in the past there was no explanation. Many people believed diseases were caused by angry gods.

Deadly Rider

In the past, diseases were so devastating that outbreaks were given frightening names, such as plague and pestilence. These names are also given to one of the four horsemen of the apocalypse – four terrifying riders who, according to the Christian Bible, will descend on the world on its final day of judgement.

The Worst Outbreaks

Modern doctors call the worst outbreaks of disease *pandemics*. These spread far and wide, killing millions. Throughout history there have been many pandemics. One of the worst was the Black Death of 1346–1353, carried by fleas, which killed 75–200 million people worldwide.

It's the Pits

It's hard to imagine just how bad outbreaks of disease were in the past. In many cities during the Black Death, there were too few people left to bury those who died. Bodies would be chucked into pits and left to rot.

Deadly Blisters

In 541–542 CE, the city of Constantinople (now Istanbul) was utterly ravaged by an outbreak of a terrible disease called the Justinian plague, named after the city's ruler, Justinian. Up to ten thousand people died each day, and the streets were piled high with bodies.

Tooth Truth

Scientists carried out some tests on the teeth of skeletons dug up from tombs in Germany that date from the time of the Justinian plague. They were able to identify traces of the germ *Yersinia pestis*, the same bug that caused the Black Death in the Middle Ages.

Looking Good (Not!)

If someone caught the plague, they would feel like they had the worst flu ever. Then parts of their body would turn black, and their skin would erupt with terrible pus-filled swellings called buboes — or worse still, their lungs would dissolve from the inside. Within a week they'd be dead.

The Pesky Pestis

Rats may have carried the disease to Constantinople, but the culprit was really a tiny bacterium called *Yersinia pestis*. *Yersinia* may be tiny, but it was one of the deadliest killers in history. It also brought the Black Death in the Middle Ages and a plague that killed millions in Asia in the later 1800s.

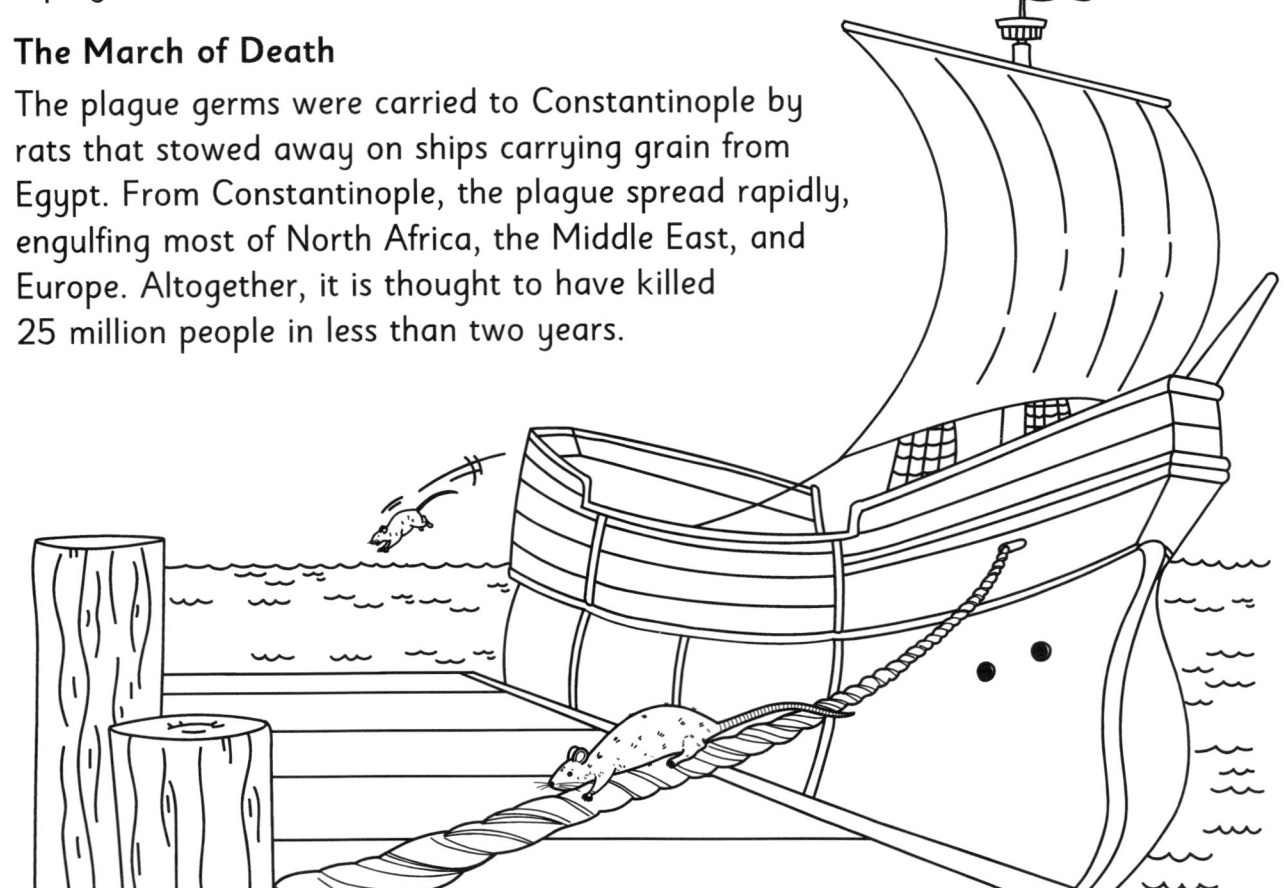

The March of Death

The plague germs were carried to Constantinople by rats that stowed away on ships carrying grain from Egypt. From Constantinople, the plague spread rapidly, engulfing most of North Africa, the Middle East, and Europe. Altogether, it is thought to have killed 25 million people in less than two years.

From *Plague!* by John Farndon, Hungry Tomato, 2017, pp. 6-11. Reproduced by permission of Hungry Tomato, Ltd.

Retrieval

Name: _____

1 In the past, what did many people think caused diseases?

_____

1 mark

2 Give **two** scary names that people gave to outbreaks.

1 _____

2 _____

1 mark

3 Look at the section **The Worst Outbreaks**. When did the Black Death end?

_____

1 mark

4 Read from the section **Tooth Truth** to the end of the text. Which outbreaks did *Yersinia pestis* cause? Give **two**.

_____

_____

1 mark

5 Think about the whole text. Tick to show whether each statement is true or false.

	True	False
The Justinian plague killed 2 million people.		
The Justinian plague was caused by *Yersinia pestis*.		
Flu is as bad as the plague.		
Rats brought the plague to Constantinople.		

2 marks

Photocopiable resource from *Complete Comprehension 5* © Schofield & Sims Ltd, 2020.

Mix it up!

Name: _____

1 *It's not nice when you get sick. But if you ever feel sorry for yourself, then this book might just make you feel a little better.*
Why do you think the text begins with these sentences?

_____

_____

1 mark

2 *But smallpox is one of the success stories ...*
What does the group of words *success stories* tell you about smallpox?

_____

_____

1 mark

3 *One of the frightening things about diseases is that people once had no idea what caused them.*
Why would this be *frightening*?

_____

_____

1 mark

4 Look at the section **Looking Good (Not!)**. What is the main point of this section?

_____

_____

1 mark

5 *Rats may have carried the disease to Constantinople, but the culprit was really a tiny bacterium called* Yersinia pestis.
Which word is closest in meaning to *culprit* in this sentence? Tick **one**.

thief ☐

captive ☐

offender ☐

germ ☐

1 mark

Unit 19

Plague!, by John Farndon

Photocopiable resource from *Complete Comprehension 5* © Schofield & Sims Ltd, 2020.

The Island at the End of Everything
by Kiran Millwood Hargrave

Unit 20 · Inference · Fiction

▽ Printable text • Modelling slides   📖 Photocopiable text and questions • pages 194 to 197

This text introduces the children to the island of Culion, a former leprosarium in the Philippines. People suffering from leprosy, or Hansen's disease as it is now more often known, were isolated there to avoid transmitting the disease to others. This disfiguring disease can now be easily treated with antibiotics, but in the past sufferers were cast out from society and forced to leave their homes. This text is linked to the Unit 19 text *Plague!*. You could discuss the thematic link between the two texts and how each provides a different viewpoint of disease.

1 Get ready

Discuss the **Key vocabulary** identified in the **Language toolkit** and then complete the vocabulary activities as desired. Please note that the selected vocabulary is a guide. Depending on the needs of your cohort, additional vocabulary discussion may be beneficial before, during and after reading. Next, display the text (pages 194 to 195) so the children can see the title and any illustrations, and encourage the children to discuss the following questions before reading.

1. **In this story the main character recounts events from the past. What features would you expect to find in a story like this?**
   Answers will vary but all the children will have both read and written recounts at some point during their primary education. General features include: use of the first person; use of the past tense; events written in sequence; use of cohesive devices (e.g. conjunctions and connectives); use of adverbial phrases to show time and place.

2. **The extract is set on the island of Culion in the Philippines. What do you know about the Philippines?**
   You could begin by asking the children where in the world they think the Philippines is. An understanding of the climate and geography of the Philippines will support them to picture the setting of the extract, so you could explore this using some of the texts in the **Reading list**.

3. **The island in the story is a leprosarium: a place where people with leprosy used to be forced to live. What do you know about leprosy?**
   The children are unlikely to know much about the topic. A basic understanding of leprosy is needed to understand the setting of the text, so you could discuss the topic in a sensitive way.

Language toolkit

Key vocabulary

brim	clutch	dusk
lapping	lepers	lush
marked	nanay	touched

Vocabulary discussion questions

- If vegetation is **lush**, how does it look?
- When you **clutch** something, how are you holding it?
- At **dusk**, what has happened to the Sun?
- Is **lapping** a gentle movement or a fierce one?
- If something or someone is **marked**, is that a positive or negative thing?
- Has a surprise ever made you **brim** with excitement?

Vocabulary activities

- **Nanay** means 'mother' in Tagalog, the main language in the Philippines. Discuss how the children can use context clues to work out the meaning of words in other languages (e.g. if they heard 'my nanay brought me a drink at bedtime', they might be able to deduce that a 'nanay' is a parent or adult family member).
- **Marked** and **touched** are synonyms, but only in a particular context. Can the children think of synonyms for both words and then work out their shared context?
- **Brim** and **clutch** can both be used to describe articles of clothing (e.g. the 'brim' of a hat and a 'clutch' bag). However, in the text they are used as verbs. Can the children think of other verbs that are sometimes used to describe objects (e.g. 'watch'; 'brush'; 'dart')?

2 First steps

Read the text together and then encourage the children to answer the following questions.

1 **Who travelled to Culion on a boat?**
Nanay, the narrator's mother. Some children may also refer to other people with leprosy who travelled there at different times.

2 **What does the white eagle on the cliff tell people?**
To stay away. You may wish to encourage the children to explain why they think people would want to stay away from the island.

3 **What is the main thing that makes Culion different to many other islands?**
It is an island of lepers. The children may focus on other elements, such as the white eagle or the setting: remind them to focus on the 'main thing'.

4 **Did you enjoy the story? Why? Why not?**
Answers will vary. The children should be able to justify their responses (e.g. *I think it's really terrible that people are forced to live on the island and their homes are burned down*).

3 Explore

- Encourage the children to imagine that they are in the same situation as Nanay. Discuss how they would feel if the events of the story happened to them or their family. Use this discussion to start a wider one about how people who have diseases are treated by society across the world. You could discuss diseases which cause disfigurement, or which carry stigma, either in the UK or in other countries. See the **Reading list** for some helpful resources.

- The island of Culion was one of many islands used across the world as 'leprosariums'. These places were used to quarantine people with contagious and stigmatised diseases such as leprosy. The children could research different places where people have been quarantined such as Culion, Kalaupapa in Hawaii or the Greek island of Spinalonga.

- The author, Kiran Millwood Hargrave, uses a wide range of descriptive language to bring her text alive. Discuss examples of descriptive language that the author uses and ask the children to think about why she has made particular word choices and what effect this creates (e.g. it helps to contrast the beautiful setting with the upsetting reason the people are on the island).

4 Skills focus   See pages 192 to 193

Use the information from the **Skills guide** and the relevant **Skills graphic** to introduce the skill of inference.

1 Model the skill using the **Unit 20 Modelling slides** and the **Modelling inference** guidance on page 192.

2 The children can then attempt the **Inference** questions on page 196.

3 Finally, the **Mix it up!** questions on page 197 offer practice in a range of comprehension skills.

Answers and marking guidance for all questions are included on pages 192 to 193.

5 Where next?

- **Speaking and listening task:** In small groups, the children could create a video campaign that encourages people to think about how they treat others, especially those who may have illnesses. They should use persuasive language and tone to call on their viewers to treat everyone equally and with kindness, regardless of any perceived differences. If possible, record their campaigns and share them with the rest of the school.

- **Writing task:** In the extract, the narrator recounts the story of her mother's journey to Culion. In it she describes the sailors who took her mother there. The children could each rewrite the story of Nanay's journey from the point of view of the sailors, focusing on their feelings towards the people travelling to Culion.

Reading list

Fiction
▶ *Beyond the Bright Sea* by Lauren Wolk
▶ *An Eagle's Feather* by Minfong Ho
▶ *Ghosts* by Raina Telgemeier
▶ *The Girl of Ink & Stars* by Kiran Millwood Hargrave
▶ *Wonder* by R.J. Palacio

Class reads
▶ *No Ordinary Day* by Deborah Ellis

Non-fiction
▶ *All About the Philippines* by Gidget Roceles Jimenez
▶ *The Germ Lab: The Gruesome Story of Deadly Diseases* by Richard Platt
▶ *Kumusta, Philippines* by Corey Anderson
▶ *Our World in Crisis: Health and Disease* by Izzi Howell
▶ *Plague!* by John Farndon (Linked text: **Unit 19**)
▶ *Tiny: The Invisible World of Microbes* by Nicola Davies

Schofield & Sims Complete Comprehension 5

Modelling inference

See Unit 20 Modelling slides

Use the **Skills guide** (see pages 20 to 21) and the downloadable **Skills graphic** to support your modelling.

1 **Why did Nanay go to the island?**
   She had leprosy.

   This question does not include a locator, so it is important to discuss identifying the key word 'Nanay' and scanning the text for it. Model reading around the key word to check whether you have located the correct section of text. This is particularly useful for this question as it will show the children that sometimes a question is about the whole text, or a theme within the text. You could discuss how we know from the text that the only people who are forced to go and stay on the island have leprosy. From this, you may wish to discuss how Nanay got to the island herself, before making the inference that she had leprosy too.

2 *You sit and clutch your bundle of things from home, what you saved before it was burned.* **Why do you think people's homes were burned?**
   They had leprosy and other people thought they could catch it from anywhere the person had been, so they burned down their houses to kill the disease.

   Model using the locator to find the correct part of the text, then read around it for context. The inference needed for this question is quite complex, so you could discuss what the children already know from the text before modelling an inference. Some may assume that people's houses were burned as a punishment. If so, draw their attention back to the main point of the text: the people on the island have leprosy and healthy people wanted to stop the disease spreading.

3 **Look at the paragraph beginning** *The island changes … .* **How might the people on the boat have felt when they saw the white eagle? Give <u>one</u> feeling and <u>one</u> piece of evidence from the text.**
   Terrified because the eagle is warning them to stay away but they are being taken there.

   Again, model using the locator to find the correct section in the text. Next, model identifying key words in the question and scanning the text for them (e.g. 'white eagle'). You may want to encourage the children to discuss how they would feel in Nanay's situation, before deciding which feeling to include in your answer. Make sure to also model finding a piece of evidence from the text to justify your response. Write your answer in a table format (see **Modelling question 4** in **Unit 5**).

4 *Someone will be there to welcome you. They understand.* **Why do those people** *understand***?**
   They have leprosy too.

   Model finding the correct section in the text and read around the locator quotation to gain a sense of context. You may wish to talk with the children about what it means when someone says 'I understand' and then relate that knowledge to the text. You could use a graphic organiser such as an 'I think/I know' chart (see page 21) to support your modelling.

Inference questions mark scheme

See page 196

	Answer	Guidance
1	Because they have leprosy.	Some children may only focus on the people being forced to go to the island. If so, prompt them to explain why the people are forced to go. **Award 1 mark for a reference to the people suffering from leprosy.**
2	Everyone with leprosy is taken to Culion in the same way.	The key point here is that everyone is taken to Culion regardless of their previous position in society. The children may explain this in a number of ways. **Award 1 mark for reference to everyone with leprosy being treated the same way.**

Answer		Guidance
3	devastated ✓ terrified ✓	Some children may choose 'frustrated'. If so, encourage them to explain why they chose this option. If they provide a good justification, you may choose to accept this response. **Award 1 mark for both correct answers ticked.**
4	So they don't catch leprosy from the sick people in the boat.	The whole sentence has been included as a quotation here to discourage the children from replicating the explanation given in it. The question is asking for the reason why the men do not want to share the other people's breath. **Award 1 mark for a reference to not catching the disease.**
5	*Impression*: beautiful *Evidence*: The text talks about the sea being as clear and blue as summer skies.	The children may focus on the positive or negative aspects of Culion. Either is acceptable as long as it is grounded in the text. **Award 1 mark for a plausible impression. Award 2 marks for a plausible impression with appropriate evidence from the text.**

Mix it up! questions mark scheme   See page 197

Answer		Guidance
1	It is beautiful and like a paradise. OR It is full of wildlife.	Some children may naturally extend their response here, as in the sample answer. However, a single adjective could be used to answer, as long as it is plausible. **Award 1 mark for a reference to the island's beauty or how it is rich in wildlife.** **Skill: Word choice.**
2	how people get to the island	If the children find identifying the main topic challenging, you could provide them with some options to choose from. **Award 1 mark for a reference to how people get to the island.** **Skill: Summarising.**
3	white stones ✓	The paragraph within which this information is located contains a lot of competing information. You could support the children further by providing them with a locator. **Award 1 mark for the correct answer ticked. Skill: Retrieval.**
4	to emphasise the contrast between the setting and the reason why people are taken there	This is a challenging question. The children may approach it in different ways, with some being able to use a deeper inference to comment on the contrast between the beautiful setting and its role. The simpler inference of emphasising the beauty of the setting still shows partial understanding. **Award 1 mark for a reference to emphasising the beauty of the setting. Award 2 marks for a reference to the beauty of the setting and the contrast between the setting and its role. Skill: Relationship.**
5	The trees are covered in fruit.	Some children may provide a definition without using the context (e.g. 'lots of'). In this case, prompt them to link their response to the surrounding group of words. **Award 1 mark for a reference to there being a lot of fruit on the trees.** **Skill: Word meaning.**

Schofield & Sims *Complete Comprehension 5*

The Island at the End of Everything, by Kiran Millwood Hargrave

This text introduces readers to the island of Culion. It tells the story of the people of Culion and how they came to the island.

CULION ISLAND, THE PHILIPPINES   1906

There are some places you would not want to go.

Even if I told you that we have oceans clear and blue as summer skies, filled with sea turtles and dolphins, or forest-covered hills lush with birds that call through air thick with warmth. Even if you knew how beautiful the quiet is here, clean and fresh as a glass bell ringing. But nobody comes here because they want to.

My nanay told me this is how they brought her, but says it is always the same, no matter who you are or where you come from.

From your house you travel on horse or by foot, then on a boat. The men who row it cover their noses and mouths with cloths stuffed with herbs so they don't have to share your breath. They will not help you on to the boat although your head aches and two weeks ago your legs began to hurt, then to numb. Maybe you stumble towards them, and they duck. They'd rather you rolled over their backs and into the sea than touch you. You sit and clutch your bundle of things from home, what you saved before it was burned. Clothes, a doll, some books, letters from your mother.

Somehow, it is always dusk when you approach.

The island changes from a dark dot to a green heaven on the horizon. High on a cross-topped cliff that slopes towards the sea is a field of white flowers, looping strangely. It is not until you are closer that you see it forms the shape of an eagle, and it is not until you are very close that you see it is made of stones. This is when your heart hardens in your chest, like petals turning to pebbles. Nanay says the white eagle's meaning is known across all the surrounding islands, even all the places outside our sea. It means: *stay away. Do not come here unless you have no choice.*

The day is dropping to dark as you come into the harbour. When you step from the boat, the stars are setting out their little lights. Someone will be there to welcome you. They understand.

The men who brought you leave straight away, though they are tired. They have not spoken to you in the days or hours you spent with them. The splash of oars fades to the sound of waves lapping the beach. They will burn the boat when they get back, as they did your house.

You look at the person who greeted you. You are changed now. Like flowers into stones, day into night. You will always be heavier, darkened, marked. Touched.

Nanay says that in the places outside, they have many names for our home. The island of the living dead. The island of no return. The island at the end of everything.

You are on Culion, where the oceans are blue and clear as summer skies. Culion, where sea turtles dig the beaches and the trees brim with fruit.

Culion, island of lepers. Welcome home.

Inference

Name: _____

1 *But nobody comes here because they want to.*
Why do people go to the island?

_____
_____

1 mark

2 *My nanay told me this is how they brought her, but says it is always the same, no matter who you are or where you come from.*
What do you think Nanay means when she says this?

_____
_____

1 mark

3 Look at the paragraph beginning *From your house ...* . How do you think the people felt? Tick **two**.

frustrated ☐   excited ☐   devastated ☐   terrified ☐

1 mark

4 *The men who row it cover their noses and mouths with cloths stuffed with herbs so they don't have to share your breath.*
Why do the men do this?

_____
_____

1 mark

5 Think about the whole text. What impression do you get of the island of Culion? Give **one** impression and **one** piece of evidence from the text.

Impression	Evidence
_____	_____
	_____
	_____

2 marks

Unit 20 — The Island at the End of Everything, by Kiran Millwood Hargrave

Photocopiable resource from *Complete Comprehension 5* © Schofield & Sims Ltd, 2020.

Mix it up!

Name: _____

1 *... filled with sea turtles and dolphins, or forest-covered hills lush with birds that call through air thick with warmth.*
What does this group of words tell you about the island?

_____

_____

1 mark

2 Read from the paragraph beginning *From your house ...* to the paragraph ending *... They understand.* What is the main topic of this section of the story?

_____

_____

1 mark

3 What is the eagle made from? Tick **one**.

white flowers ☐

white stones ☐

white pebbles ☐

white petals ☐

1 mark

4 *... the oceans are blue and clear as summer skies ...*
A very similar group of words is used at the beginning and end of the story. Why do you think it has been repeated?

_____

_____

_____

2 marks

5 *... the trees brim with fruit.*
What does the word *brim* mean in this group of words?

_____

_____

1 mark

Photocopiable resource from *Complete Comprehension 5* © Schofield & Sims Ltd, 2020.

Unit 20 — The Island at the End of Everything, by Kiran Millwood Hargrave

Unit 21

Inference — Fiction

The London Eye Mystery
by Siobhan Dowd

▽ Printable text • Modelling slides   📖 Photocopiable text and questions • pages 202 to 205

Mysteries abound in literature, and children's books are no exception. Whether the mystery concerns a missing person, a murder or a stolen object, these stories capture children's imaginations. The extract in this unit is taken from a story about two siblings, Ted and Kat, who play the role of detective as they try to solve the mysterious disappearance of their cousin, Salim. The air of mystery in this text is reflected in our final text, taken from *The Last Chance Hotel* (Progress check 3). Once the Progress check has been completed, you could compare and contrast the two texts.

❶ Get ready

Discuss the **Key vocabulary** identified in the **Language toolkit** and then complete the vocabulary activities as desired. Please note that the selected vocabulary is a guide. Depending on the needs of your cohort, additional vocabulary discussion may be beneficial before, during and after reading. Next, display the text (pages 202 to 203) so the children can see the title and any illustrations, and encourage the children to discuss the following questions before reading.

1 **This text is a mystery story. What features would you expect to find in this type of story?**
   The children are likely to have encountered mystery stories or mysterious settings at some point. You could discuss what a mystery is in a general sense, as well as applying this to specific texts. Examples of features may include: something going missing; a crime being committed; a 'detective'-like figure; a suspenseful atmosphere.

2 **In this story, someone goes missing. Have you ever read any other texts where someone or something goes missing?**
   If the children struggle to recall specific texts, you could encourage them to think about fairy tales (e.g. Cinderella's lost glass slipper; Hansel and Gretel's stepmother leaving them in the woods).

3 **The main events of this story happen on a landmark called the London Eye. What do you know about this tourist attraction?**
   As the events of the text occur at and on the London Eye, it is important that the children understand what this setting looks like. You could share images or clips from the London Eye website.

Language toolkit

Key vocabulary

abacus	A-frame	cantilevered
capsules	force	gravity
hawsers	observation	oesophagus
operating system	orbit	spokes

Vocabulary discussion questions

- What can you make an **observation** of?
- How does **gravity** keep you grounded?
- What can an **abacus** be used for?
- What job does your **oesophagus** do?
- Can anything other than a computer have an **operating system**? Explain why.
- What things can have an **orbit**?

Vocabulary activities

- **Force** can be used as a verb or a noun. How many other words can the children think of that can also be both?
- The vocabulary used in this text recalls the topic of space. Discuss terms such as **capsules**, **force**, **gravity** and **orbit**. Ask the children whether they think these words change meaning when they are used to describe things on Earth.
- The text includes a number of building-specific terms, such as **hawsers**, **A-frame** and **cantilevered**. Discuss these terms and show the children images of buildings with these features to support the discussion. See if the children can spot these features in other pictures of buildings.

Schofield & Sims Complete Comprehension 5

2 First steps

Read the text together and then encourage the children to discuss the following questions.

1. **Who are the main characters in the extract?**
   The narrator (Ted), Kat and Salim. You may wish to clarify that the narrator's name is Ted.

2. **According to Ted, what is the best thing to see from the Eye?**
   The river Thames.

3. **When should Salim have come down from the Eye?**
   At 12.02 p.m. on the 24th May.

4. **Did you enjoy the story? Why? Why not?**
   Answers will vary. The children should be able to justify their responses (e.g. *I liked it because Salim's disappearance is a real mystery!*).

3 Explore

- The narrator in this text, Ted, has Asperger syndrome. People with Asperger syndrome are often highly invested in topics that they find interesting. Discuss with the children what Asperger syndrome is and how Ted refers to this when he talks about his body running on a different 'operating system' to other people's. You might wish to discuss how Ted's interest in the London Eye is expressed in this extract through his specific and technical descriptions.

- Ted has a fascination with the architecture and engineering of the London Eye. Show the children some famous modern buildings that are known for their architecture. You could choose some other buildings located in London, such as The Shard and The Gherkin. Ask the children to give opinions on their design and appearance. The children then could design their own unusual building, perhaps in the shape of an everyday object.

4 Skills focus   See pages 200 to 201

Use the information from the **Skills guide** and the relevant **Skills graphic** to introduce the skill of inference.

1. Model the skill using the **Unit 21 Modelling slides** and the **Modelling inference** guidance on page 200.
2. The children can then attempt the **Inference** questions on page 204.
3. Finally, the **Mix it up!** questions on page 205 offer practice in a range of comprehension skills.

Answers and marking guidance for all questions are included on pages 200 to 201.

5 Where next?

- **Speaking and listening task:** Using the text's focus on the London Eye as inspiration, split the class into groups and ask each group to prepare a short tourist campaign to encourage people to visit a famous sight in London or your local city. Each group could then present their campaign to the rest of the class.

- **Writing task:** The children could write a first-person narrative from the point of view of Salim, recounting the events of the day. They could end on a cliffhanger, just like in the extract, leaving the reader wondering what happened next.

Reading list

Fiction
- *The Beast of Buckingham Palace* by David Walliams
- *The Clockwork Sparrow* by Katherine Woodfine
- *Emil and the Detectives* by Erich Kästner
- *The Guggenheim Mystery* by Robin Stevens and Siobhan Dowd
- *The Last Chance Hotel* by Nicki Thornton (Linked text: Progress check 3)
- *Murder Most Unladylike* by Robin Stevens
- *Peril in Paris* by Katherine Woodfine
- *The Templeton Twins Have an Idea* by Ellis Weiner

Class reads
- *The Highland Falcon Thief* by M.G. Leonard and Sam Sedgman

Non-fiction
- *The Buildings That Made London* by David Long
- *The Fact or Fiction Behind London* by Adam Sutherland
- *i-SPY London* by i-SPY
- *London for Children* by Matteo Pericoli
- *London (Horrible Histories)* by Terry Deary
- *Pop-up London* by Jennie Maizels
- *The Story of London* by Richard Brassey
- *TfL: The Story of the London Underground* by David Long
- *This Is London* by Miroslav Sasek

Websites
- The BBC Teach YouTube channel has a fun 10-minute video called 'Transport, Travel and the Landmarks of London'.

Unit 21

Modelling inference

See Unit 21 Modelling slides

Use the **Skills guide** (see pages 20 to 21) and the downloadable **Skills graphic** to support your modelling.

1. **Look at the paragraph beginning *On a clear day … *. What impression does this give you of Ted? Give <u>two</u> impressions, using evidence from the text to support your answer.**

   He is knowledgeable because he talks about the effect of gravity. He is thorough because he gives a lot of detail about the capsules.

   Model using the locator to find the relevant section of the text. Although the children have encountered impression questions before, they may not have much experience of giving multiple impressions. You could point out this important distinction and explain that they need to identify four pieces of information in their answer. Some may suggest information from other sections of the text. If so, remind them that, as the question asks about this paragraph specifically, all the information should come from the same place. Model writing your answer in a table format (see **Modelling question 4** in **Unit 5**).

2. *We took Salim to the Eye because he'd never been up before.* **Why else might Ted and Kat have taken Salim there?**

   So that he could see the wonderful view of London.

   As this question uses a quotation as its locator, it is important to model finding this sentence in the text and reading around it to gain an understanding of the context. Next, model identifying the question's key words, as the children may otherwise be inclined to use the quotation as their answer. You could discuss a range of responses, deciding together which is the most plausible and why.

3. *Their faces were smiling.* **Why was this?**

   They had enjoyed their ride on the London Eye.

   Again, model reading around the locator quotation, as otherwise the children will struggle to answer. As this question relies heavily on their understanding of the London Eye, you could refer to the **Reading list** resources to support them to make an inference. You could watch a video clip of the London Eye and ask them to imagine they are there – how would they feel? Why might they smile?

4. **Think about the whole text. What impression do you get of Kat? Give <u>one</u> impression and <u>one</u> piece of evidence from the text.**

   Kat is playful because she tracks the capsule with Ted and laughs when he does.

   It is important to point out that the children need to scan the whole of the text for key information. This question is quite challenging, as the text does not mention Kat in much detail. You could scan the text together, highlighting sentences where Kat is mentioned. Next, choose one of these sentences to use as evidence, modelling working backwards to decide upon the impression this evidence gives the reader of Kat. Model writing your answer in a table format (see **Modelling question 4** in **Unit 5**).

Inference questions mark scheme

See page 204

	Answer	Guidance
1	*Impression*: observant *Evidence*: He notices all the parts of the Eye such as the spokes and hawsers.	Ted is a complex character and the children may find it difficult to give an impression of him. If so, encourage them to find a piece of evidence about him, then work backwards to think about the impression that piece of evidence gives. **Award 1 mark for a plausible impression. Award 2 marks for a plausible impression with appropriate evidence from the text.**
2	The stranger may have had a spare ticket, so he thought he'd be kind and give it to Salim. OR The stranger may have wanted Salim to go on alone so he could kidnap him.	The children may focus their response on the stranger's kindness or, if using more complex inference, they may link the offer to Salim's later disappearance. Either response should be accepted. **Award 1 mark for a plausible reason.**

Answer		Guidance
3	guilty because Salim used the ticket to go on the Eye and then he disappeared	The locator is a direct quotation. You could remind the children to read around it to gain a better understanding of the context. **Award 1 mark for a plausible feeling. Award 2 marks for a plausible feeling with appropriate evidence from the text.**
4	(to get into the picture)	The inference needed is relatively simple, as the end of the sentence gives the necessary information. However, some children may make an inference from the quotation alone. **Award 1 mark for the correct answer circled.**
5	anxious because they could not find their cousin and he should have come down by then	Some children may respond with feelings that Ted and Kat have at different points in the text. However, only accept explanations that refer to the correct part of the story. **Award 1 mark for a plausible feeling. Award 2 marks for a plausible feeling with appropriate evidence from the text.**

Mix it up! questions mark scheme

See page 205

Answer		Guidance
1	thirty minutes/30 minutes/half an hour	This question does not have a locator but the relevant information is given in the first paragraph. You could provide a locator for some children, if needed. **Award 1 mark for the correct answer. Skill: Retrieval.**
2	sealed	Some children may discount 'sealed', as it implies 'closed tightly' rather than just 'closed'. If so, remind them that a synonym has a similar, rather than an identical, meaning. **Award 1 mark for the correct answer. Skill: Word meaning.**
3	*Similarity*: They both like going on the Eye. *Difference*: Ted thinks that London looks like London, but Kat thinks London looks like toy-town.	This is a challenging question as the children must find a similarity and a difference. For the difference, they must show both sides of the comparison, rather than giving an implicit comparison (e.g. 'Kat thinks London looks like toy-town'). **Award 1 mark for one similarity or difference. Award 2 marks for one similarity and one difference. Skill: Comparison.**
4	Nowhere to Be Seen	Some children may reword the original title (e.g. 'Mystery on the London Eye'). If so, encourage them to use their own words, thinking about the main events of the text. **Award 1 mark for any plausible title. Skill: Summarising.**
5	I think Ted and Kat will go looking for Salim, because Ted says at the end that he has a different operating system so he was able to figure out the mystery.	The children's predictions will be influenced by their background knowledge. Some may pick up on the fact that Ted says that he solved the mystery, while others may focus on Ted's forensic approach. Accept any plausible prediction that is linked to the text. **Award 1 mark for a plausible prediction. Award 2 marks for a plausible prediction plus an explanation linked to the text. Skill: Prediction.**

The London Eye Mystery, by Siobhan Dowd

In this extract Ted and Kat travel with their cousin Salim to visit the London Eye. When they are offered a free ticket, Salim goes on alone and something mysterious happens.

My favourite thing to do in London is to fly the Eye.

On a clear day you can see for twenty-five miles in all directions because you are in the largest observation wheel ever built. You are sealed into one of the thirty-two capsules with the strangers who were next to you in the queue, and when they close the doors, the sound of the city is cut off. You begin to rise. The capsules are made of glass and steel and are hung from the rim of the wheel. As the wheel turns, the capsules use the force of gravity to stay upright. It takes thirty minutes to go a full circle.

From the top of the ride, Kat says London looks like toy-town and the cars on the roads below look like abacus beads going left and right and stopping and starting. I think London looks like London and the cars like cars, only smaller.

The best thing to see from up there is the river Thames. You can see how it loops and curves but when you are on the ground you think it is straight.

The next best thing to look at is the spokes and metallic hawsers of the Eye itself. You are looking at the only cantilevered structure of its kind on earth. It is designed like a giant bicycle wheel in the sky, supported by a massive A-frame.

It is also interesting to watch the capsules on either side of yours. You see strangers looking out, just like you are doing. The capsule that is higher than yours becomes lower than yours and the capsule that is lower becomes higher. You have to shut your eyes because it makes a strange feeling go up your oesophagus. You are glad the movement is smooth and slow.

And then your capsule goes lower and you are sad because you do not want the ride to end. You would like to go round one more time, but it's not allowed. So you get out feeling like an astronaut coming down from space, a little lighter than you were.

We took Salim to the Eye because he'd never been up before. A stranger came up to us in the queue, offering us a free ticket. We took it and gave it to Salim. We shouldn't have done this, but we did. He went up on his own at 11.32, 24 May, and was due to come down at 12.02 the same day. He turned and waved to Kat and me as he boarded, but you couldn't see his face, just his shadow. They sealed him in with twenty other people whom we didn't know.

Kat and I tracked Salim's capsule as it made its orbit. When it reached its highest point, we both said, 'NOW!' at the same time and Kat laughed and I joined in. That's how we knew we'd been tracking the right one. We saw the people bunch up as the capsule came back down, facing northeast towards the automatic camera for the souvenir photograph. They were just dark bits of jackets, legs, dresses and sleeves.

Then the capsule landed. The doors opened and the passengers came out in twos and threes. They walked off in different directions. Their faces were smiling. Their paths probably never crossed again.

But Salim wasn't among them.

We waited for the next capsule and the next and the one after that. He still didn't appear. Somewhere, somehow, in the thirty minutes of riding the Eye, in his sealed capsule, he had vanished off the face of the earth. This is how having a funny brain that runs on a different operating system from other people's helped me to figure out what had happened.

From *The London Eye Mystery* by Siobhan Dowd, David Fickling Books, 2010, copyright © 2007 by Siobhan Dowd. Reproduced by permission of The Random House Group Ltd.

Unit 21

Inference

Name: _____

1 Read from the paragraph beginning *The next best thing to look at ...* to the end of the story. What impression do you get of Ted? Give **one** impression and **one** piece of evidence from the text.

Impression	Evidence

2 marks

2 *A stranger came up to us in the queue, offering us a free ticket.*
Why do you think the stranger did this?

_____

_____

1 mark

3 *We shouldn't have done this, but we did.*
How did Ted feel about taking the ticket? Explain your answer using the text.

_____

_____

_____

2 marks

4 *We saw the people bunch up as the capsule came back down, ...*
Why did the people do this? Circle **one**.

| to see the view | to get out easily | to get into the picture | to see the spokes |

1 mark

5 *But Salim wasn't among them.*
How did Ted and Kat feel at this point in the story? Explain your answer using the text.

_____

_____

_____

2 marks

The London Eye Mystery, by Siobhan Dowd

Photocopiable resource from *Complete Comprehension 5* © Schofield & Sims Ltd, 2020.

Mix it up!

Name: _____

1 According to the text, how long does it take to go round in the London Eye?

_____

1 mark

2 Look at the paragraph beginning *We took Salim ...* . Find and copy **one** word that means the same as 'closed'.

_____

1 mark

3 Think about the whole text. Compare Ted and Kat's feelings about the London Eye. Give **one** similarity and **one** difference.

Similarity	_____ _____
Difference	_____ _____

2 marks

4 Think about the whole text. What would be an effective title for this extract?

_____

1 mark

5 What do you think will happen next in the story? Explain your answer using evidence from the text.

_____

_____

_____

2 marks

Photocopiable resource from *Complete Comprehension 5* © Schofield & Sims Ltd, 2020.

Unit 21 — The London Eye Mystery, by Siobhan Dowd

The Last Chance Hotel
by Nicki Thornton

▽ Printable text • Modelling slides   📖 Photocopiable text and questions • pages 207 to 209

The Last Chance Hotel is a wonderful, magical murder mystery in which the main character, Seth Seppi, is a kitchen boy who dreams of bygone days when the hotel was loved and his father was in charge. Nicki Thornton's masterful characterisation ensures that we know just how much Seth loathes his nasty employers. This extract centres on the arrival of famous guests to the Last Chance Hotel, so named because it is in the middle of nowhere. It is linked by its mystery and magical themes to the Unit 21 text, *The London Eye Mystery*, and the Unit 18 text, *The Nowhere Emporium*. After the Progress check has been completed, you could discuss the links between the three texts and explore the authors' approaches to these themes. **For guidance on running this task, see page 11.**

Progress check questions mark scheme

	Answer	Guidance
1	He's loud/bossy/angry.	To explain the effect of the author's choice of words on our impression of Henri, the children need to understand the meaning of 'barking'. Some will only associate barking with a dog, so you could discuss the double meaning of the word before they answer this question. **Award 1 mark for a reference to Henri being loud, bossy or angry. Skill: Word choice.**
2	spindly	You may wish to remind the children that a correct response will involve only one word. **Award 1 mark for the correct answer. Skill: Word meaning.**
3	Seth — kitchen boy; Henri — chef; Tiffany — daughter of the owners; Horatio — owner of the hotel	The children need to read the text closely as there are numerous names and roles mentioned throughout. Some may assume Seth is the chef because he cooks elements of the food. If so, remind them that the introduction to a text always includes helpful information so they should reread the introduction before finalising their answers. **Award 1 mark for three lines correctly drawn. Skill: Retrieval.**
4	*Feeling*: unimpressed *Evidence*: He says "Is *that* our VIP guest, Dr Thallomius?"	Some children may pick up on the nuance of "Is *that* our VIP guest …" and understand that Henri has stressed 'that' to show his disapproval. Others may focus on the sentence "Not very impressive.". Either is acceptable evidence. **Award 1 mark for a plausible feeling. Award 2 marks for a plausible feeling with appropriate evidence from the text. Skill: Inference.**
5	Seth says Mr Kingfisher has a very large/luxuriant moustache, but Henri says it is a ridiculous moustache.	The children may quote details from the text, as in the sample answer, or give a more general comparison of the characters' descriptions (e.g. 'Seth likes his moustache but Henri doesn't'). Both are acceptable, but the children must refer to both Henri and Seth's descriptions to be awarded the mark. References to one (e.g. 'Seth likes his moustache') with an implication about the other are insufficient to show comparison. **Award 1 mark for a reference to both Seth and Henri's descriptions. Skill: Comparison.**

Progress check 3

Name: _____

1 *... Henri Mould, the balding head chef, bent double with old age, barking out orders ...*
What does the group of words *barking out orders* tell you about Henri's personality?

_____
_____

1 mark

2 Look at the paragraph beginning *"Seth – those tarts! ... "*. Find and copy **one** word that means the same as 'scrawny'.

_____

1 mark

3 Draw lines to match each character to their role in the story. One has been done for you.

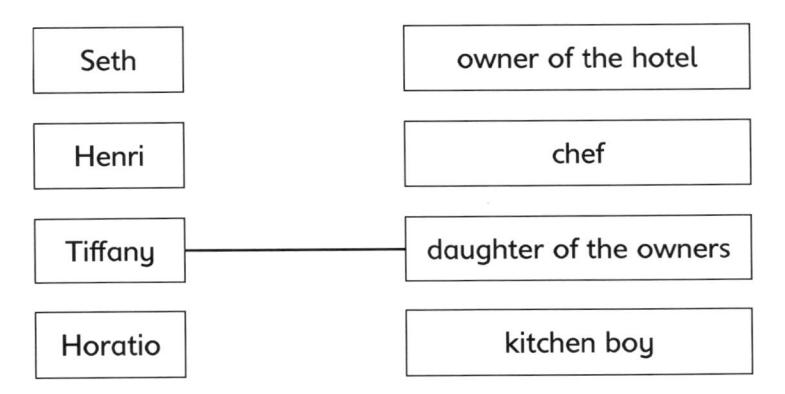

Seth		owner of the hotel
Henri		chef
Tiffany	——	daughter of the owners
Horatio		kitchen boy

1 mark

4 Look at the paragraph beginning *Henri moved across the kitchen ...* . How does Henri feel about Dr Thallomius? Give **one** feeling and **one** piece of evidence from the text.

Feeling	Evidence

2 marks

5 Look at the paragraph beginning *"And the chap with him ... "* and the paragraph beginning *"That'll be Mr Gregorian Kingfisher."*. Compare how Seth and Henri describe Mr Kingfisher. Give **one** difference.

_____
_____

1 mark

The Last Chance Hotel, by Nicki Thornton

Seth Seppi is a kitchen boy who works at the Last Chance Hotel, a hotel which very few people visit. He hates his employers and dreams of the past, but the arrival of some famous and unusual guests intrigues him.

In the kitchen of the Last Chance Hotel the loudest sound you were likely to hear was the gentle bubble of a lone egg coming to the boil.

But today, the air was alive with yells from Henri Mould, the balding head chef, bent double with old age, barking out orders as he hobbled around the kitchen.

"Seth – those tarts! Out of the oven. Now!" yelled Henri, causing kitchen boy Seth to twist around on his spindly legs and hurtle to the other side of the kitchen. All around him, the air was filled with the smell of garlic butter and roasting meat, and cloudy with a dust of flour, herbs and spices. Steam ballooned, jellies set and saucepans bubbled.

If ever Seth Seppi wished he could be even the tiniest bit magic it was now. Because a spell to split himself into three was surely the only way he was going to get through all the tasks he'd been set by his three nasty bosses – crotchety Henri and the two owners of the Last Chance Hotel, snappy and spiteful Norrie Bunn and her oily, penny-pinching husband, Horatio. It felt like the hotel had been preparing forever for these special guests that Mr Bunn had been bouncing on his toes about, and today was the day they were due to arrive.

"I need more pepper. Quickly boy!" screeched Norrie Bunn from the stove, sending a long dribble of peppercorn sauce flying across the kitchen as she launched a dripping spoon in Seth's direction. Her long, brittle grey hair was tied back from her pointy face as she sweated over the sauce, trying not to sneeze.

At least the Bunns' monstrously unpleasant daughter, Tiffany, was at her posh chefs' school, far away from her favourite entertainment – tormenting Seth.

Mr Bunn burst into the kitchen flapping his hands and squealing, "They're here! They're here!" like a small kid announcing Christmas, before rushing back out into the lobby.

Even more startling, Mr Bunn was wearing a cherry-red waistcoat and stripy trousers, rather than the familiar drab grey suit he had worn every day for years.

Norrie Bunn tugged off her apron and, smoothing down her long grey hair, rushed to attend to her guests in the lobby.

Seth managed to be the first to reach the crack in the kitchen wall where it was possible to see through to the lobby and sneak a glimpse of the arriving guests. As he put his eye to the hole, he could hear the sound of keys being jangled and Mr and Mrs Bunn, on their best behaviour, greeting the new arrivals.

Henri moved across the kitchen with unusual sprightliness, poked Seth out of the way with a very sharp elbow and peered through the crack. "Is *that* our VIP guest, Dr Thallomius? The one we've put in all this hard work for? Not very impressive. All this work," Henri groaned as he pressed his paunch tenderly, "gives me gas."

Seth had not expected their VIP guest to look like a miniature Father Christmas. Dr Thallomius had white hair, a round tummy and eyes that twinkled, but he must have only come up to Seth's shoulder.

"And the chap with him – what a peacock." Henri continued his spying. "Guess that's his security he's insisted on bringing with him. Security! Looks about as good at security as a chicken. What a ridiculous moustache."

"That'll be Mr Gregorian Kingfisher." Seth had glimpsed a young man in a bright green, tight-fitting suit, with well-combed dark brown hair, a very large and luxuriant brown moustache and a sprinkle of freckles across his nose. "He's the one who asked for a room with a picture of people playing sport."

Guests often made special requests, but it was the first time anyone had been fussy about the artwork in their room. These guests were so fascinating. Seth had never known this many people staying. Probably because outside the hotel the whole world was nothing but never-ending trees.

From *The Last Chance Hotel* by Nicki Thornton, Chicken House, 2018. Reproduced by permission.

Discover *Complete Comprehension* for Year 3

Unit	Target skill	Title	Author	Genre
1	Summarising	The Pebble in My Pocket	Meredith Hooper	Non-fiction
2	Retrieval	Stone Circles	Dawn Finch	Non-fiction
3	Relationship	My Brother Is a Superhero	David Solomons	Fiction
4	Inference	The Magic Finger	Roald Dahl	Fiction
5	Summarising	Sugar: The Facts	The NHS	Non-fiction
6	Retrieval	Prawn Pizza	Jane Sowerby	Non-fiction
7	Word choice	The Iron Man	Ted Hughes	Fiction
Progress check 1	Mixed skills	The Selfish Giant	Oscar Wilde	Fiction
8	Inference	The Ice Palace	Robert Swindells	Fiction
9	Retrieval	A House of Snow and Ice	Stephen Whitt	Non-fiction
10	Inference	The Heavenly River (Chinese Myths and Legends)	Shelley Fu	Fiction
11	Comparison	New Year Celebrations	Jane Sowerby	Non-fiction
12	Word meaning	Night Comes Too Soon	James Berry	Poetry
13	Inference	Tom's Midnight Garden	Philippa Pearce	Fiction
14	Word meaning	The Story of Tutankhamun	Patricia Cleveland-Peck	Non-fiction
Progress check 2	Mixed skills	Secrets of a Sun King	Emma Carroll	Fiction
15	Word choice	The Butterfly Lion	Michael Morpurgo	Fiction
16	Retrieval	Wild Animals to Be Banned from Circuses in England by 2020, says Government	*The Independent*	Non-fiction
17	Word meaning	Alice's Adventures in Wonderland	Lewis Carroll	Fiction
18	Inference	The Madhatters	Aoife Mannix	Poetry
19	Inference	Stig of the Dump (Extract 1)	Clive King	Fiction
20	Prediction	Stig of the Dump (Extract 2)	Clive King	Fiction
21	Retrieval	Norse Mythology	Neil Gaiman	Fiction
Progress check 3	Mixed skills	Discover the Vikings: Warriors, Exploration and Trade	John C. Miles	Non-fiction

Schofield & Sims

For further information and to place your order visit www.schofieldandsims.co.uk or telephone 01484 607080

Discover *Complete Comprehension* for Year 4

Unit	Target skill	Title	Author	Genre
1	Summarising	Roman Britain	Ruth Brocklehurst	Non-fiction
2	Retrieval	The Time-Travelling Cat and the Roman Eagle	Julia Jarman	Fiction
3	Retrieval	Volcanoes in Action	Anita Ganeri	Non-fiction
4	Word meaning	Tsunamis on the Move	International Tsunami Information Center, Hawaii, USA	Non-fiction
5	Word meaning	Russian Doll	Rachel Rooney	Poetry
6	Inference	The Little Daughter of the Snow	Arthur Ransome	Fiction
7	Retrieval	The History behind Christmas Traditions	*The Telegraph*	Non-fiction
Progress check 1	Mixed skills	A Christmas Tree	Charles Dickens	Fiction
8	Relationship	The Moomins and the Great Flood	Tove Jansson	Fiction
9	Inference	For Forest	Grace Nichols	Poetry
10	Retrieval	The Borrowers	Mary Norton	Fiction
11	Prediction	Max and the Millions	Ross Montgomery	Fiction
12	Inference	My Secret War Diary by Flossie Albright	Marcia Williams	Fiction
13	Inference	The Amazing Story of Adolphus Tips	Michael Morpurgo	Fiction
14	Inference	The Secret World of Polly Flint	Helen Cresswell	Fiction
Progress check 2	Mixed skills	Heatwave Raises Lost 'Atlantis' Village from Its Watery Grave	*Daily Mail*	Non-fiction
15	Retrieval	Threats to African Elephants	World Wide Fund for Nature (WWF)	Non-fiction
16	Inference	The Great Elephant Chase	Gillian Cross	Fiction
17	Retrieval	Black Beauty	Anna Sewell	Fiction
18	Word meaning	Charlotte's Web	E.B. White	Fiction
19	Word choice	A Series of Unfortunate Events: The Bad Beginning	Lemony Snicket	Fiction
20	Word meaning	Little Women	Louisa May Alcott	Fiction
21	Comparison	Everything Castles	Crispin Boyer	Non-fiction
Progress check 3	Mixed skills	Sir Gawain and the Green Knight	Michael Morpurgo	Fiction

Schofield & Sims

For further information and to place your order visit
www.schofieldandsims.co.uk or telephone 01484 607080

Discover *Complete Comprehension* for Year 6

Unit	Target skill	Title	Author	Genre
1	Inference	Who Let the Gods Out?	Maz Evans	Fiction
2	Retrieval	To Asgard!	Rachel Piercey	Poetry
3	Summarising	Hidden Figures	Margot Lee Shetterly	Non-fiction
4	Relationship	The British (serves 60 million)	Benjamin Zephaniah	Poetry
5	Inference	War Horse	Michael Morpurgo	Fiction
6	Word meaning	For the Fallen	Laurence Binyon	Poetry
7	Prediction	Sky Song	Abi Elphinstone	Fiction
Progress check 1	Mixed skills	The Snow Queen	Hans Christian Andersen	Fiction
8	Inference	Tin	Pádraig Kenny	Fiction
9	Retrieval	The Wonderful Wizard of Oz	L. Frank Baum	Fiction
10	Inference	Welcome to Nowhere	Elizabeth Laird	Fiction
11	Retrieval	Malala Yousafzai: 'Nobel Award Is for All the Voiceless Children'	*The Guardian*	Non-fiction
12	Inference	The Crooked Sixpence	Jennifer Bell	Fiction
13	Word meaning	Cogheart	Peter Bunzl	Fiction
14	Comparison	Alice's Adventures in Wonderland	Lewis Carroll	Fiction
Progress check 2	Mixed skills	The Hunting of the Snark	Lewis Carroll	Poetry
15	Summarising	What's So Special about Shakespeare?	Michael Rosen	Non-fiction
16	Retrieval	Macbeth	William Shakespeare	Play
17	Word meaning	Deforestation for Palm Oil	Rainforest Rescue	Non-fiction
18	Word choice	The Explorer	Katherine Rundell	Fiction
19	Inference	Pig-Heart Boy	Malorie Blackman	Fiction
20	Retrieval	Marius the Giraffe Killed at Copenhagen Zoo	*The Guardian*	Non-fiction
21	Word meaning	Evolution Revolution	Robert Winston	Non-fiction
Progress check 3	Mixed skills	Charles Darwin: History's Most Famous Biologist	Kerry Lotzof	Non-fiction

Schofield & Sims

For further information and to place your order visit www.schofieldandsims.co.uk or telephone 01484 607080